STATE, RELIGION AND POLITICS

STATE, RELIGION AND POLITICS:
Selected Writings of Satyapal Dang

Satyapal Dang

GYAN

GYAN PUBLISHING HOUSE
NEW DELHI - 110002

State, Religion and Politics : Selected Writings of Satyapal Dang

Rs. 750

ISBN : 81-212-0850-5

Published in 2004 in India by
Gyan Publishing House
5, Ansari Road, Daryaganj
New Delhi-110 002

Phones-23282060, 23261060, Fax-23285914
Email : gyanbook@vsnl.com
Visit our Website at: http//www.gyanbooks.com

Laser type Setting by: Tact Computer Graphics, Delhi
Printed at : Delux Offset Printers, Delhi-110035

Contents

Preface

Vijay Pratap Singh, S.P. Amritsar (II) had burst open the kidney trade scam going on in Amritsar exposing many a crime that were being committed in the name of saving lives of patients who needed kidney transplants and were willing to pay any amount to a gang headed by a kidney surgeon for getting hold of poor people and getting their kidneys for them by any and every means committing many illegalities and crimes in the process. Not a few police officers, Advocates, Magistrates and others were involved. A section of doctors and the rich saw nothing wrong in it while public at large and majority of the medical profession were opposed to it even though not very vocally. I joined the battle to put an end to the illegal kidney market and to get the culprits punished for legal methods to save lives of those needing kidney transplants.

Mr. Amit Garg of Gyan Publishing House, New Delhi 110002 asked me if I had written or could write a book to be published by them on the topic of kidney market in Amritsar.

Selection is entirely mine. Topics dealt with are varied but all are topical and are likely to remain so, for quite some time. There are in this book some of my writings on topics like Ram Janam Bhumi and Ram Mandir in Ayodhaya on the one hand and Kashmir on the other. Corruption including that of Prakash Singh Badal and the fight against it as also morality and ethical values, etc, of course. There are also writings about topics like need of Communist unity, etc. Kidney market too of course, is there.

It is not necessary to mention others topics. What I would like to tell all readers of this book is that, it has always been my endevour not to twist even unconsciously FACTS to suit any preconceived views or ideas of mine or my ideology. On the other hand, I have always tried not to hesitate to change and amend my views if FACTS so warrant. I hope readers will find that these writings bear me out and that this is what makes them worth reading.

Before I end I must thank the staff of my publishers and specially Shri Ajaib Singh Chahal who helped not only in the matter of proof-reading but also in editing.

Satyapal Dang

Dated: 20/4/2004 (Satyapal Dang)

I

On the National Level

1. Ayodhya Visit—An Experience

I was in Faizabad on October 2, 1990 in connection with a seminar on communalism. In response to a strong request of mine, my hosts helped me to visit Ayodhya on October 3 morning.

Except for the fact that a few years ago Ayodhya was constituted into a separate municipality, the two can be considered one city even today. Faizabad has a population of about two lakhs–40 per cent being Muslims. Ayodhya has a population of about 25,000 of whom about 3 or 4 thousand are Muslims.

People of the twin towns have long traditions of communal peace and harmony. More than one person told me that communalists did not have much mass following. Here are the two examples they gave.

After a month-long and hectic preparations, the Vishwa Hindu Parishad (VHP) held a Virat Hindu Sammelan in Faizabad on September 25, 1989 at Khastrya boarding house. Only a few hundred attended—and about 90 per cent were from outside.

As for Ayodhya is concerned, the VHP had never held a public meeting there except on the occasion of some mela or religious festival or the other. Even November 9 has been chosen for laying the foundation stone of Ram Mandir in place of Babri Masjid because lakhs of pilgrims visit Ayodhya on that day every year, it being Devsthan-Ekadashi.

(a) Left has Strength

Left has good strength in the district of Faizabad. Both CPI and CPM(M) have one MLA each in the UP Assembly from this district. Once CPI had as many as five. One CPI sympathizer said: "But for their internal fights, communists would have been in a position to sweep the polls in our district."

The first place I visited in Ayodhya was the Babri Masjid-Ram Janmabhoomi. It is a very small masjid. It is far from having the grandeur one would imagine it to have, considering its name. Both outside and inside there were police pickets.

In the main part of the masjid was the idol of Shri Ram with some pictures of some Hindu gods on both sides. Interestingly, a big picture of Thakur Gurdit Singh, Faizabad's city magistrate in 1948, was there on one of the interior walls of the building.

A big picture of the then collector K.K. Nayyar had been painted on the wall opposite Shri Ram's Murti (idol). On the wall also was written his brief life sketch, the main point being that he had helped liberate the Ram Janambhoomi.

What this gentleman had done was to help place in the masjid a Murti of Shri Ram one night in 1949 and had advised those who did this to start Akhand Ram Kirtan so that the then Prime Minister Jawaharlal Nehru could not get it removed. The appearance of the Murti was propagated as proof of the site being the birth place of Shri Ram.

It is this Murti which is still there while cases regarding the dispute remain pending before courts. Nayyar had to resign his job. He joined politics and was also an MP (Jana Sangh) for one term. Some told me that after the 'service' he rendered, he and his family became very much rich.

Except on special religious occasions, the number who come to the masjid-temple is few. On special occasions visitors are mainly from outside UP.

Baba Lal Dass, one of the government appointed priests to worship the deity, was good enough to have a detailed discussion with me. I asked him as to how could anyone be sure that Shri Ram was born at this very place when Kaushalya Bhawan was supposed to be at a distance of about 200 yards and when the Dasarath Mahal was about 500 yards away. His reply was that originally all three and many other places constituted one huge complex—even though today they are separate ones with many buildings in between.

Next place we visited was 'Sita Rasoi-Ram Janam Sthan'. It is a separate building altogether though close by. If words have any meaning, the whole of Ayodhya can be called 'Ram Janambhoomi' while 'Janam-Sthan' would mean exact site where Shri Ram was born. When I raised this point with the priest here, his answer was: "Shri Ram was born at the site of the Babri Masjid but was brought here when he was 6 days old and was thereafter kept here."

This really did not answer my point but I did not consider it prudent to press the same further. He also told us that after Shri Ram got married this place became kitchen of Maharani Sita.

We then visited Kaushalya Bhawan. The pujari here seemed to have received modern education. He told us that the present structure had come up only some hundred years ago and the original Bhawan was no longer in existence.

He was of the view that Shri Ram was born at the site of Babri Masjid because there was then a special room in which the Mahranis delivered their children. According to him, it was a separate and independent building from the beginning. The way he answered the questions, he did not seem to believe in all that he was telling us.

From here we went to the Dasarath Mahal—now a big temple in which Ram Pooja was going on in the typical manner of big Hindu temples with bells, gongs and all that. We came back to the nearby Babri Masjid and visited the 'dharamsala' known as 'Shri Ram Chritar Manv Trust'.

Here yatris from outside can stay. It has 90 rooms—40 of them with attached bathrooms and kitchens. At a time about 200 can stay conveniently but upto 500 can be packed. The accommodation is of four types. The foundation stone was laid in 1958 and the dharamsala was completed in 1965.

All this information was given to us by (Pandit) Radha Shyam Pandey—the in-charge. He happened to know intimately one of the friends accompanying me. Panditji insisted and did not let us go till we had tea with him. In reply to a question of mine, Panditji told us that before the construction of dharamsala, the site was a (Muslim) graveyard and was known as 'Laddo Mal ka Ahata'—perhaps no longer being used as such when the foundation stone of dharamsala was laid. No dispute arose. There are some in Faizabad who hold the view that the Babri Masjid was originally for Janaza prayers for the dead. Baba Lal Dass, however, had vehemently argued that Babri Masjid had been constructed after demolishing a Ram temple.

(b) Untenable Argument

Baba Lal Das did not realize that he was contradicting himself when he said: "Look, it does not look like a masjid at all". I told him that I had seen other masjids like this. In any case, if it was constructed after demolishing a temple, surely it could have been easily a common type of masjid.

One of my friends could not help remarking: "If it does not look like a masjid, it does not even remotely resemble a Hindu temple."

To be fair to Baba Lal Dass, he showed us some pillars which according to him were of Hindu architecture. These according to him, had some images of Hindu gods engraved on them, which had been damaged and even broken.

Whether these pillars conclusively prove the existence of a temple at any time at the site of the Babri Masjid is, quite debatable for more than one reason. But should one go about demolishing mosques and Hindu temples because it is thought that hundreds of years ago they were constructed by demolishing Hindu temples and Budh Jain temples respectively?

The answer which the common Hindus of UP give, becomes clear when they respond positively to the argument: "Let a really grand Ram temple be constructed in Ayodhya but why demolish a mosque? Afterall the temples, mosques, gurdwaras, chruches—are all abodes of god."

Of course, nothing can convince those who have political vested interests in the dispute.

Close to the Babri Masjid is the office of the VHP. It contains the model of the temple proposed to be constructed. It has also many huge-size pictures—some quite provocative. One such picture depicts 1,72,000 Hindus having been killed while defending Ram Janambhoomi.

Another picture claims that Guru Gobind Singhji had visited Ayodhya and had succeeded, even though temporarily, in liberating the Ram Janambhoomi. The in-charge was quite assertive in explaining the VHP case. However, he would not tell of another very authentic fact.

The most imposing temple in Ayodhya is the 'Hanuman Garhi Mandir'. It was constructed by a Muslim—Mansoor Ali, nawab of Avadh.

Hindi *Nav Bharat Times* of September 29 (Lucknow edition) carried the terms of a reported agreement arrived at Lucknow between Home Minister Buta Singh and VHP. Some other newspapers have characterized it as a false report while according to Boota Singh, Shahabuddin and some other Muslim leaders have welcomed it.

The report in the *Nav Bharat Times* was shown to us by Baba Lal Dass who did not hide his unhappiness about it. According to the agreement, the government was to allow Ram Shila Pooja functions to go on all over India; the VHP was to take to Ayodhya a limited number of Ram Shilas on November 9; the foundation stone of a Ram Mandir was to be laid some distance away from the disputed site, provocative slogans were not to be raised, etc.

(c) 'Shila Pooja' Planned

After all, there was still no undertaking that the Babri Masjid would not be sought to be demolished even subsequently. 'Ram Shila Pooja' functions going on in the country continued to be accompanied by provocative slogans communalizing the whole atmosphere. Some VHP leaders have denied any agreement.

In any case, many VHP and even some BJP leaders continued to assert that Babri Masjid would be demolished come what may, if not on November 9, then subsequently. The 'agreement' therefore did not resolve the problem. It did not even help very much to lessen communal tensions.

At best it was an effort to postpone the dispute till after the elections because that would suit both the Congress(I) and the non-left opposition. Not all leaders of VHP-RSS-BJP combine were willing to oblige even to that extent. The left and all other secular forces therefore continued their campaign for amity and some mutually agreed solution.

Another dangerous aspect of the matter needs to be noted. One Mukhtar Abbas Naqvi had been declaring that his (Muslim) organization would demolish the Babri Masjid. Recently he has even set a date—November 10. Nobody took him seriously.

For one, he was a shady character in Allahabad with no following. He had visited Ayodhya once or twice—with only RSS boys accompanying him.

In Ayodhya and Faizabad, there are Shia as well as Sunni Muslims. All are united that Babri Masjid be not demolished though another Ram Mandir may be constructed at some suitable nearby place in Ayodhya. However RSS-VHP-BJP combine seems to be making a serious effort to exploit traditional Sunni-Shia differences for its aim of demolishing the Masjid.

No less a person than Balasaheb Deoras came out with a statement when I was in Faizabad-Ayodhya that they were negotiating with Shia Muslims. Not satisfied with gruesome Hindu-Muslim riots, the RSS seems to be planning to bring about Sunni-Shia riots.

The democratic movement must take serious note of this too and take appropriate timely steps.

(d) Faizabad Seminar

Last but not least about the seminar to attend which I had gone to Faizabad. It had been organized by a very broad-based committee of leading citizens. These included the zila parishad chairman, two vice presidents of nagar palika, leading advocates, doctors, intellectuals and public workers belonging to both communities.

It was presided over by renowned scientist (plant pathology) and vice-chancellor of Acharya Narendra Dev Technological University, Faizabad, Professor Uttam Chand Upadhyay. The university has only post-graduate classes and does research work. Prof. Upadhyay has chaired many international seminars organized by UNESCO.

In his brief concluding remarks on the first day, the vice-chancellor denounced communalism of all hues in no uncertain terms and called upon people to steer clear of it as it could only hinder the progress of the country. He called for respect for all religions and all places of religious worship.

The highlight of the first day of the seminar was the speech of Mahant Phalahari of Raj Gopal temple of Ayodhya. He said in simple and religious terms:

"Those who are exploiting the Ram Janambhoomi-Babri Masjid dispute for political ends are not truly religious people. They must be unmasked. Compassion for humanity is being devoured by demon of communalism. Teaching that wants every human being to be treated as human being is being dealt severe blows.

"Animal instincts are coming on the top because we want to resolve our differences through fights. Let us not forget that international anti-Indian forces are encouraging communalism."

He added: "In mohallas and even in trains and on small railway platforms, devout Hindus and Muslims live and even offer prayers and namaz side by side. Why cannot that be done in a masjid or a mandir?"

All in the big audience—Hindus and Muslims both—listened with great attention to this speech and applauded it loudly and for long.

This writer felt quite sorry for not being able to listen to the earlier speeches because his train had reached late. The organizers had reserved his railway seat on October 3rd itself and therefore he could not attend the seminar on the second day too. Even then it was an inspiring experience and memorable visit.

2. Heartwarming Communal Harmony

I was in Haryana from October 11 to 13, 1989 to participate in the anti-communal campaign organized in view of the dangerous situation in the country resulting from the VHP campaign to construct a Ram Mandir in Ayodhya after demolishing the Babri Masjid there.

Along with Raghbir Singh, secretary Haryana state council of the CPI (and also general secretary of Haryana Trade Union Congress), I visited Jind, Nirwana, Asandh, Panipat and Sonepat.

We addressed bar association meetings at Jind and Panipat, a well-attended public meeting at Nirwana, two big hall meetings at Panipat and Sonepat and another hall meeting at Asandh.

Invariably, there was general support for our slogan against demolition of any religious place for constructing a place of worship of another religion.

There was general approval when we asserted that this would violate the true teachings of every religion and also endanger the unity of the country.

A sense of relief and happiness could be seen on the faces of many in the audience when we said: "Let another grand and big Ram temple be constructed in Ayodhya but without demolishing the Babri or any other masjid."

The support which the VHP-RSS-BJP combine seemed to be getting for some time for its compaign regarding Ram Shila Pooja, etc, definitely started declining rapidly. This was the result of people becoming aware of the real design behind it and its dangerous potentiality for communal peace and the very future of the country.

This was quite visible in Panipat when we were there. The Ram Shila procession consisted of one hired band team, one gutka team and about 15 to 20 persons only.

It is this fact which has made not only the Prime Minister but also the opposition stalwarts V.P. Singh and Devi Lal to at last take a stand against the demolition of the Babri Masjid, even though the stand is as yet half-hearted.

Again, this very reality has forced BJP leader Atal Bihari Vajpayee to say that they too would not like to demolish the masjid and that it should be lifted and shifted to some other place—a slogan which too must be rejected and for obvious reasons.

While in Haryana, I came across some very interesting and instructive facts.

In Sonepat there is a Mazar called 'Mama-Bhanja (uncle-nephew) Mazar Sharif'. It seems long long ago an uncle and his nephew were murdered by some bad elements. Both Muslims, they were equally popular in both the communities.

Their dead bodies were laid to rest in one common grave on the top of which was installed a Shiv Ling. This Mazar, next door to a masjid, is worshipped to this day both by Muslims and Hindus and has become a symbol of Hindu-Muslim unity.

Raghbir Singh told me another revealing fact. Village Batbhal near Faridabad is entirely a Muslim village. It has no Hindu family but has a Hindu temple. Sometime back the government acquired lot of land including the land below the temple for some development project.

On the ground that a Hindu temple was not needed in the village, the government wanted to demolish it. The Muslims objected. They argued: "It must have been constructed by our Hindu great grand-grand fathers. Moreover, sacred place of one religion is sacred for all religions."

The government would not agree. The Muslims of the village went up to Supreme Court and won. The Hindu temple is still there.

There are villages in Haryana like Lakhan Majra on New Delhi-Jind road and Israna on Panipat-Rohtak road which have well maintained gurudwaras without there being even a single Sikh family in the village except that of the granthi—notwithstanding the doings of the terrorists in Punjab.

Masjid in Panipat

Ghaggri in Haryana, typical dress of women of the area, has virtually disappeared. Most common now is shalwar. Sari takes only a second place and that too a poor second. And this when terrorists in Punjab not infrequently threaten to kill Sikh women if they wear saris.

In Panipat, an old freedom fighter Budh Ram told us that there is a Babri Masjid in the town. When Raghbir Singh sought to refute it, he produced a school history book in Hindi. The page on Babar contained the following: "During his regime, Babar got constructed palaces and Masjids. Of these, Babri Masjid in Panipat and Jama Masjid in Sambhal are still there". Significantly, there was no mention in the book of the Babri Masjid at Ayodhya.

Budh Ram told us where the Babri Masjid was in Panipat and we went to see it. There was no one to look after it. It was in pretty poor and even dilapidated condition. Within the masjid land, many buffaloes were grazing.

However, the masjid must have looked grand at one time. It has many gumbads and one meenar. One young Sikh boy was sitting on one of the gumbads and appeared to be doing some painting. Just above the main entrance on the gate, were carved two lotuses—on the two sides of the entry. Something clearly Hindu even in a mosque.

Facts like the above have a lesson for those who are raising the dangerous slogan: "Hindustan mein rahna hai, to Hindu ban kar rahna hoga" (if you want to live in India, you have to live like a Hindu). Living side by side peacefully, people of different religions are bound to imbibe many things from each other, enriching our composite culture.

Such traffic of course cannot be one way. However, if one religion is sought to be imposed on others and if RSS will regard Muslims as Indians only if they begin burning on pyre their dead instead of burying them, surely that is the road to ruin and disaster for the country. It must be opposed tooth and nail.

A well-meaning Delhi-based journalist has recently put forward a proposal: "Let Muslims agree to give up Babri Masjid in return for an assurance that no other mosque would be demolished". In the same article, this journalist has noted the fact that the VHP has a list of 3,000 mosques which they would like to demolish.

Surely, this journalist cannot be unaware of the fact that only recently, one of the frequently shouted slogans in Delhi by the VHP was: "Ram Krishna Vishwanath, teenon ek sath"—a war cry for demolishing three mosques simultaneously—the one in Ayodhya, the one in Mathura and the one in Varanasi. And this notwithstanding the fact that many years ago an agreement was reached as far as Mathura dispute is concerned.

Let it not be forgotten even for a moment that the slogan of a Ram Mandir in place of Babri Masjid has nothing to do with any love for Ram. In short run, it is playing the Hindu card for votes. In the long run, it is a part of a plan to turn India into a Hindu theocratic state.

It is not an accident that the slogan for demolishing the Babri Masjid on 9.11.1989 was raised along with the slogan of turning India into a Hindu Rashtra from one and the same place, i.e, the Kumbh Mela at Prayag. The fight against both the slogans is one and the same. Appeasement of communalism—of any hue—only strengthens communalism of all hues and must therefore be avoided.

Last, but not least, it was a proud privilege to have the opportunity of being a guest of Ram Ditta of Panipat. Coming from a poor family, by dint of hard work, he had become a small transporter by 1980 or so.

It happened in 1982. A bus coming from Punjab and going to Delhi was stopped by a Hindu crowd just near his office. All Sikhs including women and children were taken out. Men began to be beaten up and given blows with lathis etc. Some would have been even lynched to death.

Ram Ditta saw this and rushed to the site along with his 10-12 labourers—all Hindus from UP. The crowd was pushed back. The Sikhs were escorted to his office, were given tea, etc as well as first aid in case of those who needed the same. They were taken home by the comrade and made to feel fully safe.

The office of Ram Ditta was attacked by a crowd but the attack was beaten back. Among those thus saved was Pritam Singh, manager of a bank branch in village Sodhapur and Professor Amar Singh of Kurukshetra university.

It was told that a young daughter of the professor joined the CPI. She would say: "Communist are real human beings". This reminds me of another fact told by Comrade Raghbir Singh about his village Dhansoti in tehsil Panipat.

The village has a population of about 3,600. There are Hindus as well as Muslims. Till today, the village has neither a temple nor a mosque though people do believe in religion. This is the very village in the entire area from which not a single Muslim migrated in 1947 and in which people of both religions have always lived peacefully and like brethren.

Raghbir Singh said: "Mosques and temples can be there if the people want but then it must be ensured that they are not misused by vested interests to spread communalism which is negative of true religion."

3. Advani, Why Defend Hindu Theocratic State?

The views expressed by the BJP president, L.K. Advani during his recent visit to Kolkata in January-February 1990 have attracted more than usual attention. In a forthright manner, he affirmed BJP's opposition to the Anandpur Sahib resolution of the Akali party. Advani said, "acceptance of the resolution would tantamount to accepting a theoratic sub-state in secular India."

He further said: "We have agreed to greater powers to the states and the formation of inter-state council according to the recommendation of the Sarkaria Commission, but are opposed to the devolution of powers to any particular community or religion."

All this is welcome. It would seem that Advani has said almost the same thing which the left has been saying. Advani, however, should have clarified one thing.

He cannot be unaware of the fact that ever since the release of Simranjit Singh Mann, extremists and separatists in Punjab have been laying thick one argument: "If BJP can demand Hindu Rashtra in India, why should anyone object if we demand Khalistan outside or within India"? This argument does carry weight with many.

BJP leaders would of course say that their party does not demand Hindu Rashtra. They would be right in saying that but only technically, even if we forget the fact that not long ago Advani himself said that he did not mind BJP being called a Hindu party.

Neither Advani nor any other leader of the BJP can deny the fact that BJP is only the political wing of the RSS and that its policy is controlled and is determined by the RSS. And that RSS stands for Hindu Rashtra, i.e, for a Hindu theocratic state in India.

Some BJP leaders try to argue that Hindu Rashtra and Hindu Raj are two different things. They further point out that neither the RSS nor the Vishwa Hindu Parishad stand for Hindu Raj. They stand for Hindu Rashtra.

An ordinary mortal cannot understand the difference between the two. Moreover even the VHP has been talking of Hindu Raj. This was so, for instance, in its leaflets distributed in the VHP rally at Boat Club, New Delhi, in preparation for the Shilanyas at Ayodhya.

It is also argued that by 'Hindu' they mean 'Indian'. Does any one in India take Hindu and Indian to mean the same thing? If they really mean that, why don't they use the term 'Indian Rashtra' or 'Indian nation'. Not very long ago, some well-meaning friends of the RSS requested Balasaheb Deoras, the RSS supremo, to use the term

'Indian Rashtra' instead of 'Hindu Rashtra'. Deoras flatly turned down the suggestion.

BJP has been firmly opposing the demand for a Sikh theocratic state outside or inside India. But their refusal to come out against the concept of Hindu Rashtra only brings grist to the mill of Khalistanis and the supporters of Anandpur Sahib resolution. Unless they do that, some one can well argue: "Advani does not want a Sikh sub-state in India but does want whole of India to become a Hindu theocratic state." In Kolkata, Advani did talk of 'Indian nation'. He appealed to the people to consider Muslims as part of Indian nation. The appeal was misdirected.

The overwhelming majority of the Indian people do consider Indian Muslims as a part of Indian nation. It is only the RSS which refuses to do this unless Muslims get 'Indianised' by which they mean 'Hinduised'. Earlier the term used was invariably 'Hinduised'. For some time now the term 'Indianised' is used only to confuse the people. Advani appealed to the Muslims to recognize that 'Ram Rajya' was not a Hindu symbol but an intrinsic party of Indian culture and heritage.

Shri Rama definitely is a Hindu symbol. At the same time it is also true that religion does contribute to the culture of a country and therefore to its cultural heritage. India's culture is a composite culture and a very rich one. Original residents of India and their religions have contributed to it. Aryans too have. And Muslims too. In India, people belonging to different religions live side by side—in the natural course and voluntarily. They have been and would get influenced by each other in their life styles and even in religious affairs. In Uttar Pradesh, I have seen Muslim (married) women using sindhoor. In Bengal, at some places many Muslims fraternise with their Hindu brethren at the time of pooja and right in the pooja pandals.

Many more examples can be given—which would prove such traffic both ways. Such traffic, however, can take place only voluntarily. Any attempt to force it on any religious community cannot but prove counter- productive and can only strengthen fundamentalism.

If Advani really wants to strengthen such voluntary traffic, he should persuade the RSS, VHP and BJP give up once and for all any talk of demolishing any mosques to build temples in the name of 'beliefs—right or wrong'.

4. Regional Parties

An outstanding feature of India's political landscape today is the existence of a good number of regional parties. In some States they are No. 1 or No. 2 parties. They have been in power in some states. In the United Front Govt. of India (1996-1998 Feb) a number of regional parties exercised Central power for about 18 months. Some have shared power with the new BJP-led Government of India, which took power in 1999.

Obviously, an objective study of the phenomenon of regional parties in India is of utmost importance.

In the very beginning, it is necessary to note that all regional parties are not of one and the same type.

(i) Tamil regional parties are a class in themselves.

(ii) National Conference in Jammu and Kashmir State is also a category by itself.

(iii) Akali party of Punjab falls in a category of its own even though like Tamil regional parties, it too has a long history. It is essentially a religion based party and its communal character too cannot be denied. It has now come to represent the interests of capitalist landlords and upper sections of rich peasants of Punjab. It remains wedded to the goal of a theocratic State with sections wanting such a State within India with a very weak Centre while some other sections have tended to want a Sovereign Sikh State. It is interesting to note that all hopes entertained by some that Akali party would materialize into a regional party of Punjab, have not materialized. There are definite social, ethnic and economic reasons for the same which explains Akali party's existence in Punjab in its present form. Alliance of RSS-controlled BJP having the aim of a Hindu Rashtra in India and the Badal-led Akali Dal having the aim of a Sikh theocratic State within India is also explained by these reasons. It is not without significance that after the fractured mandate for Lok Sabha in 1996 Akali party was the only regional party (besides the Samta party) which chose to go along with the BJP. And even today, BJP considers Akali party as its closest and most reliable ally.

(iv) Constitution of free India recognized that India's unity is unity in diversity. It granted some autonomy to almost all States and special status with greater autonomy to some others like Jammu & Kashmir. With the economic, social and cultural development of India, regional bourgeois groups too grew in strength. As regards people, there was a contradictory development. On the one hand there was growth of common Indian consciousness along with the growth of Nation-State of India. On the other hand, there was the growth of sub-national consciousness as—Bengalis, Marathas, Tamils, etc. To strengthen India's unity-in-diversity, it was necessary to make India more federal than it was originally conceived—having a strong Centre as well as strong States. Instead, autonomy for States as provided in the Constitution was eroded.

The above developments led to emergence of new Regional parties demanding greater autonomy for themselves. Such was the Telugu Desham party of Andhra. In the border State of Assam, regional party that came up was a sessionist party based on Assamese nationalism.

It may be noted here that in Punjab, Punjabi consciousness or Punjabiat (as some would like to christen it) did not grow as it should have grown in the natural course. There are reasons for the same which need to be noted. In Punjab, for reasons peculiar to Punjab, even the issue of language had got communalized—Akalis and large sections of Sikhs treating Punjabi as a part of Sikh religion and Punjab Hindus disowning Punjabi and falsely declaring Hindi to be their mother tongue. This disruption of Punjabi consciousness went to the extent that some intellectuals put forward the false, disruptive and dangerous thesis that Punjabi Hindus have betrayed Punjabiat and that Sikhs alone can be its standard-bearers. This in fact disrupts efforts for revival of and strengthening of common Punjabi consciousness and strengthens communalism of both varieties.

(v) As already stated, India's unity can be maintained and strengthened only as unity-in-diversity. Secondly, regional parties are now an essential part of India's political landscape. National parties should seek alliance with regional parties not only to be able to somehow manage majority to be able to seize power but as a matter of correct and principled attitude towards them.

Indian polity is in a mess today. If we are to get out of it and go forward towards a just society, we need a powerful front of Left and Centrist (democratic and secular) forces—parties, groups and individuals. Such a front must include not only national level Left and Democratic and secular parties but also regional level Democratic and secular Centrist parties. And this must determine our attitude to various regional parties.

5. Civil Servants and Left

The B.B. Vohra episode in 1980 and the dramatic developments concerning N.K. Singh highlight the need on the part of the Left parties and groups in the country to have an in-depth study of the position, strength and role of bureaucracy in our state structure with a view to evolve a correct attitude towards it—correct also in details and not only in the main.

There is no doubt that during the British rule, the bureaucrats, especially the top ones, exercised immense and even unlimited powers. The ICS was the steel framework of the imperialist regime. And the ICS men, British or Indian—with few exceptions—served the British rulers faithfully and loyally to the end.

It is also true that the IAS of independent India has inherited some, or perhaps many, of the traits of the ICS. Whether it is the

IAS or other top bureaucrats belonging to other All-India or State Services, speaking generally their attitude towards the common people is the same as that of the exploiting classes from which they come or to join which, they aspire. Many top bureaucrats have played not an insignificant role in sabotaging even the far-from-radical agrarian legislation enacted after India became free. Similarly, many top bureaucrats instinctively tend to support employers against workers irrespective of the merits of the disputes and the demands of the workers. Not a few of the bureaucrats in the South Block used their positions to give a pro-Western tilt to India's policy of non-alignment diluting its anti-imperialist content. There is also the fact of wrong attitude of the IAS men towards the technocrats.

While all this is true and cannot be lost sight of, it does not seem to constitute the whole of the reality.

B.B. Vohra in his student days was known not only for his intelligence and brilliance but also uprightness. An IAS man, he rose to be one of the seniormost Civil Servants in the Government of India. He enjoyed unsullied reputation. And yet he could do nothing when he was wrongly arrested, harassed and humiliated towards the fag end of his career as a Civil Servant. Officers senior to him did nothing to come to his help. They did not even raise their voice against blatant violation of rules, even when it was their duty to do so. They chose to play safe. They dared not incur the wrath of their political bosses.

Whatever be the past record of N.K. Singh or his merits or demerits as an officer or as a man, one thing is certain. He would not have been arrested/kidnapped and forcibly taken away from his home in Delhi to Haryana and would not have suffered the humiliation he did, had he given the type of affidavit as was given by Amrit Nahata. It must also be noted that his immediate senior in his service did try to come to his aid but did not succeed. Obviously, someone enjoying great political power was behind this whole episode and he had his way.

While these two instances have been highlighted by the press in a big way, many others do not come to the notice of the public.

This writer knows not a few cases in which upright officers were humiliated and made to suffer in more than one way for no fault except that they insisted on recording their honest opinions on the files even when fully prepared to implement whatever orders their Ministers gave in writing.

In one Punjab case, the technique adopted was to encourage and incite some junior officers to insult their Secretary because the Secretary would not carry out patently wrong orders of the Minister given orally, which orders the Minister would not agree to record in writing. Ultimately, this officer sought and got transfer to Delhi. On the other hand, there are many cases in which top officers would do whatever desired of them by their Ministerial bosses and in return got undue promotions and favours of other types.

What do examples of this type show? In my opinion, they show that under the Indian Constitution, even the topmost rung of bureaucracy is not that powerful as it is sometimes thought to be. A strong government with strong political will, can tame the bureaucrats and make them act according to its will, even though it would be wrong to underestimate the power and capacity of the bureaucracy. If however a Chief Minister or a Prime Minister uses the unscrupulous amongst the top bureaucrats to further his or her own selfish ends and gives them the freedom to rule beyond that according to their own whims, they inevitably become very powerful and also a big menace. The examples of the type given above also show that there are officers even in the top rung, howsoever small in number, who are upright, who are willing to take risks for principles and who are not immune to the needs and aspirations of the people. This is not surprising because some from even lower middle classes have managed to enter the top rung of bureaucracy through open competitions and because of their intelligence and brilliance. Some of these officers resist for quite long times pressures to make them 'behave' and 'act' as their bosses want them to.

When injustice is done to officers of this type, when they are harassed and persecuted, should not the Left forces raise their voice in a more effective manner than they have done hitherto? It seems clear that they should.

The Left parties and groups must also take note of what all is being done by unscrupulous politicians of the ruling bourgeois class to ensure that all the key posts in the administration are manned by officers fully loyal to them personally and individually. In this connection, the Bhinder phenomenon represents a new technique. When Indira Gandhi's party was routed in March 1977 and she lost power, Bhinder too had to face music for all that he did or was supposed to have done during the Emergency. When his wife was selected as Congress (I) candidate for the January 1980 election to the Lok Sabha, this was seen by many as compensation for personal loyalty. Back in power, Indira Gandhi promoted this trusted and personally loyal police officer and made him Commissioner Delhi Police, superseding his seniors. The message for others is obvious.

It seems to me that the Left parties should not only note all such phenomena but must also publicly criticise and expose the same.

There are other important, new features, the State being not merely a law and order State and the consequent big increase in the number of civil servants, especially in the category, which has come to be known as Class III employees. This piece, is far from being an in-depth study of the problem. Its limited aim is to stress the need for the same by experts in the field. It is therefore not necessary to examine or even to mention all such aspects. One may however note here one of the lessons which follows from what has been stated above. The wrong tendency to blame the bureaucracy when in fact, political leadership of the ruling bourgeois class is the real culprit, has to be guarded against. This wrong tendency, if not checked can only help provide cover for the anti-people policies of the bourgeois Government.

6. In Our Bharat, i.e., India

Whether or not marriages are made in heaven, a debate goes on between supporters of the right of young people to choose their own life-partners and those of arranged marriages. In the long run, the former are bound to win but arranged marriages are still going to be the dominent feature of Indian society for long. Recently, however, I have been shocked to find how fathers of marriageable girls misuse their authority to find good grooms for their daughters.

About 30 years old very handsome Krishan Kumar (not real name) is a lecturer in one of many denominational colleges in Punjab—belonging to an educational institution. For very genuine family reasons he wanted to be transferred from a far off place to a place near his parents' house. He was told that the needful would be done if he would agree to be engaged to marry a daughter of a particular Principal. He very politely refused. For two years or more he desperately tried to get his transfer ordered but to no effect.

For me this was shocking. I mentioned this to an upright MLA belonging to the party with which this DAV college has some close connection. This MLA said: "Why are you shocked? This by no means is a solitary instance of its type these days in our Bharat."

Recently, I was in Meerut for nearly a week for a holiday. One day our family was having some discussion while having tea. I narrated the above matter. My nephew's wife Raman (not real name) said: "Chacha Ji, this is nothing. Here I can tell you the names of quite a few doctors who suffered quite a lot of harassment because as medical students they did not agree to be engaged to daughters of some Professors. In some cases, it was ensured that they failed. The same thing happens here in the Army. A young bright officer is liable to be asked by a Senior of his, senior in rank as well as in age, to agree to get engaged to his daughter. If the proposal is not accepted, harassment follows. In one such case, the young officer ultimately committed suicide."

Degeneration of moral values seems to have no limit in our Bharat, i.e, India.

Here is another aspect of the same phenomenon.

Originally, some persons would go from Meerut to Hardwar and bring from there Ganga Jal ('Nectar' water of river Ganges) taken from some specific places, e.g, Neel Kanth. Ganga Jal would be in two pitchers. One person would carry these in a `vehingi'. The other would be ahead of him. He would cover the distance lying down (crawling)—but getting up with some regularity. He was called 'Paigambar'. He undertook this ritual having pledged to do this if some desire of his got fulfilled. Majority of such persons originally belonged to scheduled castes. Destination of paigambar would be some temple with 'Shiv Ling'.

During the regimes of BJP-lead Governments, some members of Sangh Pariwar, e.g, Bajrang Dal called upon traders to welcome and feed these paigambars and their companions.Many complied. Number of paigambars with companions began swelling. Now lacs perform the ritual— of course sacred Ganga Jal is carried as before but paigambars no longer cover the distance lying down. All these persons are called Kawaris. Many still do this out of their superstitious convictions while others do it for fun—a sort of picnic. Often the rush is so great that Delhi-Hardwar route gets blocked. For 4-5 days, buses are taken off the route. Once press reported that fruits in trucks on this route got totally uneatable because of 4-5 days stoppage. This ritual is observerd as a Diwali-eve event.

I got this 'interesting' information from my nephew and a friend of his. The friend confirmed that BJP-led Governments in U.P. had been encouraging this. My reaction was: "It seems BJP believes not only in money and muscle power for votes but also in the bigger power of superstitions. BJP is getting ahead of the Congress in such matters."

Diwali was fast approaching when I was in Meerut where there is holiday not only on the Diwali Day but some preceding days are also holidays. It was an unpleasant surprise for me when Raman told me that it was usual in the schools to put explosives below the cars of their teachers, in flushes of schools, etc on the last working day before the Diwali holidays. This apart, I learn from Raman that favourtism/ nepotism/and corruption is rampant even in the most prestigious (private) schools in giving marks, in sports competitions etc. Priority for favourtism was said to be in this order: First, their own children; second, those who take private tuitions from them; and third, children of rich parents from whom they get costly gifts on such occasions as Diwali. Needless to say, many meritorious students would suffer. I wonder if such teachers can be called corrupt. (My doubt arises from the fact that recently a progressive doctor friend of mine told me that private doctors can be guilty of unethical practices but not of corruption because concept of corruption is only in relation to government administration).

School timings in many Meerut schools change only after Diwali. Raman's two children had to leave before 7 AM for their respective schools. Almost every day lights would go off at 5 or 6 AM and Raman had to prepare and cook breakfast materials to be taken with them with the help of candle-light. Her husband of course helped but there was nothing that he could do with extremely erratic power supply.

More often than not, there would be no light at cooking time in the evening also and candles costing Rs.10 each would be used. In between, power would be there for about half the time. My nephew had an inverter but the same was out of order. He explained; "It is very difficult to get a mechanic to come to your house to repair any modern gadget. Lot of money is demanded. Reason is the long distance and also the fact that number of good mechanics who can do the job is far from adequate."

Kalyan Singh was still the Chief Minister of U.P. when I was in Meerut. I wonder if the power position will improve with new Chief Minister in power. In any case, I found the power supply position in Meerut to be worse than even in Punjab. Akalis can boast that they are better than their junior partners in Punjab.

II

Parliamentary Democracy

1. Nursing the Constituency

Parliamentary democracy in India has come of age. Elections to State Assemblies and to Lok Sabha have become an important part of the political life of the country. While the main contenders in the elections are political parties, quite a number of Independent candidates continue to be in the field. Many of the successful Independent legislators are keen on getting re-elected.

Besides other things, the voters do take into consideration the performance, work etc of such legislators in the preceding term. Often, the candidates of political parties too, are not new faces. In case of every old face—even though he may be a candidate of one or the other political party—the voter cannot but take into account his work, performance, etc. in the preceding term in deciding whether to vote for him or not. Even when any political party holding a particular constituency changes the candidate and puts up a new face, the work and performance of the outgoing legislator will obviously matter for the success or defeat of the new face put up by the party holding the seat.

'Nursing the Constituency' has thus come to be regarded as an important task by the Independents as well as by those who fight elections as candidates of political parties. Yet neither any political party nor any institution concerned with the study of election and other constitutional practices in India has made any serious effort to lay down as to what 'Nursing the Constituency' should mean and what it should not.

The CPI has made some efforts in this direction by means of the organizational reports adopted at its Congresses, which warn the CPI legislators against adopting certain undesirable practices. It is very necessary that comprehensive and serious attempts in this direction are made without further delay.

This necessity arises from the fact that any number of wrong, unjust and undesirable practices are indulged in, by many a legislator precisely in the name of 'nursing the constituency'. Some instances of this type may be noted here.

To use one's authority and influence as a member of the ruling party or even of an opposition party, to get allotted quotas, permits, depots etc, for his supporters in the elections without any regard for the right of others, the merits of the case, rules, etc, instead of fighting for policies and systems under which public interest would be served best.

To use one's authority and influence, to get selected for jobs, sons and daughters of one's supporters irrespective of their merits, rights, of others and rules and procedures governing the selection of candidates.

To use one's influence and authority to help one's supporters amongst the officers and other Government employees to get such stations, jobs and duties which they would like to have. There are quite a number of corrupt officers who make huge amounts through corrupt means and use part of such ill-gotten money to finance the election campaign—and sometimes other activities too—of some politician or others. These politicians in turn help them to get posts and stations most suitable for making money. Once I very strongly protested to the then Chief Minister of Punjab against the posting of a particular officer in a particular key post because of his notorious reputation. The Chief Minister agreed with my assessment but pleaded his helplessness because this particular officer had many supporters in his party.

To use one's influence and authority to help one's supporters to escape from the clutches of the law when such supporters commit some serious crimes like murder, smuggling, etc. Once a Chief Minister said to me, "How can I put behind bar the notorious smugglers and end smuggling? Whenever, legally I am in a position to take strong action against a smuggler, some legislator or the other belonging to my own party would come and tell me not to do so on the ground that the person in question had helped him a lot, in winning the election."

More instances of this type could be given but that is hardly necessary. It should, however, be added that many a legislator use their influence and power not only to 'help' their active supporters and campaigners in the manner described above but also others whom they think they can win over to their sides for future elections. There are legislators who do not hesitate to use their influence and power to involve their opponents in false cases to teach them a lesson; to force them to desist from opposing them in future elections.

It is far from being my intention to suggest that any sizable section of the legislators indulges, only in these types of practices in the name of nursing their constituencies. Even those who indulge in such obviously undesirable practices do make efforts to get as much share of developmental works for their constituencies as possible. The disease, however, has already assumed such dimensions that we can overlook it only at great cost for our people and our country.

I was surprised when one of the topmost leaders of one of the important political parties in Punjab justified rank favouritism and nepotism on the ground that: "It is not possible to say 'no' to those who are your right-hand men in all your election campaigns". Such leaders obviously preach one thing and practise another and yet express shock when a section of the youth go astray and resort to such things as copying in examinations.

I read the Report of the Commission of Inquiry consisting of Justice A.N. Mulla which was appointed by the Government of Kerala to enquire into certain allegations against certain Ministers. Justice Mulla is a retired Judge of the High Court and is well-known for his bold views and judgements. The following passage in his Report has come to me as a big shock:

"And this brings me to another aspect of favouritism alleged against the two Ministers. The allegation is that they showed favour to the members of their own political group. I have already mentioned above that exercising one's discretion in favour of a person one likes, is a human attribute and he would naturally exercise his discretionary power in favour of a supporter and not in favour of an opponent. Actually, in the functioning of the Democratic State, certain concepts and traditions have developed which approve the exercise of Favouritism even on the political plane. One of these well-known concepts is 'Nursing the Constituency'. What does 'Nursing the Constituency' mean? Can you nurse the constituency in the interest of a political party if you are absolutely impartial and you have no preference for your political supporters? In the first place, it is not humanly possible to apply the rule of merit with such precision that you always succeed in selecting the most deserving. In this world of teeming billions the competition of life has reached such a stage that for every job or post there are always a very large number of applicants with similar qualifications and no child of Adam and Eve can claim that he can pick out the best amongst them. It is the duty of a politician to strengthen the hold of his group upon the electorate and if he looks after the interests of his supporters his conduct cannot be assailed. On the other hand, if he neglects to do so he will be doing disservice to his group. Therefore so long as he escapes the three pitfalls mentioned above, exception cannot be taken to such an act of Favouritism. Of course if favour is shown to a completely underserving person, or clearly against applicable rules or repeatedly to the same individual or his relatives, then in the circumstances of the case a presumption may be raised that the rightful claims and rights of the other citizens were injured for the wrongful gain of a favourite and so it amounted to 'Misconduct'."

Notwithstanding the reservations made, the above definition of the concept, 'Nursing the Constituency' does nothing except justifying a particular type of favouritism although within limits and must therefore be rejected. (It goes to the credit of Justice Mulla that in the particular cases before him he did not stick to his own definition and examined them from a very strict and correct viewpoint before exonerating the Ministers).

To say that a political party cannot grow and increase its influence without showing favouritism to its supporters (in the nature of appointments etc), is to slander the people besides being wrong. It is wrong even from the viewpoint of winning elections. An act of favouritism may or may not win some permanent supporters but is bound to antagonize some potential supporters and even some existing supporters.

To indulge in the types of wrong practices mentioned above, is wrong for any individual and any political party. It is much more so in the case of a party, which claims to be a revolutionary party.

The entire activity of a really revolutionary party must aim at *raising* the political consciousness of the people; at strengthening the mass movement at preparing the people to fight for a classless society free from all injustices and violence for a new man. Obviously the type of wrong practices mentioned above go directly against these aims and cannot but harm the real objectives of a revolutionary party. Such practices will also result in the revolutionary party more and more losing its revolutionary character.

The question arises: What the legislators belonging to revolutionary parties should do to nurse their constituencies. Here are some ideas based on my personal experience as a legislator.

First, besides fearlessly voicing the interests, just grievances etc, of the common people and fighting for policies which would serve their interests, a revolutionary legislator must himself participate in the mass movement outside and help in building and strengthening the same. And in this, he must act as a disciplined soldier of his party. He must belong to some or the other organization of his party and must function as such. Also he should report to his voters about the proceedings in the legislature and his work there.

Secondly, a revolutionary legislator should safeguard the interests of his constituency and should try to ensure that it gets due share in such developmental works as metalling of link roads, opening of new schools, upgrading of schools, etc. However, he should not do this in a manner as will go against the interests of backward areas and constituencies. While fighting for justice and due share for his own constituency, he must also champion the cause of backward areas and constituencies deserving special attention and share of development works.

Thirdly, a very large number of victims of injustices, oppression and high-handedness seek help from revolutionary legislators. In the name of being a revolutionary, one cannot say 'no' to such cases. They have to be and should be helped. Three cautions, however, are very necessary:

(a) Sometimes unscrupulous persons falsely but cleverly pretend to have been victims of some gross injustice etc, while in reality what they are really aiming at is to perpetrate some injustice. Often it is not possible to form a definite opinion about justness or otherwise of the cause represented without knowing the version and viewpoint of some other party. Revolutionary legislators therefore should to the maximum possible extent, function even in such matters in cooperation with party organizations.

(b) The number of individual cases of injustice etc, tend to be so large as to absorb one's entire time. That should not be permitted, as without a strong mass movement, the capacity of even a most effective legislator to help in such cases will be limited. A revolutionary legislator must therefore invariably and always devote sufficient time for mass work and activities connected with the mass movement.

(c) Individual cases of injustice should be helped in a manner as will not make this help a substitute for mass activity around such injustice but wherever practicable and possible, such help should assist in organizing mass activity and mass action and should be coordinated with the same.

Fourthly, a revolutionary legislator must live a simple life. His way of living and working must not be such as to cut him off from the common people. There must be no gap between what he says and what he does. He must not seek undue favours for his relations or his supporters. In fact, he should be prepared to make sacrifices in this respect and may even ask his relations to desist from getting certain things and facilities which they may deserve but which may create misunderstanding about him and his party. In the matter of simple living, many regard the view of Comrade Achhutha Menon, a Chief Minister of Kerala, as 'Gandhian' etc. In my opinion, his views as contained in an article earlier published in *Mainstream,* are really correct and revolutionary and should be seriously studied and followed in actual practice by all revolutionary legislators.

2. The Question Hour

The Question Hour can be one of the most lively, interestng and fruitful part of the proceedings of legislatures. Every day a complete one hour is reserved for the Question Hour and except for obituaries the sessions always begin with this. Starred Questions listed for the day are taken up one by one. The Minister concerned gives the reply. Some supplementaries are then allowed. Generally, and as a matter of tradition, the member whose question has been answered by the Minister is called upon to ask one or two or three supplementaries before any other member can do the same. However, other members have also the right to ask supplementary questions and often do exercise it. I know of an odd case of a member of Punjab Vidhan Sabha who almost never gave notice of any question himself but would ask the maximum number of supplementaries in relation to questions of other members. Of course, the best and the most effective supplementaries can be asked by one who knows in detail the background and the facts related to the substantive question. Members giving notices of Starred Questions, must therefore equip themselves properly about the question concerned.

The Question Hour serves more than one useful purpose. Through the press the members and also the public get useful information regarding important as well as not so important matters. Secondly, many skeletons in the cupboards of the government can be unearthed and made public. And this can help considerably in fighting corruption, nepotism, favouritism, etc. Thirdly, it can help to pressurize the government to expedite specific development works, enquiries etc, on the basis of assurances given in the House in replies to supplementaries. In other words, the Question Hour helps to ensure accountability on the part of the government to give some real substance to parliamentary democracy.

I was a member of the Punjab Vidhan Sabha for a stretch of 11-12 years without break except when the Assembly stood dissolved. I remember that except perhaps for the day on which the Budget was presented, Visitors' Galleries used to be most crowded during the Question Hour. And many among those who watched the proceedings from the Visitors' Galleries would discuss, compare and comment upon the performance of Ministers and those who had asked questions and/or supplementaries. Thanks to the hard work and mutual cooperation, the CPI members often put many Ministers in very awkward and embarrassing position. We used to enjoy this and also the fact that Chief Ministers had to come to their help. Ministers who did not do their homework properly used to be mostly in trouble. And in every Vidhan Sabha there used to be many such erring Ministers.

Not infrequently did the government request the Speaker to dispense with the Question Hour, and the Opposition would invariably oppose that call. During the last few years the roles have been reversed in this respect and this is especially true of Parliament. It is the Opposition which requests—and much too often—for dispensing with the Question Hour. I for one have not been able to appreciate this move. In my opinion this demand only helps the government on the whole. The Opposition parties should do some serious rethinking about this. It would be quite relevant to point out here that it may prove impossible to make a Minister reply to a point made in a speech. However, it is not easy for a Minister to escape a point made through a Starred Question or a supplementary.

Members have to give notices of questions as per the rules of their legislatures. Often questions are disallowed by the Speaker. Many a time the grounds given for such a step are quite valid. New members should take the help of members with experience and/or the secretariat of the legislature. There are also pitfalls which members should avoid in connection with giving notices of questions. Let me give an instance from my own experience. I had given notice of a question on the request of some government employees. It was admitted. Some days before the question was listed, some other employees of the same department came to me and told me that the facts on which the question had been framed were incorrect and the real purpose was to blackmail an officer. I got the matter enquired into with the help of a leader of the employees in whom I had considerable faith. I came to the conclusion that I had really been duped. I resolved not to give notice of any question at the instance of any lobby or individual, not known to me without verifying the facts first with the help of our comrades. This is necessary all the more now when businessmen and some other sections have developed powerful lobbies for canvassing legislators and to make them act in a manner as will serve their own vested interests. A knowledgeable friend of mine says that there have been some MPs who would give notices of questions at the instance of such lobbies for consideration. However, this matter has another aspect. As a legislator I was able to expose many cases of high level corruption with the help of questions of which I used to give notice on the basis of information given to me by some business and other interests like those who had suffered injustice on account of corruption.

Some very valuable information came to me as a result of thieves falling out. I did make use of all such information taking care that no thief would be able to benefit.

There are some legislators who give notice of only such questions as concern some development works or public services in their respective constituencies or some specific police cases, etc. There are others who ask only such questions as are of considerable interest to the public at large. In the opinion of this writer, every legislator should try to give notice of both these types of questions.

Many legislators do not ask any Unstarred Question just because replies to these are not given in the House. In case of Unstarred Questions members giving notices get only written replies. Such outlook on the part of many legislators is wrong. Much useful information can and should be obtained with the help of Unstarred

Questions. Journalists in the Press Gallery too get these replies. Hard working and intelligent ones amongst them study these carefully and publicise newsworthy information and the public too thereby gains.

We have referred to powerful lobbies of vested interests or organized sections of middle classes for canvassing legislators. Generally speaking trade unions of industrial workers (especially of unorganized sectors of the industry), of agricultural workers and even of women hardly pay any attention to making use of legislatures. Their problems get raised only if a legislature has among its members some belonging to these sections—more effectively if such members are in the Opposition benches. That however, is not always the case. Two things are, therefore, necessary if the poor sections are to figure adequately in the legislatures and if their problems are to be focused effectively through the Question Hour. First, their organizations should pay proper attention to the task of briefing sympathetic legislators. Secondly, legislators must keep close contact with these sections and their organizations and make it a point to give notices of questions which would help. The public also needs to be educated that every question of any type cannot be raised in a legislature at a legislator's sweet will. Effective parliamentary work can certainly help the fight for justice outside but cannot be a substitute for the same. The widespread tendency to rely on legislators, that is, on political intervention for everything, big or small, needs to be countered. If that is not done, it will result in weakening the mass organizations and in the long run eroding the efficacy of even the competent parliamentarians.

We have mentioned above that often questions are disallowed by the Speaker for valid reasons and as per rules. Equally not infrequently are questions disallowed for totally wrong and unjustified reasons and without quoting any rule to justify the same. The frequency of such wrong rejections has been showing an upward trend of late. The main reason for this is that really impartial Speakers are becoming a rare phenomenon. Many are blatantly partial. More others have a soft corner for their own (ruling) party/parties and are keen to save them as much embarrassment as possible. And for this, they not only bend but even violate rules. Let me give some examples relating to the Punjab Assembly.

(a) In Mohali Punjab near Chandigarh, there is a Thapar concern called 'JCT Electronic Ltd. Mohali'. Some top brass of the concern had got printed bogus letterheads of a terrorist organization. These would issue to unions, serious threats to force them to withdraw notices of demands. These would also issue to the labour authorities ultimatums forcing them to act as per the wishes of the management. This became a scandal. The Ropar SSP registered a case against more than one officer under the TADA. The case was withdrawn by the government. No district authority can withdraw a case under the TADA after it has been registered.

The leader of the CPI group gave notice of a Starred Question which was rejected on the ground that it related to an individual. The CPI leader pointed out that it related to the action of the government; that it was a matter of great public importance and also there were more than one accused. The Speaker, however, stuck to his guns and did not admit the question. This was in 1992.

(b) The Principal of a Government Dental College had misappropriated a huge sum in connection with the purchase of dental chairs. The Minister announced with fanfare that he had discovered the scandal and had ordered a charge-sheet against the Principal and an enquiry. A Starred Question of a CPI MLA regarding this matter was disallowed on the ground that "it is a matter of ordinary administration of the department" (sic). This was long ago. No one till date has heard about the result of the enquiry. Every reader can draw his/her own conclusion.

(c) Gurbachan Singh Manochahal, leader of a notorious terrorist outfit of Punjab, was killed in an encounter at the beginning of 1992. The notice of a Starred Question was given by a CPI MLA seeking information whether a diary of his was recovered by the police and, if so, whether it contained the names of any parties and organizations which were being given financial help by him. The question was disallowed on some untenable ground (relevant papers misplaced). The MLA concerned personally discussed the matter with a responsible and concerned officer of the Vidhan Sabha Secretariat. The question was amended as suggested and was resubmitted. It has been disallowed again on the ground that: "The member is giving information instead of seeking one, and it is hypothetical". This order was communicated on December 22, 1993. Both the objections are blatantly and clearly wrong. Members can speculate about the real reason. There was once a lot of speculation that Manochahal (when alive) was a frequent visitor to the bungalow of a Home Minister of the Government of India. I for one don't want to indulge in any speculation. I prefer to believe in the dictum that a Speaker like the king can do no wrong.

(d) There is a government primary school in Jalandhar which has teachers but hardly any pupils. Someone with conscience in the government ordered its shifting to another area (Jalandhar Cantonment). Someone with some vested interest against the shifting and having powerful connections saw to it that the order was not implemented. A Starred Question was rejected on the fantastic and totally false ground that the matter concerned a local authority, but actually because someone in the concerned department did not want the issue to figure in the Vidhan Sabha. With no argument for justifying the order, an officer of the Vidhan Sabha advised that a fresh question be given notice of. This was done. The question was rejected again in October 1993 on ground the it was "partially covered by the question already disallowed during the Budget session, 1993."

Can anyone beat this? (The question was subsequently admitted in December 1993).

(e) In an ESI hospital in Amritsar, construction began for sewerage disposal for a large part of Amritsar. This created a furore among the relatives of patients and potential patients. The trade unions lodged strong protests.

A CPI MLA gave notice of a Starred Question about it. The question referred to a representation made to the Minister and sought information about the action taken. Obviously, if the question were to be admitted, the government would be on the mat when it would come up. The question was disallowed on the ground that "complaints made to a Minister cannot be the basis of an Assembly question". No rule was quoted in support of this contention. In the past any number of questions have been admitted on the basis of complaints/representations, etc, made to the Ministers/government.

Incidentally, the ESI Corporation moved the court which stayed the construction.

(f) Two Starred Questions of CPI MLAs seeking information about persons appointed as Excise and Taxation Officers and as Executive Officers of Notified Area Committee—including their names, names of fathers—and also about the procedure adopted for their appointments have been disallowed. The ground given in each of the two cases was that the matter being *sub judice*. When this ground was given all the appointments had been challenged in the High Court on the plea that these had been made in violation of the rules to appoint relatives of Ministers and officers. One can justify a particular supplementary being disallowed, but the disallowing of the questions themselves cannot be justified on the ground of the matter being *sub judice*. The information sought for, if given, was likely to expose nepotism. Soon after, in the case relating to the EOs, the High Court set aside all the appointments.

More examples can be given but that is not necessary. It would be useful to mention other reasons which are usually given to disallow inconvenient questions. These are: the question is 'vague and imprecise'; 'is of excessive length'; 'relates to internal working of a corporation which is an autonomous body' (even though it may be a 100 per cent government body); 'administrative matter cannot form the basis of a question'; 'other legal remedies are available' (this plea can be put forward in relation to almost every question), etc.

There are methods by using which some Speakers try to help the government to avoid inconvenient questions even after they have been admitted.

For instance, the Speaker may grant extension without valid reasons and may not even order that the question came up before the end of the session. And after the session, the question is converted into an Unstarred one. And for long the member who had given notice of the question does not get any written reply. Often the reason given is that the department has not supplied the reply.

I know of cases in which the Speaker allowed a large number of supplementaries arising out of some unimportant questions only to ensure that the Question Hour is over before the turn of an inconvenient question comes. As if watched by the whip of the ruling party, even those of its members ask supplementary questions who usually don't open their mouths. And the Speaker becomes unusually 'generous'.

Every Minister often asserts that the supplementary does not arise out of the main question. The Minister may be right. However, on several occasions, this is only an excuse to withhold some inconvenient information. A really impartial Speaker will force the Minister to reply. An obliging or subservient one will uphold the Minister's objection even when it is clearly wrong.

These don't exhaust all the tricks of the trade. Three important lessons need to be drawn.

One, ways and means must be found to ensure that the Speakers are really impartial. It is not an easy job given the rapid degeneration of moral values. The question, however, is urgent and important. Pushing it under the carpet will be quite dangerous not only in relation to the Question Hour but for the very system of parliamentary democracy.

Secondly, a legislator must not only know how to speak well but must be a good fighter who is polite, reasonable, knows his facts and the rules and can be firm.

Thirdly, where necessary steps should be taken to get the relevant rules amended, the ones which are not satisfactory. In this connection the experience of the CPI group in the Punjab Assembly has not been happy. A number of suggestions were sent by the CPI group for amendments. Hardev Arshi of the party and a member of Rules Committee for the year 1992-93 repeatedly requested for holding a meeting of the Committee. Not a single meeting was held. For the year 1993-94, the Rules Committee had not even been constituted despite reminders by the CPI group leader. This again emphasizes the need for having really impartial Speakers.

3. Mr. Speaker

It does not have to be argued that in the working of the parliamentary institutions, the Speaker occupies a very crucial position. The way the Speaker acts and exercises his authority can make all the difference to the functioning of the House over which he presides. Let us go back to some of the most renowned Speakers in India to have an idea of the qualities which a Speaker should possess.

Vithalbhai Patel was the first Indian and the first elected Speaker (then called President) of the Central Legislative Assembly. He had defeated his rival candidate by a majority of two. The rival candidate had the backing of the then (British) government of India. Patel believed that as Speaker he must observe complete impartiality. He emphasized that 'he was responsible to the Assembly and no other authority'. He asserted 'complete independence of the Chair from the influence of the executive'. Immediately after his election he severed his ties with the party to which he had belonged. He stressed that he was no longer a partyman and requested the leader of his former party to absolve him from all party obligations. He held the view that he must not let his 'conduct be influenced by any political party or by his own personal sympathies'. On the basis of this principle that he upheld, he went to the extent of refusing to resign his office when the Congress asked him to do so. At the next general elections he contested as an Independent candidate and was returned unopposed.

G.V. Mavalankar was the first Speaker of the Lok Sabha. He had been elected by a margin of three votes. He too was regarded as completely impartial. Even though he did not resign from the Congress, he stressed that a Speaker should not attend party meetings or participate publicly in the discussion of controversial issues. His successor, Ananthasayanam Ayyanagar, too did not quit the Congress party but he did resign from the Congress Parliamentary Party. Mavalankar, Ayyanagar and Hukam Singh all supported the principle of resigning from the party provided there was a convention that the Speaker's seat would not be contested. Even though no such convention had developed, Lok Sabha Speaker Dr Sanjiva Reddy who held office from 1967 to 1969 resigned from the Congress to which he had belonged for 34 years. Speaker Reddy expressed the categorical view that:

> "Speakers had an obligation to resign from their parties after their election to the Chair, even without a guarantee of electoral protection". It was out of the need of the Speaker being impartial that the idea arose that the government should consult the Opposition before deciding his nominee for Speakership. If one were to sum up the qualities of a Speaker, one would say: "He should be intelligent with adequate experience and tact and, above all, completely impartial with no desire to become the Prime Minister, a Chief Minister or even a Minister."

If we really had such Speakers, vast powers conferred on them to disqualify members under the amendment to the Constitution of India (popularly known as Anti-Defection Law) would be fully justified. Unfortunately, we no longer have Speakers of the right type and this power has been and is being misused by Speakers to save the office of Chief Ministers of their parties, their own office and even to become Chief Ministers themselves. Often the powers are misused to increase the majority of the ruling party and to weaken the Opposition. The most scandalous behaviour of some Speakers is so recent that it is not necessary to recount any example to substantiate the contention.

Even in relation to the functioning of the House, Speakers these days are generally highly partial and that is one of the important reasons for disorderly scenes in the Assemblies.

Let me illustrate on the basis of my observations of the functioning of the Punjab Vidhan Sabha which was elected in February 1992.

Question Hour is a very important part of the work of the Assembly and in a way most interesting and also instructive. It is during the Question Hour that often very important information is elicited, many scandals are exposed; some grievances of the people are brought into focus and sought to be removed and very often Ministers are put on the mat. A Speaker who is not really impartial misuses his position to help the government in more than one way. Not a few very important but inconvenient questions from the standpoint of the government are disallowed by the Speaker on one pretext or another and even on the ground that the question deals with a delicate matter. Sometimes, when a very inconvenient question is listed and the government does not want it to come up, the Speaker goes on allowing too many supplementaries on preceding questions so that the Question Hour is over before that inconvenient question figures in the course of the proceedings. If its turn does come, the Speaker readily accepts the request of the government for extension of time to furnish a full reply. Here it should be explained that no question can be admitted without 15 days notice, which period is considered necessary for the government to get all the information even from the districts. However, in case of inconvenient or embarrassing questions, not unoften extension is granted even when all the required information is available in the Secretariat itself. Also, there is no insistence from the Chair that the reply must be given during the session itself, leave aside a directive fixing the day during the session on which the reply must be given. One could give many examples but I would present only two.

During the 1994 Budget session of Punjab Vidhan Sabha there were two Starred Questions relating to the Chief Minister's Flood Relief Fund to which more than Rs. 10 crores had been contributed. The fund was started immediately after the July 1993 floods. Only a few lakhs were used for flood relief. Highly objectionable rules which enable the Chief Minister to use the fund for other purposes and which are silent on some very crucial matters were framed. One Question was by two CPI MLAs and another by a dissident Congress-I MLA. Extension was asked for both, in one case twice. Both came up finally on the last day of the session on April 4, 1995. Again extension was sought and granted despite strong protests. All the information asked for in the two questions was available in the Punjab Government Secretariat itself. There was no pulling up of the Minister concerned. The opportunity of supplementaries was, of course, thus negated. At least in the case of the CPI members, even a written reply has not been received till to day despite repeated reminders. In the case of another very inconvenient Starred Question which would have exposed scandalous irregularities in hospitals attached to the Government Medical College, Amritsar, something similar happened. The question did not come up during the Question Hour. Ultimately, it got converted into an Unstarred Question. It took almost one year for the CPI member who had asked the question and dozens of reminders to get a written reply which hides more than it informs.

The two examples given above raise another important issue, that is, relating to the privileges of legislators. In India, following the example of the House of Commons, these privileges have not been codified. It is the Speaker who decides whether a question of privilege is involved whenever a notice of any Privilege Motion is given. When information sought by a member is deliberately withheld by a Minister to avoid being embarrassed as in the above two cases is it or is it not a breach of privilege of a member?

After all, the right of citizens to get information (except that which endangers national security) is one of the most essential ingredients of a genuine democracy. It applies with greater force to the right of the legislators to get information. When the same is deliberately denied, it should surely be considered as breach of privilege of the members. In connection with a number of experiences like those cited above, CPI members gave notices of breach of privilege against the Ministers. Every time the Speaker ruled:

> "No question of privilege is involved. However, the Minister concerned is being requested (again) to send his reply without further delay."

Initially, this helped to get replies. However, that is no longer the position now. In the opinion of this writer, the issue involved deserves to be discussed in a conference of Speakers. Incidentally, the Chief Minister of Punjab could boast that till then not a single motion of breach of privilege has been admitted in the State Assembly during the three and a half years against any Minister or officer. Many are of the view that this fact does not do any credit to the Speaker. Let me give one example. A police officer had misbehaved with one MLA when he was performing his duty of helping some people. A notice of breach of privilege was given. After obtaining a report from the police department itself, the Speaker ruled it out though there were weighty reasons for its admission.

Notices of Call Attention Motions are one of the means by which members—whether belonging to the Treasury Benches or the Opposition—can raise matters of urgent public importance in the House. Rules of Procedure and Conduct of Business of the Punjab Vidhan Sabha provide that the Speaker can allow not more than three matters to be raised in a day by such motions. No motion may be signed by more than three members and a 48-hour notice is necessary for its admission. The Minister concerned has to reply to such a motion as is admitted by the Speaker. Each signing member can ask one question but no debate is permitted.

Any good Speaker should interpret these rules liberally as that would be in the public interest. It would also help in avoiding disorderly scenes. However, the tendency on the part of the Speaker(s) has been to admit as few Call Attention Motions as possible. During the Budget Sessions one of the reasons given for rejection is that the matter can be raised during the general discussion on the Governor's Address or on the Budget. This reason cannot be accepted as valid because neither the Chief Minister nor the Finance Minister nor for that matter any other Minister is bound to reply to various points in their speeches. And more often than not even very important points are not replied to. Of course, other untenable reasons too are often given for rejecting Call Attention Motions.

For many years there was a convention that every Call Attention Motion given notice of, would be sent to the concerned department. Often that helped to some extent even if later on it was disallowed by the Speaker.

An adjournment motion to discuss a definite matter of urgent public importance requires a notice of two hours before the commencement of the sitting. The general practice has been to reject all such motions and this rejection often leads to walkouts.

Every Thursday is the non-official day in the Punjab Vidhan Sabha. Generally, there are non-official days only during the Budget Session because the Beant Singh Government followed the practice of not having any other session for more than two to three days. While non-official resolutions have been admitted and discussed during the Budget session, not a single non-official bill was discussed in any of the four Budget Sessions of the Punjab Assembly. Two non-official bills prepared with much labour were given notice of by CPI MLAs for the 1994 Budget session. One related to minimum wages. It did not involve any extra expenditure. And yet the Speaker disallowed it on the ground that it was a Money Bill and prior permission of the Governor had not been taken. The other sought to amend the Hindu Succession Act in relation to Punjab. Similar amending acts had been passed by at least three other States. Even though this fact was brought to the notice of the Speaker, the Bill was disallowed with the totally untenable and extraordinary argument that it would be better if steps were taken to get the Hindu Succession Act amended by Parliament.

Legislation is supposed to be one of the most important functions of the Assembly. The government has been following the practice of using its majority to pass even very important and lengthy bills without adequate discussion. Seldom do the few members who are keen to study the bills before they are moved get time to do so. The Speakers have been obliging the government by dispensing with the required 15 days notice.

The House has a number of committees—one of them is the Rules Committee which can recommend to the House changes in the

Rules of Procedure and Conduct of Business of the Punjab Vidhan Sabha. The Committee is nominated by the Speaker. The present rules do need important changes.

Late Ajnala did nominate the Rules Committee for the year 1992-93. Some concrete proposals for changes were submitted by the leader of the CPI Group. Despite repeated requests, no meeting of the Rules Committee was called by the Speaker in his capacity as its *ex-officio* Chairman. The new Speaker adopted the practice of not constituting the committee at all.

We will now like to refer to the controversy regarding the Zero Hour. No doubt the rules don't provide for it but for years it has been there. Immediately after Question Hour and before other business of the House starts, members raise at this Zero Hour some matters of great public importance. The Minister may or may not respond. The Beant Singh Government was keen to dispense with the Zero Hour. Ajnala ruled that rules did not provide for Zero Hour but he would allow issues to be raised under the garb of points of order. Of course, after they were raised, he would give the ruling: "It is no point of order". Speaker Harnam Dass Johar, during the 1994 Budget session went one step ahead and ruled: "If a point of order is held to be no point of order then the press would not report even its subject matter."

This ruling was violative of the rules and was also an attempt to do away with the Zero Hour. A very determined Opposition was able to force the government to relent on this issue and the Speaker had to beat a retreat. Incidentally, one of the suggestions made by the CPI leader for amending the rules was that the Zero Hour should be formalized.

How far away have we travelled from the ideas of Vithalbhai Patel, Mavalankar and Reddy—at least with regard to Speakers of the State Vidhan Sabha—would be clear from the following instances from Punjab.

The Speaker, Harnam Das Johar, held a gala dinner at official expense to celebrate the completion of two years of Beant Singh

Government and its achievements. Many eyebrows were raised and a number of Opposition MLAs did not join to record their protest. A clever device was thought of when the government completed three years. Now the function was to celebrate the completion of three years of the Punjab Vidhan Sabha, something which had never been done before. The object, of course, was to eulogise the Chief Minister.

Indian Express (Chandigarh edition) of February 27, 1995 carried the followed news: The Vidhan Sabha Speaker, Mr Harnam Dass Johar, expressed the wish that Mr Beant Singh stays in power for 15 years more so as to consolidate the gains of development set in motion by him.

This was at a State-level cultural rally at Ludhiana organised to mark the completion of the week-long celebrations of his government's three years in office. Nor is this all.

The above quoted report continued: Mr Joha went to the extent of asserting that he would never allow Opposition MLAs to disturb order in the Assembly. This speech was reported in many other papers too. And this was on the eve of the 1995 Budget session of the Assembly which began on February 28, 1995. Leaders of all the Opposition groups in the Punjab Vidhan Sabha took strong umbrage at such pronouncements. They met the Speaker and lodged their strong protest. He told them that he had never said any such thing. He assured them that he would issue a contradiction. He never did.

The example set by the Speaker was naturally followed by the Deputy Speaker, Ramesh Dogra, of the Congress-I. Being only a Deputy, he seems to believe that he can surpass the Speaker. Along with a battalion of Punjab Ministers, he too actively canvassed for the Congress party candidate in Gidderbaha constituency. On May 15, 1995, he attended the election meeting of the Chief Minister at village Bhalawna and joined party workers in house-to-house convassing. He also briefed newsmen about the huge gathering in the election meeting and the party's position in that meeting. (*Indian Express*, May 28, 1995).

It is time that someone like the Speaker of the Lok Sabha or the Chairman of the Rajya Sabha takes effective steps to restore the dignity of the office of the Speaker of the State Vidhan Sabhas. In the meanwhile it is to be hoped that they too will not be afflicted with the same disease.

4. Random Thoughts of a Former Minister

It was in 1957 that I first contested elections to the Punjab Legislative Assembly. The constituency was different from the one from which I had won for the first time in 1967. It included some working class areas like Haripura but did not include such strongholds of CPI, as Chheharta and the neighbouring villages. On the other hand it included many parts of Amritsar in which we had no base whatsoever. The Amritsar City Committee of the CPI was quite clear that there was absolutely no question of winning the seat. In fact, it would be a great thing if we could manage to save our security deposit.

Why then was it decided to contest the seat? The main consideration was that the Communist Party could neither support the Congress nor the Jan Sangh and if there was no candidate of our own, our supporters would get divided between the bourgeois Congress and the communal Jan Sangh. It was felt that such a position would weaken our base even in the working class areas in the constituency.

In 1962, the constituency was the same as in 1957. For the same reasons, it was decided again to contest from it. Both times, it was decided to put me up as the Party candidate. I naturally agreed as a disciplined member of the Party. Some experiences of these two elections need to be re-called.

During the course of the election campaign, our base would be much more vocal and active. Processions and rallies organized by the Party would be joined in by our supporters from the neighbouring areas too. Even in localities in which we had no base at all, large number would come to attend our public meetings and would listen to us. All this would create an illusion in the minds of many comrades including even many leading ones that we had good chances to win.

Actually results used to disillusion and even disappoint very much our comrades. The actual results both times more or less justified the assessment made at the beginning by the City Committee of the Party. The results both times proved that the common people were quite wise and knew between whom the real contest lay. Some of our supporters too would not vote for us because they thought they would only be 'wasting' their votes. Knowing that CPI could not win, some of our supporters would decide to vote for the 'lesser evil' between the real contestants. Of course, there were many who were our supporters not on political level but on the trade union level. They would not vote for us in any case.

The experience of not only these two elections but of all the subsequent elections too would make clear that a system of elections based on proportional representations would reflect the will of the people more truly and more correctly.

A question that got posed was whether we should permit bogus voting by letting some over-zealous comrades and supporters impersonate for voters who had died or who were not present on the day of voting. Jan Sangh was quite an expert at the job and the Congress too had no qualms of conscience on this account. Notwithstanding this, our party in Amritsar took a firm decision in these and subsequent Assembly elections fought by it against this malpractice. It needs however, to be admitted that we could never prevent it fully, but in our case the malpractice would be indulged in on a smaller scale than by our bourgeois opponents. In the case of the bourgeois parties, I am sure that no effort whatsoever is made to check it. In fact, more often than not, it is encouraged.

It has been my opinion since long that the introduction of proper identity card is essential to eliminate or to reduce to the maximum possible extent quite a few of the malpractices which have come to prevail on quite a big scale.

The main argument of the Government of India against the introduction of the identity card system throughout India was the big expenditure that it involve. The argument overlooked many other benefits that would accrue from such a system. For instance, it can help remove to a considerable extent some of the malpractices in the Public Distribution System. It can also help to decrease the misuse of hotels by anti-social elements, etc.

Another question that arose related to transporting of voters to polling booths. Law prohibits voters being provided transport by the candidates and political parties. The bourgeois parties flout this law on a very big scale. They hire taxis, scooter-rickshaws and cycle-rickshaws. We decided against it. We would appeal to the voters to walk the distance. In the beginning we got good response from our voters. The truth, however, is that with every subsequent election, it began to be felt more and more that we too must make arrangements for transport and this was done too—though on a much smaller scale than would be done by bourgeois parties. We have generally not gone beyond cycle-rickshaws—and only sometimes some scooter-rickshaws.

The law banning the providing of transport is nowhere observed. Should it then be repealed? Our opinion is that conditions should be created to enforce it. For that two things are necessary. The number of polling booths should be increased further. Their location should be fixed more carefully and rationally. Secondly, on the day of polling, all transport except the specifically exempted and those having special symbols for identification should be banned.

An important test faced the Communist Party in Amritsar during the first two elections. There were feelers from the Jan Sangh that they would leave the constituency to be contested by us and would support us against the Congress if we agreed to support them in other constituencies of Amritsar in which CPI had no candidate of its own. It is a matter of pride that our party in Amritsar rebuffed the feelers with the contempt they deserved. There was no vacillation or faltering whatsoever. In fact, it would not be wrong if I say that our party in Amritsar has not compromised in any elections or on any principle for the sake of winning the seat. One wishes that this could be said of the two Communist Parties as a whole.

Before 1967 elections came, the Assembly constituencies in Punjab had been re-constituted. From the Amritsar (West) Constituency, many (though not all) of our weak areas got excluded. And some of our strong areas got included. The latter included Chheharta and villages like Ghanupur. Our comrades were jubilant. But the Congress was unhappy. Congress and CPI would obviously be the real contenders with Jan Sangh and the Akali party trailing far behind the two. The Congress began efforts to bring about changes in the proposed Amritsar West Constituency. Our party in Amritsar decided to make every possible effort to ensure that the proposed constituency remained finally as it was. Our case was fairly strong on merits. The Party succeeded in this. Mention must be made of two political figures who helped us considerably. One was Justice Gurnam Singh of the Akali Party. The other was Pandit Amar Nath Vidyalankar, a Congress leader and a very prominent figure in INTUC. Our appeal to him was very simple. We argued that the constituency as proposed would help a trade unionist to go to the Assembly and therefore in the interest of the working class he should help to ensure that the proposal was not amended (as was being sought to be managed to increase the chances of the Congress party). He said that he would help us to the maximum possible extent. I must say that he amply kept his promise. I do not think one can find such a broadminded Congressman in the Congress-I of today.

We got enrolled a fairly good number of genuine eligible voters who had not been included in the first instance. The Congress too put in a very large number of applications of new voters—many not residing in the constituency and a large number of Armymen posted in the constituency but not eligible for being enrolled. We filed as many objections as we could. Many of our very correct objections were rejected and there were many from outside the constituency in the final list. The Returning Officer was hell-bent on enrolling as voters the clearly non-eligible militarymen referred to above. After all, it had already been announced that the Congress candidate from the constituency would be the then Chief Minister. Only a thinly veiled threat of going to the High Court made him change his mind and act legally. It may also be mentioned that many included in the final list from villages outside the constituency who came to vote for the Congress candidate were successfully persuaded by our comrades and volunteers not to. This was done by frightening them with legal consequences and telling them that they were likely to be prosecuted for impersonation.

As was the wont even then, the Congress misused its ruling position to a very great extent. For instance, any shopkeeper had only to ask to become a depot holder if he promised to support the Congress. The road of the main bazaar in Chheharta was metalled within days without caring for and even violating many statutory obligations. Any number of more instances of the type could be given. But nothing helped.

The Chief Minister was defeated by a big margin. This, however, gave us an exaggerated idea of our strength. Actually, in the constituency, Congress and CPI are almost equally strong. What made a big margin possible was the anti-Congress wave in North India in 1967 and also the Communist Party's electoral agreement with the Akali Party led by Sant Fateh Singh. Landlords, and a section of rich peasants did not vote for CPI—even the pro-Akali ones—despite this alliance but majority of Akali voters did. Hardcore of the Jan Sangh too did not vote for us despite the anti-Congress wave.

Neither the Akali led United Front nor the Congress got an absolute majority. The Front was able to win over some Independants and thus got a razor thin majority in the Assembly. There were serious differences inside the Akali Party as to who should be the leader of its Assembly Party and hence the Chief Minister of the first non-Congress Government in Punjab and the first Chief Minister of Punjab reorganised on linguistic basis with Haryana having become a separate state and some areas of the erstwhile Indian Punjab having gone to Himachal. All the non-Akali constituents of the United Front favoured Justice Gurnam Singh and that did help him to become the Chief Minister. CPI-M decided to keep out of the Ministry but to support it from outside. Harkishan Singh Surjeet was made the convenor of the Coordination Committee of the Front. The Committee was to guide the Government in all policy matters.

There were differences inside the leading decision-making body of CPI in Punjab. Some of us were against joining the Government. By majority it was decided to join it. There were differences also as to who should be the one Cabinet-rank Minister in the Government. I and some other comrades favoured Comrade Teja Singh Swatantar who was a veteran leader of the Party and an experienced legislator. The main argument against him was that he was a member of the Upper House and since the Party stood for the abolition of the Upper House, the Party's Minister should be from the Assembly. That is how the majority decided that I should be in the Cabinet, even though I had no prior experience of any parliamentary work whatsoever. In the Cabinet, that was my weakness. Our strength lay in the fact that the Government was also dependant on our group in the Assembly even though it was a small one.

I joined the Cabinet only in April 1967 even though the United Front Government had assumed office in February. Electoral agreement with the Akali Party had been on the basis of some sort of an agreed programme. Before the Government took power a programme for it was agreed upon. The Government fell in October 1967.

The experience of being in this Government though quite short was interesting. Some aspects of this experience deserve to be recalled.

Before the election, both the Communist Parties had been demanding state-wise food zones. For various compelling reasons, the Government of India adopted this policy. Food and Supplies Department had been entrusted to me. A major policy question which confronted the new Government was fixation of procurement price for the new wheat coming into the market. There was total agreement that the price must be remunerative but there were differences as to what would be the remunerative price. Some Ministers coming from landlord families put forward formulas which were wrong on the face of it. For instance, one such formula provided depreciation of tractors, etc for calculating the cost of wheat only at a rate admissible for the full year. There were similar other clever devices to justify the demand for a profiteering price instead of a remunerative price. After much discussion an agreement more or less on an ad hoc basis was arrived at. It was about Rs. 22 per quintal higher than the price at which peasants had been forced to sell their wheat previous year.

Peasants now were more than satisfied with the new price. What was necessary now was to ensure that they actually got it and that the big traders were not able to corner the crop. The only way to ensure this was to make certain that the State agencies themselves purchased most of the marketed surplus. This was done successfully. Peasants were happy. Consumers had to pay more for a month or so than they had to in the previous year. However, when the price of wheat and atta even in retail was not allowed to shoot up as it had done the previous year, and when in fact it remained at a more or less much lower level throughout, they too felt happy and satisfied. The big traders who had purchased some in the hope that prices would shoot up this year had to suffer losses.

It was not smooth sailing all along. The Congress Government of Himachal Pradesh demanded that their traders be allowed to make purchase from markets in Punjab. This was firmly refused. A virulent propaganda was started in Himachal against CPI. It was propagated that CPI was out to starve the people of Himachal. CPI leaders from Himachal came to discuss the matter. They were informed that the Government of Himachal had been offered as much wheat as it wanted on State-to-State basis but it would not entertain the idea on the untenable ground that it was not in a position to build up a public distribution system. They were told of another decision. We had allowed every Himachali residing and working in Punjab to purchase and send two quintals each for his family in Himachal. The District authorities were told to ensure smooth and quick implementation of the decision. By and large this was done. The number of beneficiaries was very large indeed. Himachal Pradesh comrades were satisfied, agreed with our viewpoint and were able to meet the propaganda offensive against CPI in Himachal.

One Jan Sangh Minister wanted that the flour mills in Punjab be allowed to sell at least resultant atta to private traders of Himachal.

This was not agreed to as it would have turned out to be the thin end of the wedge for large-scale smuggling of wheat. All efforts to buy wheat from markets on private accounts also failed.

An Akali leader (not a Minister) and a big landlord wanted that he be allowed to take out of Punjab a big quantity of his wheat as he was residing outside the State while his agricultural land was in Punjab. A policy decision was taken that all such persons would be allowed to take out only two quintals in each case for consumption by their families. The policy was correct but the Akali leader was far from satisfied.

This policy decision had an interesting fallout. An elder brother of mine with his family residing in UP had land in Punjab. He too had obtained a permit to take to UP two quintalsof wheat out of his produce in Punjab. Our comrades as well as an IAS Officer brought to my notice that the Jan Sangh leaders were propagating that my brother had been given a permit for more than 10 quintals. I asked this very officer to immediately seize all records, to go into the matter thoroughly and to report the truth to me without any hesitation and fear. His report was that the permit issued was only for two quintals and only that much had been taken. I took up the matter with Jan Sangh leaders. After they satisfied themselves with the help of some officers in whom they had full trust, they expressed regrets that some of their leaders had done false propaganda and assured me that they would get it stopped.

Another interesting incident. I got information from our comrades that a landlord IAS Officer (not connected with any of my departments) was illegally smuggling his wheat out of Punjab through Chandigarh Union Territory. I asked a top police officer of the rank of the DIG in whose integrity I had full faith to enquire into the allegation. He said: "Sir, the matter will be properly enquired into but I am sure, your information will be proved wrong. I know the officer. He is not of that type". My reply was: "Let us see. I know our comrades who have given me the information". His report vindicated our comrades. I could only complain to the Chief Minister against this landlord IAS Officer which I did. My respect for this upright DIG Police went up still further. I had known of his unshakeable uprightness since long out of his experience with us as trade unionists.

Thanks to the wrong policies of the Government of India, price of sugar in the open market had shot up very much. Quota for the public distribution was not adequate. It was decided to stop all supplies from this quota to cold drink manufacturers, halwais, etc. A particular cold drink manufacturing firm mobilized strong support and the matter was raised in a meeting of the Cabinet. Many wanted sugar to be allotted out of the quota meant for the public distribution system. I remember some circles close to our party too had put in a word for the firm. I remained firm and luckily the Chief Minister supported me. That clinched the matter.

However, I had some problems with the Chief Minister. Once, when I was on tour, he acceded to the request of Food Inspector of Jalandhar district to cancel his transfer which had been ordered by the Director, Food and Supplies and which was fully justified. Before I spoke to the Chief Minister taking exception to his orders, I had found out the reason given to him and that the reason was based on an utter falsehood. The Chief Minister cancelled his order and assured me that thereafter he would leave matters concerning my departments to me.

Labour was not one of my departments. The fact of a trade unionist being in the Cabinet however did encourage the organized workers and make them believe that it was an opportunity to win some of their just demands. In a number of cases, one of the most important demands for linking DA with the cost of living index was conceded even without a strike and in some cases after short duration strikes. In a few cases, the employers adopted an adamant attitude. They had the support of and encouragement from within the Cabinet. One Minister openly but falsely accused workers on strike of one mill, of goondaism when in fact it was the employer who had resorted to goondaism. In another case, strikers were severely lathicharged. I went to the Chief Minister ready to resign. The Chief Minister assured me that instructions would be issued immediately that the police must not interfere as long as workers remained peaceful. In both cases strikes got settled to the satisfaction of the workers.

For reasons of space, I will now briefly give some instances regarding another aspect of being a Minister. The question of correct relationship between the party and the party's Minister in the Government arose in my mind in a big way. The party leadership wanted a particular comrade to be appointed Chairman of an Improvement Trust. I was not against non-officials being appointed Chairmen provided this was done generally on the basis of competence and incorruptibility and irrespective of political affiliations. I also felt that the Government was not going to last and our comrade would not have enough time to prove his worth because he would be removed as soon as the Government fell. I was for accepting the view of the Department to have officials as Chairmen. Party leadership let me have my way. In another case, however, I had to appoint a particular Municipal official as an Executive Officer against my own judgement and in deference to the decision of the concerned party committee.

A very upright officer (IAS) once told me that a particular comrade of ours was making a lot of money misusing my position in the Government. I knew this comrade and told the Officer that he had obviously been misinformed. He got the matter probed and was good enough to inform me that he had really been misinformed. In another case, however he turned out to be right. Some comrades wanted me to transfer a Food Inspector to a place only 8-10 kilometres away from his existing posting, and the plea was that it would be convenient for his family. This was not convincing. The Director Food was requested to check up. He informed me that the official was corrupt and wanted to go to the nearby centre because the post which he wanted would enable him to make money which was not there. I asked the comrades to go deeply into the matter. After some days I was told by them that what the Director had told me was correct. Once a young woman comrade came to me: "I have done something which I now think may not be correct". She had collected some money for the party with the help of some officials of the Food Department. A load was off her chest when she returned the money to the persons who had given it. On one occasion at least I was sharply criticized for not showing proper respect for the leadership of the party.

Something about experience with the bureaucracy. Once an IAS officer in one of my departments had asked me: "Sir, will you prefer an honest but an inefficient officer or a dishonest but efficient officer". I asked him: "Cannot honesty and efficiency go together"? "Rarely", was his short reply. He himself in my opinion did combine both the qualities in his person. His honesty can be judged from the fact that if he would use his official car even for a kilometre for some personal reason, that would be entered as such in the log book and the expenses involved debited to his personal account. I must admit that when I first learnt about it, I felt a little ashamed because I had not been scrupulous to that extent.

In the very first days of Ministry, a top ranking officer came to me with a file to know what notings should be made on that. My reply was: "You recommend in accordance with your own views. I assume that I have a right to over-rule that if I disagree, I would like to have the benefit of your views."

The Secretary of one of my departments had told a leading comrade of ours. "We have seen a number of Ministers who start with some ideas of their own but soon get adjusted to routine and become dependants on the bureaucracy". Later on, this officer had to concede that Communists were of a different type.

An IAS couple was attached to me—each being Secretary of one of my departments. Both were very intelligent. However, they had different ideas of Secretary-Minister relationship. One would argue endlessly in his effort to get his views agreed to by the Minister. The wife would be content with recording her opinion and at best a short discussion with the Minister if she disagreed with the latter's orders.

The Chief Secretary during the entire period of the United Front Ministry was from the I.C.S. steel-frame of the British period. He came from a big landlord family. One thing I remember about him is that one day he ordered all ordinary citizens out of the lift in the Secretariat, which only Ministers and officers are supposed to use but which actually is used by many others. Those ordered out included my wife. Of course, he did not know her identity nor did she tell him.

The upright officer referred to above, met me in my MLAs flat in which I had continued to live during the period of my Ministership, immediately after the Government had resigned, having been reduced to a minority. He asked my views about the bureaucracy. I had replied: "It is not so strong as I had thought it would be."

One of the things I have regretted was sanctioning of discretionary grants to the extent of the provision after it became clear that the Government was going to fall. It was not proper and ethical. Its implementation was stopped by the new Government—I think correctly.

Gurnam Singh had submitted resignation as soon as defection of about 19 legislators led by Lachhman Singh Gill from the Akali Party became known. It was a graceful act on his part. Gill became the new Chief Minister whose Government was supported by the Congress from outside. There was justified widespread public anger against the Congress for engineering the defections. The Akali leadership put the entire blame on the Congress. It is strange that the Akali Party has never seriously considered as to why its members get enticed and why it splits again and again when it gets power.

Next elections came in 1969. Anti-Congress wave was still there. And that helped us to win again with a good margin. An Akali-Jan Sangh Ministry was formed but it too did not last very long.

During the 1972 elections to Punjab Assembly we had an electoral alliance with the Congress in accordance with the All-India line of our party. It was an easy victory, even though many from the rich supporters of the Congress did not vote for us.

Given the balance of forces in the particular constituency and the Congress-CPI alliance once again, we won the seat comfortably even in 1977 notwithstanding the backlash of Emergency. The Akali Ministry was dismissed in 1980 alongwith many others by Indira Gandhi just as many Congress Governments had been dismissed in 1977 by the Government of Morarji Desai in which the Akalis shared power. The Akalis correctly assailed Indira Gandhi for this undemocratic act and even falsely charged that it was motivated by anti-Sikh considerations. But they have always justified the precedent set by Morarji Desai.

I had interesting experiences as a legislator sitting in the Opposition benches. Most interesting perhaps was the fact that a measure proposed by us would be supported by the Akalis (and also the Congress) if they happened to be in Opposition but the same would be strongly opposed when they would happen to be in government. Similarly, whosoever was in power, our group would have plenty of material to expose high-level corruption. Whenever there was a change of Government, we would have the impression that the new government was more corrupt than the earlier one. Treatment meted out to upright officers would be more or less the same. I know of one such IAS officer who got himself shifted to Delhi because of the humiliation he had to suffer at the hands of a junior officer at the instigation of his Minister. His only fault was that he dared tell his Minister that he would put his own views on the file, that the Minister could overrule him and that he would loyally carry out the orders of the Minister. I know of a number of Ministers who would take money even for ordering transfers of officers. Amongst the Akali Ministers, those with the Congress past were most experts in making tons of money.

1980 and 1985 elections to Punjab Assembly were really the two elections fought without any favourable wave. We lost both though with very small margins. Both times there were some adverse factors. The composition of the constituency is such that our electoral alliance with the Akalis in 1980 harmed us in this constituency. In fact the more our leaders asserted that there would be a non-Congress Government which meant an Akali Government, we lost more votes. This happened especially because of the rise of extremism in Punjab during the Akali Ministry and the failure or refusal of the Badal Ministry to provide adequate protection to Nirankaris and to ensure their religious rights.

There have been serious differences in our party in the matter of electoral tactics—in relation to both the Congress and the Akali Party. Life however made the leadership take a unanimous decision in favour of no truck with the Akalis (together with no truck with the Congress) in the 1985 elections. This in fact, was the only election which we fought on our own strength. There was no BJP candidate but the majority of their supporters voted for the Congress. We were able to maintain our base amongst the Sikhs in the main and the Akali candidate's illusion that all Sikhs would vote for him and he would win 'because Hindu votes would get divided', turned out to be an illusion. He fared very bad as the third but he did poll more vote than we had thought, he would, Congress won by an extremely narrow margin.

It needs to be stated that the decision not to have any truck either with the Akalis or with the Congress and to fight the elections in alliance with CPI-M alone was widely welcomed by the party as a whole. The fact that we could win only one seat (Jalalabad) caused no regrets. It was generally recognized that the number of legislators was not a correct indicator of our strength amongst the masses.

A few words about fund collections. Our collections came mainly from the common people and those amongst middle classes who politically supported us. We would make it a point not to take money from anyone who would like to contribute by way of investment or who was an anti-social element. The working class would contribute with amazing generosity. In every election we would spend much less than other candidates but much more than the legal limit. However, there was no violation of law because every time the entire fund was raised in the name of the party and the entire election expense would be met by the party and there is no legal limit as far parties are concerned. Law in this respect needs to be changed. In every election, the party saved substantial amount. This does not mean that no measures are necessary against money power in elections. My own view is that State should at its own cost provide free of charge many facilities to all party candidates just as it already provides the voter lists. There should be no Independent candidates. Genuine independent candidates are extremely a rare phenomenon now. Some in fact rely on the support of one party or the other. Quite a few enter the field either at the instance of one party or the other to weaken a rival or to make money by blackmailing one candidate or the other. A system of proportional representation will help to do away with many such evil practices, as already noted.

Personally I have always had a sort of allergy to fighting elections. One reason is the requirement of elections to go to everyone to make a formal request including persons whom you would otherwise loath to meet. Perhaps this is an un-democratic trait of mine but it is there. An added reason is that whether you win or lose, you are saddled with a very heavy responsibility to help people in many big and small genuine problems of theirs and to refuse to help when the demand made is wrong and unjust or could mean injustice for someone else. In the constituency in question, we have a fairly strong party machinery to help. Even then, I have been finding the responsibility too heavy perhaps on account of my age and health. Few find it possible to believe that I really want to be out of election battles. One of the top leaders of the Punjab Communist Party today once told me: "All pretend not to be keen on fighting elections but all really are."

I do not think so. I believe that despite plenty of opportunism and parliamentarism which have crept into the Communist movement, there are really good examples to follow even in this field. There is Comrade Achhuta Menon who insisted that he be not asked to contest elections in view of his health even when after winning he would once again stand the chance of becoming Chief Minister. He succeeded in opting out. There is also Master Hari Singh whose request not to be made to contest was not accepted and who just disappeared until the last date for filing nomination papers was over. And surely, there are many others of that mettle. Their example needs to be followed by many of us.

5. Bogus Voting and I-Cards

To eliminate bogus voting altogether and to that extent purify our electoral system, T.N. Seshan, the then Chief Election Commissioner of India, set for himself the task of introducing voter identity cards with photos. The idea was that no voter should be able to vote without producing his/her identity card. The idea was good and the determination of Seshan to achieve his objective was well known. Many, therefore, hoped that bogus voting would become a thing of the past in the near future notwithstanding strong resistance to the idea from some powerful quarters having vested interest in large-scale bogus voting. Unfortunately, the hope has been belied and crores of rupees spent on the project appear to have gone down the drain.

During the Punjab Assembly elections in February 1997, bogus voting took place on a bigger scale than ever before. In Amritsar, two new phenomena were noted. Earlier, bogus voting was resorted to by activists and supporters of political parties. This time 'professionals' too did the job. One such person told a journalist that he had already voted 12 times and earned Rs. 300. And there were still two hours left for polling to close. Second, some girls too took to bogus voting for money. Bogus voters could be and were easily spotted by many while rubbing off their ink-marks with the help of some chemical outside certain booths before going to others to vote again in the name of someone else. The Policemen on duty nearby just watched. Presumably, it was not their duty to check bogus voting.

Even most of those voters who had been issued identity cards did not take these with them when they went for voting. This was just not necessary. Anyone whose name was there on the voters' list could vote whether or not he/she had the identity card. And if the name was not on the list one could not vote even with the identity card. This was ruled by the Bombay High Court and very rightly. Unless every eligible voter had been issued an identity card, to insist on such a document for voting would result in many being deprived of their legal right to vote. And this possibility would be there not merely because of inefficiency or sabotage in the matter of preparing identity cards. It is something in-built in the system.

If the system of identity cards as well as voters lists is to remain, the possibility of the names of many being there on the voters list but with no identity cards issued to them would always be there. That would be so because many would get themselves enrolled as voters making use of the very last opportunity, not leaving time for their identity cards to be prepared and issued to them. Not that it is impossible but we just do not have the required high level of efficiency. It is this aspect of the matter that Seshan overlooked.

In the opinion of this writer, it is better to devise a system of voting only on the basis of identity cards and not only for the earlier mentioned reasons.

The way voter lists are prepared contributes towards bogus voting. During the recent elections to the Punjab Assembly, names of about 200 voters belonging to one area of Amritsar (West) constituency were found there not only at their correct addresses but at two other addresses in nearby streets in each case. There were minor discrepancies in names – at one place 'Lal Chand S/o Ram Parshad'would be there while at another it would be 'Lal Chand S/o Ram Prashar'. In the case of women, at one place the name of her husband, would be there while at another her father's name would be mentioned. Thus, each of these genuine voters (firm supporters of a particular candidate) would vote for two-three times by just removing the ink-mark.

This was not the only example. The practice is fairly widespread. Some unscrupulous parties/candidates manage this with the help of staff deputed to prepare voters list. They get away with all this because most of the political parties and candidates concern themselves with the voter lists only after elections are announced. At least this writer has more than once demanded investigation into such cases for giving deterrent punishment to the dishonest and corrupt officials involved. There has been no response whatsoever, even though with growing consumerism and consequently growing corruption this malpractice is increasing instead of decreasing.

The million dollar question is, can we do away with the system of voter lists and have voting only on the basis of identity cards? This is not difficult. Moreover, I understand that such a system does prevail in some European countries.

Each identity card should not only have a photograph of the person concerned but also his/her residential address and date of birth. It should be possible to get the change of address, if any, recorded in the identity card. With such cards every eligible voter can vote at his/her polling booth and the voter lists would just not be necessary. Of course, to prepare such cards for all in the country may take few years. But once these are there, there would be no need to have the voter lists. Moreover, these can serve as really multi-purpose identity cards. The system would not only result in doing away with bogus voting altogether but would also benefit the citizens in many other ways. It would also help fight crime.

The succeeding Election Commissions have as yet not shown any keenness to have a proper system of identity cards. It is not also a question of crores already spent. It is also a question of not throwing away the baby with the bath water. Let the Election Commission discuss the whole issue at an all parties meeting and take a definite, considered decision. Political party leaders should have the necessary briefing from their grassroots-level workers to be able to make good suggestions.

6. Electoral Reforms

Urgent need of electoral reforms has been felt since long. All political parties whether in power or opposition have been talking about it. And yet there has been no serious effort to undertake the job. At best, there has been some tinkering with the problem.

Through its 'National Agenda', the BJP-led government too has promised electoral reforms. Nothing will come out of this too unless strong public opinion builds up irresistable pressure and is clear as to what specific reforms are needed. Let us have a look at the actual experience and draw necessary conclusions.

Experience

According to reports in the press, as in many previous elections, in this election too, many voters when they went for voting found that their names were missing. This phenomenon has been very much on the increase since some years now.

Another connected phenomenon is the inclusion of many names of persons in voters lists when such persons have never been there and in fact, reside in some neighbouring constituency. Naturally, this takes place on a much bigger scale in case of Assembly constituencies and local body wards. These two phenomenon are the result of collusion between unscrupulous potential candidates and even parties on the one hand and unscrupulous and corrupt elements amongst government employees and officers responsible for preparing voters lists, dealing with objections etc, etc.

Some say that if voters are vigilant when lists are prepared, revised and finalized etc, the voters lists will become truthful. In theory this may be correct but it cannot and will not work in actual practice, at least as things stand today.

Bogus Voting

Correct lists are an essential pre-condition for really 'free and fair elections'. How can that be ensured? The only solution is to do away with the system of lists and to replace it with a system of voting on the basis of identity cards. Such a system is needed also to get rid of the phenomenon of bogus voting.

To begin with the main form of bogus voting was: Some voters voting in their own names as well as in names of those who had died or had migrated to far off places and had not come for voting. Ink put on fingers of voters before being allowed to vote could be easily removed with the help of a chemical. Those who indulged in bogus voting were activists/supporters of some parties. Erstwhile Jan Sangh (later BJP) was considered to be the most experienced in the matter. Congress came next. Communists did not indulge in it. The phenomenon has now assumed alarming proportions.

In this and some earlier elections too, many candidates employed persons to do bogus voting. Such persons were paid per bogus vote polled by each of them. Some responsible communists in an earlier election argued with me in all seriousness that if we are to fight elections without adopting such wrong methods as are adopted by bourgeois parties, we might as well give up fighting elections because we would not be able to win any. To my mind, if communists start indulging in such methods they will cease to be communists. That will also mean battle for free and fair elections being given up. What needs to be done is to intensify the battle for identity cards and doing away with the system of voter lists. It is true that as a result of Seshan's scheme for identity cards, crores of rupees seem to have gone down the drain. This is because the scheme was conceived in haste and was sought to be enforced in even greater haste. Preparing identity cards with photos, dates of births, sex, residential addresses etc, should be continuous process. Identity cards should be multi-purpose cards to be needed not only for voting but for many other purposes too including for post middle stage admission in educational institutions and for proving identity for getting various government facilities and concessions. Obviously, such cards will have to be prepared and given to people at an age 2 to 4 years before the age for voting. Such identity cards will dispense with the need for voter lists.

Objections

One objection often raised is: what will happen when the cardholder changes his residence and goes to a new place. Given the present day advanced technology, getting the correction made should not be difficult at all. Another objections is: 'almost half of our population is still illiterate. Voters will lose their cards and will thus, be deprived of the right to vote'.

Objection is without much weight. If the cards are multipurpose cards, tendency to lose them will be minimized. Also, there can easily be a system of getting duplicate cards on payment of a small fee.

It is also argued by some that the system of identity cards would be costly. It is not so. In fact it may prove to be cheaper if the money saved by doing away with voter lists is taken into account. System of multi-purpose cards when once there, will prove beneficial in some other ways also. Government employees including teachers will not be required very often to do extra duties like preparing voter lists, etc. That will help to increase efficiency in government offices and the standard of education in our educational institutions. It will also help in fighting crime.

The fact is that major political parties have developed vested interests in bogus voting and therefore they don't want a system of voting on the basis of identity cards only. It is a question of overcoming this non-vocal but powerful opposition.

Till such time as a proper system of identity cards comes into force, complaints about defective voter lists must be thoroughly enquired into. Officials who deliberately did this must be given deterrent punishment. Hitherto, all such complaints however serious and even when absolutely correct on the face of it have been hushed up. This prevailing practice must go.

Inking

Another measure is very essential, if bogus voting is to be eliminated. Some ink has to be discovered or invented which will not get rubbed off, for at least a week, by any means. In the meanwhile, policemen on security duty should have the legal duty to nab and prosecute any voter found trying to rub off the ink on his finger. Also, it should not be the discretion of presiding officers to let off bogus voters. Some minimum deterrent punishments should be provided in law for all electoral offences.

Buying Votes

Buying votes with money, liquor and other types of inducements has become another important factor vitiating free and fair elections and distorting the will of the people.

In *panchayat* elections in Punjab, illicit liquor is provided openly by opposing candidates through a system of '*piaos*' as in done by some social organizations to provide water to people on roads etc, in summer.

During the 1997 election to Punjab Vidhan Sabha, liquor (illegal) and legal was provided on a very large scale and fairly openly. Complaints lodged did not result in effective action; whenever action was taken, no prosecutions were launched.

During 1997 Punjab Assembly elections and a little earlier in the Amritsar Corporation Election, foreign liquor was supplied even to middle class people to get their votes. Sarees etc, were openigly distributed to women.

What needed is, special law providing deterrent punishments and effective action by effective and really impartial Election Commissions—Central as well as state Commissions functioning with the help of really effective and impartial official and non-official observers. The need of such Election Commissions and such observers with adequate legal powers is brought out by the fact of direct purchase of votes with money.

Brar's allegation

In 1999 elections to the Lok Sabha, Akali candidate Sukhbir Singh Badal (s/o Chief Minister Parkash Singh Badal) was defeated by a narrow margin by Congress candidate Jagmeet Singh Brar from the Faridkot parliamentary constituency. Both on the eve of and on the polling day as well as after the polling day, Brar had alleged open purchase of votes by Badal. I checked up this allegation with the help of more than one absolutely impartial persons. To my horror, I was told that there were counters to which voters were taken, given Rs. 200/- each and made to swear on a religious oath that they would vote for Badal with officials and even top trusted bureaucrats taking active part in the operation.

Votes are 'won' with the help of sops/collective bribes also, e.g, by promising a Dharamsala, paving of streets, etc, in case of victory. In some cases, this is done even before polling.

In the 1998 parliamentary elections, one BJP candidate is reported to have promised a bridge of boats over a river badly needed by farmers living in India but having their agricultural land on the other side of the river. In the previous elections, Congress candidate had been making the same promise but it was never implemented. BJP candidate this time therefore promised: "Even if there is no BJP government, I will get the bridge constructed. I will ensure that the bridge is provided with the help of local area development funds at my disposal, *even out of my personal funds*."

A serious discussion is needed as to how winning of votes by such promises, not all meant seriously, can be prevented. Perhaps, it is necessary to introduce a concept of a post-election illegal gratification just as there is already a concept of post-marriage dowry.

Violations

All that has been stated above constitutes violation of the Model Code of Conduct. There are, however, many other types of violation of the Code too. Here are some instances from Punjab in connection with the last held Lok Sabha elections.

1. Sukhbir Singh Badal, Member RS, on the eve of the beginning of the election process made a speech in a village in his constituency. He expressed his inability to provide funds for a particular project demanded by the villagers as fresh elections were going to take place. Meeting was in fact an election meeting.

   The Deputy Commissioner concerned (Faridkot) was prompt enough to announce the necessary funds. News appeared in papers. The Chief Election Commissioner issued a notice and called for an explanation. What happened thereafter remains a mystery. The Deputy Commissioner was not even transferred. Badal suffered defeat in his own district but he led in Faridkot distt. 'Credit' for this may go to the Deputy Commissioner.

2. Some police officers were transferred and some were given promotions/extensions. According to press reports, Congress lodged a complaint with the Chief Election Commissioner not only about this but many other violations too. Nothing happened. *Tribune* of 8-2-98 carried a very prominent news that one particular SSP was openly helping the Akali candidate. Details were also given. Nothing happened, it seems.

3. There were reports in the press about some 'clever' violations of Code of Conduct. For instance, Chief Minister in his speeches

in villages would say: "I know your needs. I cannot make any announcement just now (in view of the Code of Conduct). I will communicate my decision to the Sarpanch in his ear."

Gift to big land owners

Akali-BJP government has been supplying electricity free of charge to owners of tubewell for irrigation of agricultural land including in case of big landlords, some of whom benefited to the extent of Rs.75,000 a month or so.

6. Some Suggestions

To make good the losses, the Punjab State Electricity Board has been finding ways and means to get bigger amounts out of the pockets of domestic and some other categories of consumers, enhanced bills caused great resentment. Fearing loss of votes PSEB Chairman (an Akali leader) as also the Government announced that those getting these enhanced bills did not need to pay and that these would be written off/reduced after elections. News to this effect appeared in the press more than once.

Other examples of such 'clever' violations can be given. No notice of these was taken by the Election Commission of India or by any other authority.

Advocate General of Punjab was repeatedly issuing press statements on various election issues including such issues as apologies by Sonia Gandhi. I am aware of the fact that Advocate General is not a government officer and can carry on a political (election) campaign. However, it is obvious that it is highly undesirable and the Election Commission should have at least taken note of this moral violation of the Model Code of Conduct. It did not. At least for future, the matter needs to be considered seriously.

Criminalisation

Politics in our country including Punjab, has been criminalized. On the other hand, criminals have become politicians and they fight elections, become MPs and MLAs and even Ministers. It is necessary to keep out of legislatures politicians turned criminals as well as criminals turned politicians. Chief Election Commissioner declared his determination to keep such elements out of 1998 Lok Sabha elections. He could not possibly do that. One or two were kept out because they had been convicted and under the law their nomination papers had to be rejected.

According to a report in '*Outlook*' of February 23, 1998, "an eminent panel identifies 72 lok Sabha candidates are facing criminals cases". They could not be debarred because they had not yet been convicted.

Same or some other eminent panel went on to soon identify the number of criminals as well as the number of convicted criminals who were in the 12th Lok Sabha. A blanket law to debar all those being tried for criminal offences is not there, it should not be there. The reason is that, sometimes very upright persons have to face criminal offences for daring to lead a perfectly justified strike or an economic struggle or political agitation. Such cases often are even altogether false.

Money Power

Money-power distorts elections in a really big way. And that perhaps is the most difficult problem to be resolved.

Some argue that elections require huge amounts of funds and that also is the root cause of corruption. Therefore, elections should be state funded. Both the propositions are exaggerated if not altogether wrong. Remedy suggested can prove worse than the disease.

As regards funds needed for elections, political parties can and in any case should be in a position to raise necessary money from the people. Let me give one example. CPI has contested Punjab Assembly elections in 1967, 1969, 1972, 1977, 1980, 1985, 1992 and 1997, i.e, all the elections ever since 1967. In all these elections funds were raised from the common people and supporters of the party and nothing from any smuggler, black marketeers, etc. Even candidates only gave small personal donations.

No money was spent on buying any votes with cash or liquor or in any other manner. In every election party saved money because the entire amount raised as election fund could not be spent. Saving was there whether election was won or lost.

It is wrong that the root cause of corruption are the huge funds needed for elections. Truth is the other way round. Huge funds are spent on elections (legally as well as illegally) by candidates who are in the field to 'win come what may' so that they can make tons of money, many times more than they spend.

There are upright people in politics (majority once, minority now). Upright persons don't have to spend such amounts as will force them to become corrupt. Those for whom politics is a lucrative profession and corruption is no sin, do spend huge amounts. If elections are state funded, they will have more money to be used illegally (to buy votes, etc) at their disposal because all legally required money will come out of the state exchequer.

State may fund the elections only partly and that too in kind as for instance by supplying voter lists free of charge, by allowing time on mass media, by printing and giving voter slips etc. Some funding of this type is necessary to enable poor candidates/parties to be able to fight elections on level-playing ground as far as legal expense is concerned.

Secondly, maximum limits should not be excessive; should include all expenses including those spent by candidate, parties, relatves and friends. These limits should be strictly enforced. Of course, illegal expenditures must be prevented. This too requres really powerful and impartial Election Commissions having adequate number of observers with adequate powers.

Some steps have already been taken by the Election Commission to cut out some needless expenditure. For instance, wrting on walls without prior permission of the owners has been prohibited. Number of vehicles to be used for propaganda has been limited. More such steps can be decided and legally enforced. It needs to be stated that most effective way of election propaganda are village, and Mohalla meetings as well as public meetings, rallies and processions and of course house to house canvassing. Most of the other means serve no purpose except causing nuisance for the public.

Question of vehicles being used to transport voters is an important one. Measures taken so far have not produced much results. They can easily be bye-passed/negated. For instance, many cars are used as taxis. They are hired and when caught it is denied that they are taxis.

Voters in hired vehicles are told before hand that if checked they should say they are going to pay the charge from their own pockets. In my opinion, polling booths should be much nearer the voters than they are at present. Maximum distance now fixed must be reduced. It is entirely practical because many more suitable buildings have come up. This will dissuade voters from demanding to be transported.

Non-official Forums

Besides legal measures, there should be non-official forums to educate the voters to exercise votes keeping in view interests of the country and the people and the big harm giving votes for money, liquor etc, does to the both. School and college text books which deal with electoral systems etc, should deal with such aspects also to bring up the new generation with correct outlook.

As regards non-official campaign, Left should take the initiative. Surely, many good people will come forward to join and even lead the campaign. If democracy is to be saved in this country, this job is a must. Of course, propaganda for this must be carried on otherwise too, i.e, through public meeting, etc held for other political issues and through general political conferences which are held from time to time

Muscle Power

Muscle power is another very serious problem vitiating electoral mandate. It has to be fought on two fronts. One, by fighting for adequate security forces headed by officers who would really ensure their correct functioning and not helping one party or the other. Secondly, by organized strength of those non-official forces which are honestly against the use of muscle power. Fighting rigging by counter-rigging will prove counter-productive in the long run.

Election Commission

As we have already seen, really independent Election Commissions can go a long way to ensure free and fair elections. It is suggested that the Election Commission of India should be appointed by a committee consisting of the Chief Justice of India, Prime Minister of India and Leader of opposition in the Lok Sabha or some such body.

State election Commissions should also be made by constitutional authorities and should be appointed by similar state-level bodies/ committees.

Multiplicity

Problem of too many candidates has also become a problem leading not only to inconveniences (3 feet long ballot papers, etc.) but also to distortion of the will of voters. Problem arises because of too many independent candidates.

A study of experience of elections uptodate reveals that the number of serious independent candidates has gone down very much. Of the serious independent candidates, most have the support of one party or the others. Most of the independent candidates now are there for very wrong reasons.

Some are there at the instance of some candidate because the calculation is that the independent candidate being sponsored will wean away some potential voters of the rival candidate. Some are there to get some facilities. Some seek only some fame which can help in their businesses or to become professional "social workers" who charge fees for every service rendered.

This explains the phenomenon of number of independent candidates going up and up while the number of successful independent candidates has been going down and is now negligible.

In 1952, there were 849 independent candidates for the Lok Sabha. Of these 36 won and 503 constituting 59.25 per cent lost their deposits. In 1996 there were10635 independent candidates; only 9 won. As many as 10603 constituting 99.70 lost their deposits.

No doubt, steep increase in the amount of security deposits for 1998 Lok Sabha elections has resulted in considerable decrease. However, number is likely to go up again. Moreover, security deposit amounts must not be raised to such an extent as to keep out serious candidates supported by parties who have limited financial resources or even poor candidates not supported by any party.

It has been my view for quite sometime that in case of Lok Sabha and Assembly elections no independent candidates should be allowed unless he has the support of some political party which because of giving this support is not putting up any candidate with its official symbol.

In case of Panchayats and local bodies, independent candidates have very much relevance. In fact they should have at least as much relevance as candidates of parties. Actually, some local elections should not be contested on party basis at all.

When Chheharta used to be a separate town and not a part of Amritsar, CPI never contested elections to its Municipal Committee on party basis. It used to form a broad front which would put up not only CPI men/women as candidates but also genuine independents having some political sympathy with the Congress although Congress was the main rival of the front and it used to put up official Congress candidates.

During 2 decades (1952-1972) all the elections were won by the Front which never lost more than 2 seats out of 9 and later 13. CPI has the same outlook as far as Panchayat elections are concerned. Unfortunately bourgeois parties are not cooperative in this matter.

Religion and Castes

We have so far dealt with the question of some needed reforms. Many others will be suggested when the matter is taken up by any new Government of India. However, it is necessary to discuss another question of vital importance for free and fair elections. It is of preventing (mis)use of religion and casteism for garnering votes.

It is a fact that votes were sought by taking holy books like Geeta, etc to houses of people during house-to-house canvassing and getting voters to swear by them to vote for particular candidates. Extent of this varie from place to place. Meetings were held in places of worship and even in presence of idols and holy books and appeals for votes were made. Election commission has since barned these practices.

Akali party invariably asks for votes in the name of the Panth, i.e, Sikh religious community. This definitely implies a religious appeal. Sikhs vote for different parties, e.g, Akalis, Congress, Communists, BSP, etc. Many Sikhs are not supporters of any party but decide in every election for whom to vote. 'Panth' means Sikh religious community as a whole. When Akali party, a political outfit, appeals for votes in the name of Panth it definitely exploits religion. Similarly, if Muslim League asks for votes in the name of Islam, it amounts to exploiting religion.

Having in manifestos pledges for defending genuine religious rights of religious minorities on all India scale or on state basis and also speeches on these lines is one thing but asking for votes in the name of religion is quite another. In the opinion of this writer, appeal for votes by the RSS-controlled BJP in the name of Hindutva which covers such matters as demolition of Masjids, constructing Mandirs in place of demolished Babri Masjid or Masjids which Sangh Pariwar may demolish henceforth clearly amounts to exploitation of religious sentiments of the people. I am aware of a judgement of the Supreme Court which almost rejected this view. *It is my belief that sooner or later this judgement will have to be reviewed by the Supreme Court.*

Sub-sects

Apart from such unmistakable exploitation of religion to garner votes, there are also clever ways of doing so. These are indulged by semi-religious sects also. Here is one most recent instance. Originally Congress(I) candidate in the Bhatinda Parliamentary Constituency in Punjab belonged to Dera Sucha Sauda, a sect which claims over 5 million members. There is a large number of them in Bhatinda constituency. On the last date for withdrawal of nomination papers, in view of an understanding between Congress and CPI, the Congress candidate belonging to this sect was asked to withdraw as Congress had decided to support the CPI candidate. The candidate did withdraw but there were clear and strong indications that the Head of the sect had issued orders that all belonging to the sect must vote for the Akali candidate. This was alleged but was denied. A report in the *Tribune* of 18-3-98 however, proves that orders did go out. Here are relevant extracts: "The Dera (Sucha Sauda) sect hitherto religious, was said to have declared its support for the Haryana Lok Dal (Rashtriya) in Haryana and Akali Dal in Punjab. However, Baba Gurmeet Singh in an interview to TNS at the sect headquarters said: 'he still continued to be apolitical and had nothing do with politics'.

However, he admitted that it was the unanimous decision of the Sangat to vote unitedly. But, he reiterated that he had nothing to do with the decision. The Baba said that he had advised the Sangat that whatever decision it took, it must remain united. He said his followers had sought his advice. As he was above politics and belonged to all, Sadhus from the Dera went to different places and helped the followers to arrive at a consensus and decide for whom to vote... Baba Gurmeet Singh admitted that Parkash Singh Badal had come to the *dera* before elections. He did seek my *ashirwad* and I said my *ashirwad* was to everybody and added that even Rajindar Kaur Bhattal, the PPCC President, Hans Raj Swan (BJP candidate from Sirsa) and some others had come to him for his *ashirwad*. He said his *ashirwad* was for everybody and it was the people who had to decide.... that nobody was special to him. Krishan Lal (a full time Sadhu and manager of the *Dera*) said that Baba had nothing to do with the decision of the Sangat (to vote for HLD (R) and Akali party). He insisted only that, whatever decision was taken, it should be unanimous so that the Sangat remained united.

The Report in the *Tribune* also refers to the allegation that Badal had made a huge contribution to the *Dera* for enlisting Baba's support. This was strongly denied. The manager of the *Dera* had said that *Dera* had huge assets of its own and that no donations of any kind were accepted by it.

The *Tribune* report cannot leave any doubt in the mind of any impartial person that in the name of 'keeping the *sangat* united', followers in Punjab and Haryana were ordered to vote for Akalis in Punjab and HLD (R) in Haryana. According to the report, success of Mr Sukhbir Singh Badal, the son of Chief Minister Parkash Singh Badal is attributed (by many) to the last minute support declared by the sect leader, Baba Gurmeet Singh.

Margins of Akali victors in Bhatinda as well as Faridkot constituencies were not big. Possibly Akalis would have lost both these seats but for the united support of the Sangat of this *Dera*. And it is not only this sect whose support is sought and is given in this manner. Whatever party may be supported in this manner, it clearly amounts to exploitation of religious sentiments.

It is high time that Election Commission of India takes note of all this and takes/recommends to the Government of India and state governments effective steps to end misuse of religion in any subtle form.

Likewise, casteism has also to be driven out of electoral field. Question of reservations being an issue in elections cannot be helped but casteist appeals for votes must be monitored with a view to take action in accordance with law. If the law as it exists today is inadequate, it must be amended and made adequate.

Last but not the least, as things stand today really free and fair elections in India are still a far cry. Unless effective steps are taken at Government as well as non-official levels, things will become worse and we may reach the point when people will lose faith in the system with serious consequences for the country. It is time for all who want parliamentary system of democracy to survive in India to act decisively.

7. Open Letter to CPI National Council Members (*Mainstream* of 20 November 1999)

The CPI is in the throes of a major crisis (which has indeed engulfed the Left as a whole) in the wake of the 13th Lok Sabha election results. This letter, by a veteran CPI leader of national standing commanding esteem and respect among all sections of the public for his extraordinary honesty, integrity and fearless struggle against Khalistani secessionism-cum-terrorism in Punjab, is of considerable significance in that context.

—Editor

Dear Comrades,

I hope you will not mind this letter from one who was a member of the National Council (NC) of the CPI for many years. When you meet in December 1999, you will surely review the last election of the twentieth century to the Lok Sabha, particularly the CPI's own dismal performance. I believe that it will be useful if the NC takes into consideration views of the ranks and even fellow-travellers including Left intellectuals.

Personally, I am convinced that it will not be possible for the NC to draw correct lessons unless it also reviews its electoral line over the years. You will recall that a minority of 10 to 15 members has been differing with the officially adopted electoral line. This minority held the following views though these did not always get expressed very clearly:

1. Seats in legislature were important, but of primary importance was work among the masses including militant struggles on one hand and constructive work as well as service of the people on the other.
2. Anxiety to get more seats must not lead to sacrificing principles. Long-term interests of the movement must not be sacrificed for short-term gains.
3. Agreements with non-Left parties in the electoral field are not impermissible. These agreements, however, must be based on

mutually agreed common minimum programmes with the correlation of forces being such that these would be honestly and sincerely adhered to.

4. Overall adjustments without any common minimum programme with the main aim of getting some more seats somehow is sheer opportunism which can seriously damage the long-term interests of the Left and of the country. It was asserted by some of us that this opportunism for the sake of seats would in the long run eat up the mass base of the party and undermine its capacity to win any seat. It would even lead to a situation where no main non-Left party would make any adjustment with the CPI as it would not stand to gain from it.

5. No doubt, the first-past-the-post system of elections is very disadvantageous for smaller parties. To ensure minimum representation some local adjustments with Centrist parties were considered permissible by the minority.

The big majority rejected the above line again and again. Instead, a line of total adjustments with one party or the other was pursued on State levels and sometimes even national level. The extent to which we went in pursuit of some seats somehow would be clear from the following:

1. In UP we had a good mass basis in at least some districts amongst agricultural labourers. Our electoral alliance with late Chaudhary Charan Singh and his party contributed a good deal towards our losing this base. Let me recall one fact. Dalits, afraid of kulaks and their *lathials*, would not dare come out to vote even though the State was being ruled by the Congress. Anyone shaking hands with them was bound to antagonize the agricultural labourers.

2. In Punjab, joining hands with the Akalis to defeat the Congress had a similar effect, I think it was in 1980 that the CPI and CPI-M joined hands to fight the Assembly elections with no agreement either with the Congress or Akalis. The CPI won only one seat and the CPI-M none. Yet the ranks of both the parties felt stronger and were happy.

3. If we look up the old files of *New Age*, the weekly organ of the CPI, we would find that in Tamil Nadu we alternately supported the DMK and AIADMK characterizing as progressive once DMK and the next time AIADMK. It could not but affect our credibility.

4. The line of winning seats somehow blinded us to the casteist character (and also other negative features) of Laloo Prasad Yadav and Mulayam Singh Yadav. We saw in them strong and true anti-communal forces when at least Mulayam Singh Yadav was widening the gulf between Hindus and Muslims—pushing Hindus in UP towards the BJP. By helping these casteist leaders we helped replacement of poverty by casteism as the rallying slogan for the poor. The failure of the Left to fight the caste system after India became independent, too contributed to that process.

5. From the time of the 1991 elections to the Lok Sabha we saw in the V.P. Singh-led Janata Dal our real (Centrist) ally shutting our eyes to its negative aspects. For example, its alliance with the BJP in 1990, the Janata Dal Government of Karnataka being the first to abolish land ceiling, its having more or less the same economic policy as the Congress, the V.P. Singh government's approach considerably strengthening terrorism in Punjab, etc.

   The line of winning seats somehow very much eroded the Communist moral values for which once they had commanded respect of the tallest in the country. I have seen important leading comrades arguing that electoral battles cannot be fought without giving liquor/money to sections of voters. When E.M.S. Namboodiripad became the Chief Minister of Kerala in 1957, Communists had a majority of only two in the Assembly. Offers of lakhs of rupees could not bring about defection of even one CPI MLA. The party then was united. Can either of the two parties claim today that in this respect it is still made of the same mettle? The reality, as all know, is far from it.

6. Till the eve of the 1999 Lok Sabha elections, the Communist parties were still respected as being qualitatively different from the non-Left parties insofar as corruption is concerned. When

we embraced a King of corruption on the one hand and a Queen of corruption on the other, we lost in this respect too. Parliamentarism has also resulted in the CPI as also the CPI-M maintaining opportunist silence on crucial controversial questions. For example, the question of Akali opposition to the quota system for recruitment in the Army, the question of reservation for Jats in the matter of Central Government jobs, etc. It is not necessary to dwell more on this.

Let me, however, briefly point out how opportunism in the electoral field (outside West Bengal, Kerala and Tripura) has also vitiated CPI-CPI-M relations. The CPI-M had never agreed to the CPI proposals to reach mutual agreement and then jointly negotiate with other potential partners. It would negotiate separately and would even try to gain at the cost of the CPI. At a later stage the CPI too adopted the same tactics. The CPI-M at one time did not hesitate even to support the BJP/Jan Sangh candidates against the CPI on the ground that the BJP and not the CPI was in a position to defeat the Congress. One has to be thankful for the fact that in this respect at least the CPI did not pay back the CPI-M in the same coin. Even in the 1999 elections, there were allegations that the CPI-M worked against CPI candidates in some constituencies. In the interest of Communist unity itself, the CPI should take the issue to the ranks of the CPI-M in a proper way.

Coming back to the question of electoral tactics in general, it is high time the CPI as also the CPI-M review their entire post-independence past and draw appropriate lessons. That will also help them to see why corruption has made considerable foothold in both the parties; why both the parties are becoming unscrupulous for winning elections; why Communist leaders and cadres are becoming ease-loving; why mass struggles and service to the people have taken a backsea; why we are unable to do all that is necessary to renovate Marxism as also Leninst principles of organisation, etc. In short, why the Communists instead of becoming a big national force are becoming irrelevant.

It is not yet too late. If we stop talking of a 'third (electoral) front'; if we have a perspective of a Left democratic front; if we realize that this will not emerge unless the Left is on the way to become a big force; if we stick to basic moral values and don't sacrifice principles; if we really treat mass work and service to the people as primary, it will not be long before the Communists are in a position to change the very face of India. This path may lead of fewer seats for sometime to come, but will yield rich dividends even in the matter of seats in the long run.

Please excuse me if you think that is sheer impertinence on my part to address this letter to the National Council. Of course, I don't claim to be very wise and I may turn out to be wrong. But I do believe that given my convictions as at present, by writing this letter I am, only doing my duty.

III

Punjab Problems

Hindu Organisations and Punjab Politics

1. In 1989 the entire country was worried about the situation in Punjab. It was rightly considered as a threat to the very unity and integrity of India. It is generally well recognized that a great deal of responsibility for the this situation lay with forces of Sikh separatism and communalism aided and abetted by Imperialism which is making all-out efforts to destabilise India. The role of Hindu communalism and Hindu organizations in bringing about such situation is not understood and recognized to the extent it should be. If the crisis in Punjab is to be overcome successfully and the game of extremists and terrorists having the backing of imperialism and the military regime of Pakistan is to be defeated successfully and with minimum of sacrifices, it is necessary to fight also Hindu communalism with full force. And that cannot be done unless the role played by it so far is understood and realized. The aim of this piece is not to make a detailed and exhaustive analysis of that but only to help understand it generally and broadly.

2. The anti-national and even anti-Sikh demand for 'Khalistan' is based on the totally wrong, unscientific and dangerous concept of Sikhs-a-separate-nation. All those who propound this false thesis bring grist to the mill of separatists and protagonists of another partition of India. Some confusion is created by the fact that the Punjabi translation of the word 'NATION' is 'QUOM'. The same word has also been used for 'Religion'

(and also for 'Caste'). Sikh religious community has in the past often been referred to as Sikh Quom. This is taken advantage of by the separatists to argue that Sikhs are a separate nation. They can be refuted by pointing out that Jat Sikhs would often say their 'quom' is Jat, etc. That, however, does not prevent them from sowing confusion by misusing the fact that the word 'quom' has been used also to mean religion. Be that as it may, the fact remains that it was the British rulers and their spokesmen who made persistent efforts to plant in the minds of the Indian people and to encourage the false and dangerous concept of nation being based on religion. There is ample material to support this contention. The Muslim League led by Mohd. Ali Jinnah had been encouraged to demand 'Separate Pakistan' by arguing that (Indian) Muslims constituted a separate nation. This false argument was directly and greatly helped by the RSS thesis of Hindu Rashtra. It is a fact of history that Hindu communal organizations like the RSS and Hindu Mahasabha too believed and propogated religion-based-nation idea. They considered the Hindus to be a separate nation. And this could not but help those who argued that the Muslims constituted a separate nation.

The RSS which unlike Hindu Mahasabha has not ceased to exist after independence, has continued to believe in and propagate the Hindu-Rashtra concept. And this undoubtedly has directly helped the Sikhs-a-separate nation concept and hence indirectly the demand for 'Khalistan'.

Late Romesh Chander of Hind Samacher Group of Papers son of Lala Jagat Narain was in no way hostile to the RSS and BJP. He was in fact quite friendly to both. In an editorial written on the eve of Bala Sahib Deoras' visit to Punjab in 1982-83, he had strongly pleaded that the RSS should give up the slogan of Hindu Rashtra and instead adopt the slogan of 'Indian Rashtra' (Bhartiya Rashtra). Bala Sahib had rejected the appeal and had argued that 'Hindu Rashtra' meant and included every 'Indian'. This had not convinced even Romesh Chander and he made this clear in an editorial of his dated 25-8-1983.

The truth is that Golwarkar had made amply clear and in so many words that the non-Hindus in India would be second class citizens. The real RSS thesis is that only a Hindu Rashtra can be a really Indian (Bhartiya) Rashtra. The RSS is not prepared to give up this concept. Nor can the BJP dare repudiate it because it depends on the RSS for its very existence. And this RSS thesis had played considerable mischief in Punjab too. It has to be fought if the fight against the thesis Sikhs-a-separate-nation and the slogan of 'Khalistan' have to be fought successfully.

3. No serious student of Punjab politics will now deny that much mischief in Punjab politics has resulted from the fact that the question of linguistic re-organisation of states and of language in Punjab got mixed up with religion and communalism.

British India's division into provinces had not been done on the basis of geographical, historical, economic and linguistic basis. This division was done with a view to keep people backward and to divide and rule. The Madras Presidency for instance included Tamil speaking as well Telegu speaking people while many Telegu speaking people were in the Princely state of Hyderabad. The pre-independence Punjab included Punjabi speaking as well Hindi or Haryanvi and Bagri speaking people. There were also a number of Princely States like Patiala, Nabha, etc, which were inhabited by Punjabi speaking people. As a part of the efforts to defeat the British game, the Indian National Congress made a firm commitment to reorganize the then provinces on linguistic basis. After India won her independence and the Congress became the ruling party, it tried to go back on this commitment. Reorganisation of Indian states on linguistic basis came only after bitter struggles. Except in the case of Punjab, there were united struggles. These had achieved success by 1956 or so.

In Punjab, the Akali Party led by Master Tata Singh came out with the demand for a 'Sikh Suba'. Later on it was modified to a 'Punjabi speaking province in which the Sikhs should comprise at least 60 per cent of the population'.

The immediate and also long-term interests of Punjab demanded that while opposing this communal demand, people should heave been sought to be united for the re-organisation of Punjab on a linguistic basis, irrespective of which community would constitute what percentage. Only the Communists tried to do that. The Hindu communal organizations like Jan Sangh, and also the Congress opposed even the correct concept of a Punjabi speaking state. Instead, they demanded Maha Punjab in which Sikhs would constitute a very small minority.

It needs to be mentioned that even when Sant Fateh Singh delinked the demand for Punjabi Suba from religion (even though only very partially) and even when Prime Minister Indira Gandhi agreed to re-organise Punjab on linguistic basis, the Jan Sangh continued to oppose it. Jan Sangh and RSS workers definitely had a hand in the disturbances which took place in Punjab when the present Punjab and Haryana came into existence as separate states of Indian Union.

All this strengthened communalism in Punjab—Hindu as well as Sikh. It increased the communal divide.

4. As has already been mentioned, even the question of language in Punjab got mixed up with religion and communalism. The role of Hindu organizations and Hindu communalism in this respect had played much havoc in Punjab.

All Punjabis—Sikhs as well as Hidus—speak Punjabi language. During the British rule Punjabi was not made the medium of the instruction even at the primary level in government schools. It was not made the language of administration even upto the district level. Sikh religious scriptures were and are in Punjabi written in Gurmukhi script. Punjabi in Gurmukhi script was taught in Sikh private schools. Hindu private schools generally had Hindi as medium, even in the lower classes. Punjabi those days was written in Persian script too. It was written in Dev Nagri script too but on much lesser scale.

After independence, the Akali Party championed the cause of Punjabi language and its natural script Gurmukhi. But they went about it as if these were parts of Sikh religion. This was disservice to the cause of Punjabi. Hindu communalists on the other hand disowned Punjabi even while speaking Punjabi in their homes, at their shops with customers, etc. They even argued that Punjabi was only a dialect of Hindi and was not at all a separate language. With this argument they justified their call to the Hindus to record Hindi and not Punjabi as their mother tongue during the census. They would not own Punjabi even with the option to write in Dev Nagari script. Jan Sangh was in the forefront of this compaign. Hindu Congressmen and even leaders often did not lag behind. Only the Communists denounced this communal campaign and tried to counter it. They were not a big force and they then had their main bases in the Sikh peasantry. Overwhelming majority of Hindus were carried away and got recorded Hindi as their mother tongue.

This further strengthened communalism of both hues. This was also one of the factors responsible for the fact that re-organisation of old Punjab on linguistic basis into Punjab and Haryana was faulty and some problems remain unresolved even till today.

For the solution of 'Punjab problem' on a lasting basis, it is necessary that Hindu Punjabis too must own Punjabi as their mother tongue. It is also necessary that the Punjabi language and religion must be completely divorced.

In 1967 and again in 1969 Akalis and Jan Sangh shared power. Their partnership could not last long because of their respective communal bases, besides other factors. It, however, needs to be noted that the Jan Sangh toned down its opposition to Punjabi.....Even though it did not actively compaign for it, it did help to change the situation for the better. During the 1981 census, many more Hindus got recorded Punjabi as their mother tongue. This change for the better in the attitude of the Hindus on the question of language has been continuing. It received a setback with the rise of Sikh terrorism and separatism in Punjab. It has received a further setback as a result of linguistic survey carried out in 83 villages and two towns of Abohar and Fazilka in January 1986 under the orders of Mathew Commission. This Commission was set up under Rajiv Longowal

Accord to decide some Hindi speaking contiguous areas to be given to Haryana (with village as a unit) in lieu of Chandigarh to be given to Punjab. Many Punjabi speaking Hindus were keen to go to Haryana because of continuing terrorism in Punjab. They, therefore, declared Hindi to be their mother tongue.

The problem therefore remains. Communists have been consistent champions of delinking Punjabi language and script from religion and all Punjabis recognizing Punjabi as their mother tongue.

Interestingly, RSS Chief Golwarkar stood for Punjabi but he allowed Punjab RSS and Jan Sangh to 'defy' him in this respect. Neither RSS nor BJP can be expected to become genuine, whole hearted and active champions of Punjabi language. That increases the responsibility of Hindu Congressmen who in the past to a great extent failed to act in a secular manner in respect of this matter. It is to be hoped that they have learnt some lesson from past experience including the recent one.

The Arya Samaj in Punjab had been born with anti-Sikh prejudices and bias. These too have to be overcome.

5. All religions have much in common. Hindu religion and Sikh religion perhaps have much more in common than any other two religions. There are historical reasons for the same. It can even be said that Sikh religion arose out of Hindu religion. That does not, however, do away with the fact that Sikhism has grown into an independent and separate religion. It is so recognized in the Constitution of India. The RSS, however, has a theory that the Sikhs are a part of the Hindus. There are others too who hold this belief and propagate it. This increases the fears of the Sikh elite that Sikhs may get absorbed in Hinduism and may lose their separate identity. This fear is exploited by those who propagate the false thesis of separate political identity of Sikhs. This thesis can only lead to the thesis Sikhs-a-separate nation. The Sikhs have a separate religious identity but not a separate political identity. To deny the former only helps the communal and separatist forces. Some of the topmost BJP leaders of Punjab concede in private that it proves

counterproductive to argue that the Sikhs are a part of Hindus. Some of them belong to RSS. However, they seem to be in no position to make the RSS give up its stand.

The RSS position denying Sikhism as a separate religion is wrong and has contributed towards widening the Hindu-Sikh rift.

6. The main strategy of the separatist forces has been to widen the Hindu-Sikh gulf and even to bring about Hindu-Sikh riots leading to migration of the Hindus from Punjab and of the Sikhs into Punjab from the rest of India.

Methods adopted towards this end are well known. They have included burning of shops, murder of innocent persons as well as of prominent figures including murder of the Sikhs who dare oppose, sacrilege of religious places, hurting religious sentiments, etc.

It should be obvious to anyone that similar measures from the Hindu end, independently or as counter measures, would produce exactly the same results. Communalism of one variety actually helps the variety which it claims or pretends to fight. Similarly, measures of the type mentioned above resorted to in the name of opposing Communal/Chauvinist/Separatist forces produce the same results. In a situation of this type, there can be no successful 'Hindu defence or Sikh defence'. Only through Hindu-Sikh unity, can both be defended successfully. Rejecting this sound and tested thesis, some new Hindu communal organizations have come up in Punjab.

One is Hindu Suraksha Samiti (HSS). It first came up in Patiala and then spread to some other places in the state. Interestingly, it was started by a protégé of a Congress leader who is now in the Akali Party. The protégé himself was till then considered a very shady character. Quite a number of Hindu Congressmen aligned themselves with this organization at one stage or another.

The other is the Shiv Sena which wants every Hindu to have a Trishul.

Below we give some instances to illustrate the type of role played by these organizations.

(a) On 16-8-1982, a number of Hindu as well as Sikh shops were set on fire in Patiala. Those who had burnt the Hindu shops had made the necessary preparations in a Gurdwara. Those who burnt the Sikh shops had made preparations from within a Hindu temple.

(b) In February 1984 the Akali party had given a call for one day state-wide bandh for 'Punjab demands'. Other parties declared support. All joined the bandh for varying reasons, including anxiety to avoid clashes. But for some incidents, the day passed off peacefully.

Soon after, the Hindu Suraksha Samiti gave a call for a one day state wide bandh in Punjab to protest against the arrest of its founder leader. Even if the arrest were to be considered unjustified, in the prevailing situation, this call was very wrong and had the potential of much mischief. Jarnail Singh Bhindranwala and the All India Sikh Students Federation declared their opposition. The sentiment dominating the Hindu middle class urban youth was: "We must show that we too are a force...The Sikhs too must observe bandh as the Hindus did when the Akalis called for one...". There were many unfortunate incidents including deaths. In Amritsar, a crowd inspired mainly by some Hindu Congressmen damaged the Golden temple model at the Railway Station. A picture of Guru Ram Dass, founder of Amritsar, was burnt down. Privately some 'justified' it as retaliation against the sacrilege committed in the Sitla Mandir some time earlier. Actually it had the same effect, i.e, widening Hindu-Sikh gulf.

This bandh resulted in the collapse of the negotiations in Delhi which had started a day or two earlier.

(c) The Blue Star operation was the most unfortunate event. It is a pity that it became a necessity when it came, even though it could have and should have been avoided. It deeply hurt the sentiments of the Sikhs and pained many others too. Big damage done to the Akal Takht could not but make this hurt much more acute. The feeling of relief amongst the Hindus at the big blow to the terrorists who had converted the Golden Temple into an arsenal was natural. It was, however, very wrong and unfortunate that in some places sweets were distributed at the news of the death of Bhindranwala. Initiative was taken by communal and/or immature elements amongst the Hindus. Wherever someone intervened against the move it was given up. Sweets distribution was only on a small scale but it did some damage.

(d) First time Hindu-Sikh confrontation after Rajiv-Longowal accord took place in Gurdaspur in December 1985.

A Hindu temple on the outskirts of the town was being managed by a Pujari. One tough (who happened to be Sikh by religion) had rented out some land said to be of the temple to some individuals who had put up Khokhas on the same. The Shiv Sena intervened. The authorities promised to remove the Khokhas by a specified date but the promise was not kept. The Shiv Sena decided to do the job itself and carried out a very provocative anti-Sikh announcement in the town. The tough first started Akhand Path of Guru Granth Sahib and then collected a crowd. The result was confrontation. At least one person died. Curfew had to be imposed in the town for a number of days. This was the first curfew in the state after the Rajiv-Longowal Accord.

(e) On 12-2-1986, a Hindu businessman of Ludhiana was shot dead when he refused to part with the big amount with him. The culprits might or might not have been Sikh terrorists. Shiv Sena gave a call for Hartal in Ludhiana on 13-9-1986.

Its volunteers in the funeral procession stoned a Gurdwara on the way. There was danger of the situation deteriorating rapidly. Curfew was imposed. This was the third curfew in the state after Rajiv-Longowal Accord.

Let no one consider that Hindu communalists in Punjab had only been responding subsequently. In April 1981, some Sikh communal organizations had announced a procession in Amritsar to demand a ban on smoking in Punjab. Hindu communal organisation pre-empted the decision. They brought out earlier a procession to assert the right to smoke. Many anti-Sikh slogans were raised. What was the result? The anti-smoking procession originally expected to be a damp squib became a big affair and was equally communal and provocative. Congressmen got communally divided. RSS was active in the Hindu procession.

It is not necessary to give more examples. It is as clear as day light that Hindu communalists who hold the entire Sikh community responsible for the crimes and misdeeds of the extremists and seek revenge etc, only help the latter. And there are signs that in the days to come, the RSS and the Hindu Shiv Sena are going to be more active than before.

It is not without reason that the US Imperialism which has been fully backing Sikh separatists and even allowing camps in the US to train terrorists also lent support to a Hindu Sammelan organised some time ago in the US by forces which stand for Hindu Raj.

7. The Congress (I) notwithstanding the Hindu tinge from which most of its leadership suffers and the opportunism in which it indulges for the sake of votes, cannot be called a Hindu communal organization. However, we have seen that not unoften many Hindu Congressmen of Punjab have acted communally (same is true of many Sikh Congressmen of Punjab). Certain actions of Haryana Chief Minister Bhajan Lal during the crisis through which Punjab had been passing for years were, at par with the actions of Hindu communalists. As these had sunstantial impact on the political situation in Punjab, these need to be mentioned even though very briefly.

The Akali threat to disrupt the Asiad Games in New Delhi deserved strong condemnation. It had to be met firmly but tactfully. But the way in which ordinary Sikh passengers as also top dignitaries travelling to Delhi were humiliated by Haryana police was a tremendous help to Jarnail Singh Bhindranwale and the Sikh communalists. At one stage, Bhajan Lal had started acting on the theory of 'teaching the Sikhs a lesson'. Besides being a gross violation of all that Gandhiji stood for and taught in the matter of communal harmony and disharmony, what followed in Haryana as a result of this theory (even though for a short while) did have a considerable negative effect on the Punjab situation. All this strengthened those who wrongly argued that the Sikhs were a second class citizens and even slaves in India and that they must fight for their independence.

As was stated in the very beginning, this is not an exhaustive paper. It does not, for instance discuss the economic basis of Hindu communalism in Punjab. It does not also examine the reasons as to how it happened that the RSS in Punjab did not, speaking generally, work actively for Hindu-Sikh riots in Punjab even though it wants Hindu Rashtra which in fact means a Hindu theocratic state in India. In many parts of India, RSS has actively fomented anti-Muslim riots. Its 'Hindu ideology' had done a good deal of harm to Hindu-Sikh relations in Punjab as we have sought to show above. At various stages it advanced the dangerous slogan that the Hindus should arm themselves for their defence. RSS men at some places even collected money, etc for the purpose. It, however, needs to be admitted that for various economic and political reasons it did not actively work to foment Hindu-Sikh riots. The real credit for the fact that there have been no Hindu-Sikh riots in Punjab, however, lies elsewhere. To some extent the Left can claim credit. It worked tirelessly for maintaining Hindu-Sikh unity to the extent it could considering its strength. The main credit goes to the sound and healthy instincts of the common people—the Hindus as well as the Sikhs. To more or less extent, really secular forces and elements other than communists too contributed. So did sections of the Akalis.

Punjab is not yet out of woods. Recently the situation has been worsening. What has been stated above should help to draw certain lessons.

No doubt Imperialism is doing all it can to disintegrate India because India refuses to become a puppet. A key element in the strategy of Imperialism is to aid and abet those who stand for 'Khalistan'. Hindu communalism, slogans of revenge and retaliation, theory that all Sikhs must be held responsible for the misdeeds of separatists, actually help the game of Imperialism and of separatists backed by it. That is why Imperialism encourages forces of Hindus communalism too. To underestimate the need to fight Hindu communalism while fighting Sikh terrorism, separatism and Akali communalism, will be a very dangerous mistake.

This piece was written long ago for *Religion and Politics in India,* edited by Moin Shakar; published in 1989.

Freedom Struggle and Glorious Role of Punjabis/Sikhs: Bid to pit Punjab's Contributions against Rest of India Unwarranted

In the Golden Jubilee year of India's independence, sacrifices made during the struggle for freedom by the people of our country, were remembered with pride. Significant contributions made by Punjab were also recalled. If one were to say that Sikhs contributed more than their proportion in India's population, all would agree. Some, however, have been presenting a different picture. Here is what Col. Partap Singh Gill, former Lt. Governor of Goa, Daman and Diu, has said in a letter to the Speaker of the Lok Sabha as reported in the *Tribune* of 23rd September, 1997:

> ".....Out of a total of 121 freedom fighters hanged by the British, 93 were Sikhs; 2646 Indians were deported to Kala Pani—of them as many as 2147 were Sikhs. At Jalianwal Bagh, Amritsar, of about 1300 killed, 799 were Sikhs". At that time Sikhs were only one per cent of the nation's population and yet their contribution was over 80 per cent.

SGPC president Gurcharan Singh Tohra too has been giving similar figures. So has been Chief Minister Badal with the difference that he has been using the word 'Punjabis' instead of 'Sikhs' (One can only hope that Badal has not become a votary of the thesis that only Sikhs are true Punjabis). Such figures seek to create a totally wrong impression that Sikhs/Punjabis almost singlehandedly fought for India's independence and the rest of the country made only an insignificant contribution. It is therefore necessary to examine them critically.

First, no one says to which period or periods these figures relate and what their sources are.

Secondly, let us have a look at some figures contained in *India's struggle for freedom* published by the Government of West Bengal in 1987. This document of factual history was written by an Editorial Committee consisting to twenty-three veteran freedom fighters, famous historians and researchers. Its objectivity can be judged from the following observation in the book about the revolutionary movement in pre-independence India. "Punjab too had as glorious a place in the revolutionary history as Maharashtra and Bengal. In particular it spread among the Sikhs" (p.10). The book in no way understates the contribution of Punjab and of Sikhs.

According to this book, "thousands of tribal men, women and children were imprisoned at Chaibasa (in Chota Nagpur tribal area) and several were shot dead by the English (during 1830-33)." (p.2)

"15,000 Santals were slaughtered in the (Santal) rebellion of 1855 by the British imperialists." (p. 3)

When Wahabi revolt (1786-1831) reached Bengal Titu Mir and others created a free zone. While fighting to defend it, "Titu and 40 others died heroe's death. 800 rebels were imprisoned. Titu's Commander Rasul was sentenced to death, the rest to transportation to a penal settlement for life." (p.3).

Incidentally, "The first convicts transported to Andaman Islands were the Wahabis." (p. 3)

In February 1915, 5th Light Infantry of Singapore revolted. "All of them were Muslims of East Punjab and Rajputana.....They were deeply influenced by the propoganda of the Ghadar Party and the anti-British Khilafat agitation...The revolt spread like wildfire in the city of Singapore...British and Japanese soldiers recaptured Singapore and carried out general massacre." (p. 89).

In Jallianwala Bagh : "Nearly 2,500 men, women and children were killed and injured." (p. 103).

"All told, at least 10,000 Moplas were killed in the name of crushing down the (Mopla) rebellion (1921-22) and 3,000 more were sentenced to transportation for life and shipped off to Andaman (Kala Pani)." (p. 115).

"There was an uprising in Rampa area in Andhra Preadesh in 1922-24 under the leadership of Alluri Sitaram Raju. Sitaram and his co-fighters Cora, Parol and others were killed by the British. Many were given life sentences and sent to Andamans." (p. 120).

In Bombay, the Communist party and the All India Trade Union Congress gave a call for general strike in support of the (RIN) revolt (18-22 February, 1946). In Greater Bombay, 3.5 million workers responded to the call of general strike. On the other hand, the Government declared Marshal Law and handed over Bombay to the British military. The British used tanks and armoured cars to break the general strike. In the two days in machine-gun bullets, over 500 people were killed.

On October 22, 1946, "Then what happened at Vayalar (Kerala) was a Mini-Jallianwala Bagh. The soldiers opened machine gun fire, killings more than 500 workers and peasants activists." (p. 200)

It is not necessary to give more figures from the book being quoted from. We may however cite some figures given by two other prominent personalities.

At the time of the 1857-59 revolt, after the victory of the British had been already achieved, nearly 50,000 people were hanged in the most cruel manner on roadside trees. Later in peaceful protests, Satyagrahs and Gurdwaras liberation movement thousands of entirely peaceful protesters were killed while a much larger number suffered serious injuries and disabilities. In the 'Quit India' movement of 1942, over 10,000 people died in police and military firings.

From an article in *Mainstream* of 13th September 1997 by Bhagat Dogra Jagmohan Singh.

And here is just one instance of what happened in Haryana in 1857: "......167 freedom fighters (residents of Chaubisi) were mercilessly crushed to death when they disobeyed orders of the British and announced their support to the nationalist forces...Those who died included Hindus and Muslims." (From an article in *The Tribune* of 20th September 1997 by Bijendra Ahlawat).

All this should be enough to convince anyone that the figures being given by Akali leaders including the Chief Minister are doctored and the conclusion drawn that India minus Punjab/Sikhs did not make any significant contribution in the struggle of freedom are totally wrong assertions as "contributions of Sikhs/Punjabis is not being recognized. Bhagat Singh had not been given the honour due to him because he was a Sikh," etc. All this does not strengthen but weakens national unity and integration. When Khalistani terrorism was still going strong in Punjab, these very figures were cited by its supporters to justify the demand for Khalistan. The argument was: "India got her freedom as a result of sacrifices made by the Sikhs and therefore they should have a Sikh sovereign State". Patriotic Sikh masses rejected the argument. They would reply : "Our martyrs gave their lives and made many other sacrifices along with others for a free, united and prosperous India. If we made more sacrifices than our proportion in India's populatoin, that increases our responibility to defend India's freedom and unity."

As a concerted effort is on to send wrong signals at a time when there is danger or revival of terrorism in Punjab, this writer thought it necessary to put the record straight.

The Situation in Punjab

Our economy is in a bad shape. Major parties are interested in safeguarding the interests of the exploiting classes. They seek to divide the common people on the basis of religion, caste, etc, so that they don't get organized to fight against poverty, for right to education and employment, reasonable wages as well as remunerative prices for their crops, etc. Left is weak and divided, hence unable to meet the challenges, which our country faces, by massive struggles. In such a situation, it is but natural that various types of social conflicts will grow and get sharpened. And if the parties that matter are unscrupulous enough to use every means to create vote banks; to use every possible method to come to power; to mint money and still more money, these social conflicts can become a serious danger for the society. And this seems to be happening in our country.

Recently, some Dalits skinning dead animals, that being their profession, were attacked by falsely alleging that they were killing a cow. This happened in Haryana. More or less at the same time in a village in Jalandhar district of Punjab, there was a prolonged social as well as economic boycott of Dalits by the rest. The matter does not seem to have finally settled amicably even yet. More examples of this type can be given but that is not mecessary. One particular phenomenon however needs to be taken serious note of.

For some time news has been appearing in Hindi and Punjabi dailies of Punjab almost every other day about religious conversions. These are about Christian missionaries converting not Hindus but Sikh Dalits to Christianity in various parts of Punjab in all three regions, i.e, Malwa, Majha and Doaba. There are also news items about new Churches coming up in villages. Such stories are there in newspapers we get in Amritsar though generally they relate mainly to Amritsar district. There are reports about responses and reactions too, not only by the SGPC but even by some from or close to the RSS Parivar. SGPC has even appointed a committee to visit concerned villages and find out the facts and causes of these conversions.

I have gone through these reports carefully. There is not even one allegation about force/coercion having been used anywhere. Reasons given are generally but briefly as follows:

1. Hindu Dalits embraced other religions because being victims of the caste system, they were never treated as equal citizens. A similar situation is now arising as far as Sikh Dalits are concerned.

At the root of the problem is discrimination against Dalits who now want to be rid of it.

In many villages, there are separate Gurudwaras as well as cremation grounds on caste-basis (Mazhabi Sikhs, Ramadasia Sikh, etc). Even such villages as were free from this bad practice are falling prey to it. Construction of a separate Gurudwara by Dalit Sikhs in the border village Bhaini Massa Singh has started only very recently...Dalit Bakhshish Singh of this village asked as to where were those who now are shouting about conversions when the Granthi of Gurudwara Baba Jiwan Singh on the occasion of the Anand Karaj (marriage) of her daughter Harjeet Kaur begged for *Guru Granth Sahib* but was refused.

There are many villages in Gurdaspur district in which centuries old untoüchability still prevails.

In some regions, there is shortage of water and therefore water is stored in Bawaias (tanks). When need arises, people belonging to Scheduled Castes are not allowed to take any out of the stored water. Similarly even common utensils kept for use on occasion of marriage, etc are not issued to Scheduled Caste families.

2. For years together, SGPC has not organized any religious gathering not only in our villages but in our whole area to preach Sikhism and its tenets.

3. Dalits are poor. Like themselves, theis children are likely to remain illiterate. Why cannot SGPC open free primary schools and even free dispensaries in rural areas?

   This question shows that by religious conversions, Dalits hope not only to be rid of humiliating discriminating but also to have a greater opportunity for their children to get education and medical care.

Opponents' View

Loud opponents of conversions allege that these are the result of:

(i) False propaganda that Christianity is capable of doing miracles. For instance, at gatherings, pictures are shown of a disease ridden person changed, from a condition of hardly being in a position to walk, returning dancing after the miracle.

This may be true to some extent at least. And of course, such a claim has no basis in reality. But then power of making miracles is claimed by priests of more than one religion, perhaps by every religion. Claims may be crude in cases of some and more refined in some other but without any basis in any case. This needs to be countered by education and developing a scientific temper.

(ii) Allegation of money-power being used is hardly being made by any one though it is not absent altogether. One convert made this allegation and added that he realized his mistake and had re-converted. I know personally two young Sikhs having become Christians allegedly for money. However, they are not Dalits but Jats.

As already stated, newspapers have also reported responses. As would be clear from the above, SGPC has not made much noise about it. Tarlochan Singh, Chairman of the National Commission for Minorities, has spoken about it. Some may be of the view that being a statutory authority, he should not have intervened suo moto in the way he has done. He has spoken as if conversions are only for money and hence illegal.

Pro-RSS elements and groups are intervening in their own way out of their alleged desire to help Sikhs who according to them too are Hindus (and therefore have no separate religious identity). The demands are as would be expected. For instance, a law banning all conversions altogether or like the one enacted recently by Tamil Nadu. Just as caste in which one is born cannot change, religion in which you are born must remain your religion all your lilfe. It seeks to negate the right to profess a religion of your choice granted by our Constitution after a very long debate in the Constituent Assembly.

It is good that as yet at least, VHP and Bajrang Dal have not tried to demolish any Church (in Punjab).

Pro-RSS and BJP elements are very much exaggerating the conversions. For instance, on March 12, 2003, one pro-BJP Hindi daily came out with a long report with the headline: "Thirty thousand families made Christians in Malwa region in one decade."

Interestingly, Punjab Christian Movement (PCM) has issued a statement from Jalandhar welcoming the decision of the SGPC to set up an enquiry to check the validity of these reports (that some Christian organizations were instrumental in the conversion of poor and Dalit Sikhs in border districts of the state). The PCM demanded an all-party committee to ascertain the factual position in border districts in this regard. This writer is not in a position to enlighten the readers about the PCM. The report about the PCM has appeared in a leading English daily of March 12, 2003.

There has been another interesting development. Almost simultaneously with the alleged recent conversions, a view has been put forward that Sikhism is not for abolition of castes but only for equality and equal rights for all castes. This may or may not be a coincidence. This view however was challenged and a debate started through the press.

What Should be Done?

Last but not the least, the important question is as to what all patriotic forces and peoples, Left or non-Left, should do in the present situation in relation to conversions.

If the SGPC and various Akali Dals including Akali Dal (Badal) firmly tell the Sangh Parivar not to interfere, there will be no serious problem.

In any case:

(i) Equal right of all persons 'to freedom of conscience and the right to freely profess, practise and propagate religion', of course, 'subject to public order, morality and health and to the other provisions of this part (III of the

> Constitution)' has to prevail. No law inconsistent with it or with other provisions of the Constitution should be sought to be enacted. In other words, right to change one's religion has to remain.

This right should become individual/personal right and mass conversions should not be there. However, this would become a reality only if caste-based discrimination is abolished amongst Hindus as well as Sikhs. A leading comrade who was born and has since been living in a village told me the other day: "About 6 years ago too, there was a sort of a wave of conversions to Christianty by Sikh Dalits. However, to escape the wrath of upper castes/classes, they did not cut their long hair and beards so that only those would know about their conversions who would visit their homes and see photos of Christ on the walls, etc."

By now Dalits are much more assertive than earlier. Those anxious that they should not change their religion should work for abolition of the caste system and ensure at least real social equality.

Morchas Not the Way

Ravi-Beas Water. The December 31,1981 agreement regarding Ravi-Beas surplus water signed by the Congress-I Chief Ministers of Punjab, Rajasthan and Haryana did evoke a negative reaction from the leadership of the Akali Dal-L, but it was in a low key. When the Prime Minister-Akali leader talks regarding the Akali charter of 45 demands broke down, the Akali Dal announced its decision to launch an agitation against the agreement. While it surprised many, the decision caused all-round concern.

The concern increased when it was announced that the main form of agitation would be preventing digging of the proposed Sutlej-Yamuna Link Canal (SYLC) as this was bound to lead to a confrontation between sections of people of Punjab and people of Haryana. The possibility of its leading to a worsening of the communal situation in Punjab too could not be ruled out. Naturally, the decision of the Punjab CPI-M to join the Akali Morcha was a much bigger surprise.

The CPI-M advanced more than one reason to justify its decision. One was that it had prevented the Akalis from launching a morcha for religious demands and had successfully persuaded them to go in for a morcha on a purely economic issue. Credit was sought to be claimed for this 'achievement' though the resolution formally deciding to launch the morcha began by talking of religious discrimination against Sikhs. Moved by an Akali leader, it had been seconded by Jagjit Singh Lyallpuri then of the CPI-M.

Soon after the adoption of this resolution, Akali Dal sources 'clarified', that besides its demand for the reopening of the accord on the Ravi-Beas surplus waters, the movement would include nine other demands. Among these nine were listed such religious demands as broadcasting of Gurbani from the Golden Temple and enactment of an All-India Gurdwara Act. There was also the demand for more powers for States as sought in the Anandpur Sahib resolution (for a Sikh-dominated Punjab in an India with a very weak Centre). The CPI-M and the CPI had opposed this resolution very strongly.

There was no public reaction from the CPI-M to this 'clarification'. The CPI-M also chose to maintain discreet silence when a top Akali leader announced that the planned movement would in fact be their *Dharamyudh* and also when Gurucharan Singh Tohra had called it India-Punjab war.

On April 24, 1982, CPI-M volunteers joined the Akali jathas at village Kapuri to prevent the digging of the canal. For various reasons, the Akali Dal decided to postpone the morcha and did not continue it after April 24. It is not known whether the CPI-M was consulted about the postponment. In any case, the announcement was not a joint one. However, indications were that the CPI-M would continue to take part in the morcha, if and when the Akalis resume it. It is therefore necessary to examine the arguments which the Akalis and the CPI-M had put forward. To be able to do that properly, some relevant facts and the background have to be kept in view.

By 'surplus water' is meant water over and above that which was already being used before India's partition.

In anticipation of a treaty with Pakistan and on the assumption that Pakistan would give up its claims regarding Ravi-Beas surplus waters, an accord was reached in 1955 for sharing the same as under: Punjab 7.2 million acre feet (MAF), Rajasthan 8.0 MAF, Jammu and Kashmir 0.65 MAF (Total 15.85 MAF). Availability was calculated on the basis of the flow series of 1921-45. Total of 15.82 MAF water represented average or mean availability and not actual surplus water in any single year. Thus the 1955 agreement in fact decided the proportionate shares, actual in any particular year depending upon the total actual surplus water that year.

Under the Indus Waters Treaty of 1960, the waters of Sutlej, Ravi and Beas became available for unrestricted use by India after March 31,1970. For this, India had to pay Rs. 100 crores to Pakistan.

Punjab was reorganized in 1966 and the separate State of Haryana came into existence. It demanded its share of the surplus Ravi-Beas waters out of composite Punjab's share. (Waters of Sutlej had already been planned to be utilized fully). In March, 1976, the Government of India issued an order dividing old Punjab's share of 7.2 MAF as below: Haryana 3.5 MAF, Delhi 0.2 MAF, Punjab: balance not exceeding 3.5 MAF. In case of less availability, shortage was to be borne by Punjab. Haryana's share was not to be decreased. Arrived at under the influence of Bansi Lal, Uninon Minister, the decision caused wide-spread resentment in Punjab. All political parties of Punjab opposed it. Giani Zail Singh was at that time Punjab's Chief Minister. He informed the Punjab Vidhan Sabha that he had requested the Government of India to reconsider its order. However, his Government accepted rupees one crore from Haryana towards digging the Punjab portion of the SYLC.

After the 1977 election, Parkash Singh Badal became Punjab's Chief Minister. His Government accepted another one crore rupees towards canal expenses. The preliminary notification to acquire land for the canal was also issued by his Government. Further, it was announced that construction work on the SYLC in Punjab territory would be inaugurated by Badal and the function would be presided over by Devi Lal, the then Chief Minister of Haryana. It seems there was strong opposition from within the ruling Akali Party and the construction work never started.

Badal requested the then Prime Minister to reopen the matter. Morarji Desai agreed to review the case but refused to make any change in the order. Surjeet Singh Barnala of the Akali Dal was Minister for Agriculture in his Government.

The Haryana Government went to the Supreme Court with the prayer that it should order the Punjab Government to implement the 1976 order. The Punjab Government headed by Badal filed a counter-case to get the 1976 order declared null and void. The Government of India brought about an out-of-court agreement on December 31, 1981, replacing the 1976 order. In view of this agreement, the Court dismissed all the cases before it, though the Akali leaders had made an application that the cases should not be allowed to be withdrawn.

The CPI-M led Kisan Sabha has challenged the legal validity of the December 1981 agreement in the Punjab and Haryana High Court. The case is still pending.

The agreement states that according to flow series of 1921-60 (mean) surplus Ravi-Beas water is 17.17 MAF (as against 15.85 MAF according to 1921-45 flow series). Mean supply of 17.17 MAF has been allocated as under: Punjab 4.22 MAF, Haryana 3.50 MAF, Rajasthan 8.60 MAF; Delhi 0.2 MAF; Kashmir 0.65 MAF. Shares of Delhi and Kashmir are not variable. Shares of others would increase or decrease depending upon how much surplus water is actually available.

According to the 1976 order, distribution of water between Punjab and Haryana was at best in the ratio of 50:50. The new ratio is 55:45 permanently and 58:42 till such time as Rajasthan is able to make use of the extra water allotted to it. From the viewpoint of Punjab, the new agreement obviously is better than the 1976 order. The fact, however, remains that the opposition parties were not associated or consulted at any stage before this agreement was signed. The matter was treated as if it concerned only the Congress-I. One reason was the then pending elections in Haryana and the narrow partisan electoral interests of the Congress-I. If the (mean) share of Haryana was to be decreased even marginally from 3.5 MAF, the Congress-I might suffer in the elections.

Let us now examine the main arguments being advanced by the Akalis and the CPI-M in support of their contention that even the new agreement does gross injustice to Punjab and according to Akalis, particularly to Sikhs.

1. The Akali leaders have been asserting that Rajasthan is not entitled to any share because it is not a riparian State. In support of this, they cite international law and conventions. They forget the "small" fact that Punjab and Rajasthan are not different countries. They also overlook the following: (a) Even before partition, Rajasthan was getting water from Punjab through the Bikaner Canal. (b) Without taking into account the need of Rajasthan for water from Punjab rivers, India could not have justified its demand for all the surplus water during Indo-Pak negotiations. The not-so-small amount of Rs. 100 crores was given to Pakistan out of the national exchequer. (c) Rajasthan was to bear 60 per cent of the expenditure on Pong Dam and 20 per cent of the Beas Sutlej Link. (d) The Akali leaders themselves did not raise any objection to Rajasthan' share till very recently.

   The Akali leaders also make the point that Rajasthan should not have been allotted at least the additional 0.6 MAF water under the new agreement. This is not a very big quantity and in any case for many years it will be utilized by Punjab. Differences regarding this can and should be settled through negotiations. They do not justify a morcha which will divide the people.

   It is true that the CPI-M has not come out against Rajasthan getting any share. But it is also true that it has not come out against the Akali stand. And the official organ of the Punjab CPI-M reproduced extracts from an article of Manjeet Singh Khera which supported the Akali stand though not in so many words (April 24, 1982).

2. Both the Akalis and the CPI-M argue that the ratio of shares of Punjab and Haryana should be 60:40. In this connection,

they always refer to the Punjab Reorganisation Act of 1966. Actually this Act does not provide this ratio as far a surplus waters are concerned. This ratio was provided for division of some other types of assets which were not of very great value. As far as surplus waters are concerned, the Act does not lay down any ratio or even any criteria. It leaves the matter to be decided mutually by the States concerned and failing that by the Government of India.

Many argue that water is on a different footing from ordinary assets. Some would consider the geographical/cultivable area of the two States to be the correct basis. This ratio is 53:47. Some others would want population ratio to be the basis. According to the 1981 Census, this ratio is 56:44. Still others would argue that the need of the States concerned and the interests of the country as a whole should also be taken into consideration. It is pointed out that percentage of net area irrigated to net area sown is the highest in Punjab. Differences in this regard can and must be resolved through negotiations.

3. The most important argument of Akali and CPI-M leaders runs as under: When SYLC is constructed,. Haryana will get 3.5 MAF water out of the water which in actual practice Punjab is at present utilizing – whether its own share or someone else's share. No extra water will become available. Water which at present flows to Pakistan will continue to go to that country till the Thein Dam is constructed. It is therefore certain that lakhs of acres of Punjab land in parts of Faridkot, Bhatinda, Sangrur and Patiala districts will go dry.

The argument has many flaws: Firstly, if for any reason any of the States concerned has not been able to use its full share and the unutilized part of its share has been fully or partly used by Punjab, it would not be a justification to deny the former its full share in the future too. Of course, a way out should be found to ensure that Punjab's economy is not hit. This again should be a matter of discussion in a calm atmosphere. Secondly, the argument does not take into account the following: (i) The actual share of Haryana in any particular year from Ravi-Beas surplus water would depend on the total actual surplus. If the total is less than 17.17 MAF, Haryana's share would not be 3.5 MAF but less. (ii) Haryana is already getting water in excess of its entitlement from Sutlej waters. This excess would be counted towards Haryana's share under (i) and additional water to be given to Haryana would decrease to that extent. (iii) With the construction of the SYLC, we would be in a position to utilize a part of the water now going to Pakistan. Taking everything into consideration, Punjab is not likely to suffer to any great extent.

According to figures available with the Punjab Government, actual net surplus Ravi-Beas water (excluding pre-partition use and waste) for 1980-81 was 11.65 MAF. Out of this Punjab actually used 3.62 MAF. Haryana got a total of 4.87 MAF out of waters of three Punjab rivers. Its entitlement out of Sutlej waters was 3.17 MAF. Thus Haryana got 1.70 MAF against its share in Ravi-Beas surplus waters.

If the December 1981 agreement had come into force and if the SYLC had already been constructed, the picture would have been as follows: (i) Out of 11.65 MAF, Haryana's share would be 2.5 MAF. Having already got1.7 MAF, it could claim only 0.8 MAF more. (ii) Out of 11.65 Punjab's own share would be 3.00 MAF. It would be entitled to use 0.44 MAF of Rajasthan's share. It would thus get 3.44 MAF as against 3.72 MAF it actually utilized, that is , a shortage of 0.18 MAF, even if no part of water gone waste was to become available for utilization. It is claimed by the Government side that out of wastage, 1.47 MAF would have become available for utilization while 1.2 MAF would have continued to flow to Pakistan. Out of this 1.47 MAF additional surplus water, Punjab's share would have been 0.37 MAF.

If these figures are correct, it becomes clear that the cry of lakhs of acres of Punjab land going dry is unwarranted. To say the least, it is grossly exaggerated. If the figures are doctored and are therefore challenged, the dispute has to be resolved through negotiations and with the help of impartial experts. Such matters cannot be resolved through confrontation between people of neighbouring States. Morchas on such issues can only complicate matters.

An effective morcha in Punjab on the Ravi-Beas waters issue would inevitably lead to counter morchas in Haryana and Rajasthan. That would divide the common people, and State units of most parties will get ranged on opposite sides. In Punjab, separatist forces will exploit the agitation and it may result in worsening of the communal situation. It will weaken the growing struggles of the toilers against the anti-peoples policies of the Government of India and of the State Governments. It will harm the cause of national integration. Even in relation to the matter in dispute, the Central Government is likely to be in a stronger position to dictate as a result of the morchas and countermorchas.

It is painful that the CPI-M should have joined such a morcha. It is to be hoped that the CPI-M, instead of joining the morcha, will join hands with the CPI to mobilize public opinion to force the Government of India to call an all-parties meeting at all India level but including the Akalis to thrash out differences in a calm atmosphere and also to force it to ensure early construction of the Thein Dam.

After the election in Haryana, it was not be impossible to force the Congress-I leadership to treat the matter as a national issue and not as a party affair. The Akalis too had to be forced to give up chauvinist slogans and not to treat the matter as a handle for narrow partisan interests.

Issues Bedeviling Relations

1. It is high time that the issues which have been bedeviling the relations between quite a few neighbouring states of India including Punjab and Haryana are debated frankly. These issues are mainly (1) territorial disputes and (2) Rivers water disputes.

Chandigarh and some said-to-be Punjabi speaking areas as in Sirsa (Haryana) and some said-to-be Hindi speaking areas in Punjab, e.g, Dera Bassi have been bones of contention. I remember a massive all-parties demonstration in Chandigarh, main slogan of which was: "khirea phul Gulab da, Chandigarh Punjab da". Chandigarh saw an equally massive demonstration of people of Haryana shouting equally catchy slogans claming Chandigarh for their state. Sentiments had also been worked up about other territorial claims. Much water has flowed in Punjab rivers since then. Life has made people wiser but not the leaders of most political parties guided solely by vote-bank politics.

Overwhelming majority of people of Chandigarh including Sikhs want the city beautiful to remain a Union territory. Punjabi speaking people in Sirsa etc. don't want to be taken into Punjab. Many will tell you : "If our area goes into Punjab now, we will be at the tail of the irrigation system and our agriculture will be ruined". In Haryana many will tell you : "What does it matter if a village which we think is ours goes to Punjab. After all, it will not be going to Pakistan" No demonstrations and counter-demonstrations are possible now regarding these matters. Even those who may be very much in disagreement with communists will/should agree with Lenin's view that "leaders should not only teach people but should also learn from them". All political parties national as well as regional—should agree that in relation to Chandigarh and territorial disputes between Punjab and Haryana, statues quo should prevail.

2. River water disputes are more difficult to resolve. Let us discuss disputes in this respect between Punjab and Haryana (and Rajasthan):

Punjab Re-organisation Act 1946 provided that all assets (except unused waters of rivers) will be divided between Punjab and Haryana in the ratio 60 : 40. Water's division was to be decided mutually and failing that by the Government of India. First Award given by Indian Government did not do justice to Punjab. Even the second one, did not do full justice, though injustice was less. Award of the Eradi Commission too failed to resolve the problem. Efforts are now being made to rouse Punjabi chauvinism which can lead to a dangerous situation as has developed between Karnataka and Tamil Nadu. That must be avoided as that will do immense harm both to Punjab and Haryana and also to India's unity-in-diversity and her integrity.

It must be stated bluntly and sharply that slogans like: "Punjab has no river water to spare"; "if we have any, we will sell it"…..

"These are Punjab rivers and no one else has any right over their water". "Only riparian states can claim water of any river and neither Haryana nor Rajasthan are riparian states", etc.

To the best of my knowledge and belief, not any of these slogans were raised by Akali party or anyone else till the rise of terrorism in the state. These slogans were first raised by those who came to be known as 'militants' or as terrorists. These were then taken up by Akalis and also by some intellectuals. In any case, these are not correct. Many Himachalis ask: "How can Punjab claim these river exclusively. Logically, Himachal can claim those rivers as exclusively belonging to it because they originate in Himachal. And we have the right to stop their water flowing to any other state, if and when we need can do it". Obviously no Punjabi will accept this position and rightly so.

Originally there was dispute only about respective shares of Haryana and Punjab out of share of erstwhile Indian Punjab.

As regards riparian principle, in my opinion it applies to sovereign countries and not to states within one country. No doubt, India is federal and needs to be more federal. However, it is one country and not a federation of 28 or so countries even though some states can have greater autonomy than the general pattern. Rivers water disputes have to be and must be resolved on some principle other than the riparian principle e.g, river basin principle. Secondly, when there is drought and shortage of water in a river, an upper state (e.g, Karnataka in case of Kaveri), must not act as if the lower state (Tamil Nadu in this case) has no right to water of the river at all. Water must be shared on some mutually agreed principle never forgetting that as Indians, as brothers/sisters and even as human beings we must share scarcity and prosperity in that spirit and not through unjust methods which may lead to mutual enmosity and even destruction. Punjab, Haryana and Rajasthan must avoid what happened not long ago between Karnataka and Tamil Nadu. Thanks to the Supreme Court of India and possibly the advice given by the Congress High Command to the Chief Minister of Karnataka, good sense prevailed.

Coming back to Punjab, following conclusions emerge:

1. Share of Rivers water between Punjab and Haryana must be mutually decided. If that proves impossible, let it be decided by a Bench of the Supreme Court in which no judge is either Punjabi or Haryanvi.

2. Question of SYL Canal has already been decided by the Supreme court. Also, Punjab has no moral or legal right to go back on its commitment made more than once by its topmost leaders. Even then, this matter too may be gone into by the Supreme bench which may be constituted to decide the shares of water.

3. Beant Singh Chief Minister of Punjab contended that Punjab should have a share in the waters of River Yamuna if Haryana is to have shares of surplus waters of Beas and Sutlej. The Supreme Court Bench can decide this question also.

It has to be ensured that the decision of the Apex Court are accepted by all and that there would be no agitations against these. Towards this end it is necessary for all national parties and also the regional parties to go to the people and convince them why this course necessary for the very future of our country, for its unity and integrity. All national parties must ensure that their state units are not allowed to take different and opposite stands on the same issue. Interests of the country as a whole demand not vote-bank politics but principled politics.

Motive Behind Projecting Maharaja Ranjit Singh

The Tribune of July 8, 2001 had a news item with a bold headline: 'Punjab to spread Maharaja's philosophy'. The first para of this long news report of a speech of Chief Minister Parkash Singh Badal reads: "(Shri) Badal said his Government would make earnest efforts to propagate the philosophy of Maharaja Ranjit Singh."

I am neither a philosopher nor a very competent person to analyse various philosophies. Even then I cannot resist the temptation of commenting upon Badal's frequent utterances regarding Maharaja Ranjit Singh and his rule.

Democracy was not the order of the day during the period of Maharaja Ranjit Singh. Governments were not elected by the people. Emperors, kings and maharajas wielded absolute power. Generally speaking, the institution was hereditary. That it was so was not the fault of Maharaja Ranjit Singh. In the society as it was then and in view of the nature of its economy, the prevailing political culture was natural. There were good maharajas and there were bad ones too. Maharaja Ranjit Singh was a good maharaja.

Had a Ranjit Singh been born during the days of Badal, he most likely would have been a good democrat. Badal, on the other hand, has been reducing democracy to a mere formality. He has been going all out to become an autocratic ruler concentrating all the powers in his own hands. No Minister can take a stand as per his own judgement. Nor is that all. The manner in which he distributes cheques at Sangat Darshan Darbars shows that he has assumed the powers of the Minister for Local Government, the Minister of Panchayati Raj, the Finance Minister, etc and also of the Municipal Committee, the Zila Parishads, the Block Samitis and even of the Panchayats. He is the Maharaja and can distribute government money in any way he likes. Spineless bureaucrats dare not draw his attention to rules and regulations and don't mind being reduced to the position of glorified clerks. His admirers may soon begin calling him Maharaja Ranjit Singh II. However, no one will consider him to be a good maharaja.

Maharaja Ranjit Singh is praised by one and all by saying, "he saw everyone with one eye", meaning thereby that he did not have different standards and yardsticks for different persons. In this respect, we are told that he was a democrat to the core because in a democratic form of government, all are supposed to be equal before the law. Prakash Singh Badal is just the opposite of Maharaja Ranjit Singh in this respect. Even in the matter of Sangat Darshan Darbars, when and where to hold them is decided by calculating the likely gain for the Akali Dal and BJP in the next elections. Nor is this all.

Even a rapist and also a murderer can go scot free if he is a close relation of some leader of the ruling coalition headed by Badal. I have written about the murder of a Bank manager and have alleged that the murderer is not being traced for more than two years now because the Chief Executive of the State is interested in hushing it up. Maharaja Ranjit Singh did believe in the principle that "no one is above law howsoever high he may be". But not our democratic Chief Minister.

Dynastic rule was inevitable in a particular type of society. It is obnoxious in a democracy. And once upon a time Badal was its strong critic. He flayed not only Indira Gandhi for it but also Jawaharlal Nehru. At least in relation to Indira Gandhi he was quite right. But now it is no secret that he would go to any length to establish the rule of the Badal family. What is worse is that he allowed his son (when the latter was a mere MP) to go round the State holding meetings of officers and issue orders to them as if he was already the Chief Minister the late *a la* Sanjay Gandhi at the national level. Would Maharaja Ranjit Singh, if he had been alive today, have acted like Badal!

Maharaja Ranjit Singh was secular. He himself was a Sikh but Punjab was not a Sikh theocratic State. All religions, we are told, were on equal footing. Badal is not at all truly secular. He remains a votary of the Anandpur Sahib Resolution whose declared objective is to ensure the 'political domination of the Sikhs' in Punjab. In a democratic set-up this would mean people of other religions becoming second class citizens. To achieve this objective, Badal will not even mind the RSS and the RSS-controlled BJP establishing Hindu Rashtra in India. Let it be recalled that Badal had called upon the Sikhs to go to Ayodhya for kar sewa to ensure "*Mandir Wahin Banega*" by demolishing the Babri Masjid.

Badal expressed his gratitude to Prime Minister Vajpayee for granting approval to set up a programme, a unique visual project at Amritsar, on the life and times of Maharaja Ranjit Singh......

This would be welcome if the project is manned by really objective historians and not such historians who are willing to prove whatever they are required to prove and to denounce what the rulers of the day want to be denounced even if it is absolutely true. Maharaja Ranjit Singh was a good maharaja in a particular sense. However, it is time for people to know the truth about the real economic conditions of the common people, including the common Sikhs under his rule as compared to the feudal classes.

I will make only one more point. Badal has announced that The Maharaja Ranjit Singh Chair would be set up in Guru Nanak Dev University as a part of these celebrations (i.e, bicentenary coronation celebrations of Maharaja Ranjit Singh). Let me remind the readers of the fate of the earlier Chairs. Almost all had to close down as the government stopped providing the necessary finances. These included the Guru Gobind Singh Chair, Sant Kabir Chair, Bhagat Nam Dev Chair and Guru Ravi Dass Chair. Dr. B.R. Ambedkar Chair with Harish Puri as its professor continued for some more time because Dr Puri offered to work without any salary. It may be relevant to remind the readers that when in 1988 or so Vice-Chancellor S.S. Bal retired, a Maharaja Ranjit Singh Chair was established in the University by the then government. No money was provided even after one year. Bal, a prominent historian, would have done a good job if he was provided the necessary finances. One can only hope that the second Maharaja Ranjit Singh Chair will not meet the same fate. For money, there is an army of Ministers. Chairs are established only to oblige some persons or to gain some applause and not for research work as such.

To sum up, there is much talk of Maharaja Ranjit Singh and his philosophy only to help Badal become Maharaja Ranjit Singh II and to establish the Badal dynasty. The Maharaja's name is also being misused to establish a theocratic State in Punjab within India with a very weak Centre.

Hard Look at Free Power-supply for Agriculture

The issue of free supply of power (electricity) for agricultural purposes is a hot issue in Punjab. The Akali Dal (Badal) was for it and Badal promptly implemented the commitment made on the eve of 1997 Assembly Elections immediately after he became the Chief Minister of Punjab for the third time. The experience of this had been as follows:

1. (a) Big landlords like Badal himself and Harcharan Singh Brar of the Congress were the biggest beneficiaries. The media assessed their gain as Rs. 12 lakh or so a year in each case. No one contradicted this assessment.

   (b) Landlords and rich zamindars having more than one tubewell each also gained a lot not only as a result of not having to pay for the electricity consumed by their tubewells but also by selling water, which they were getting free, to peasants who needed it for their crops; and the latter could get only by buying the water from them.

   (c) Poor peasants did not benefit in any way while middle peasants having their own tubewells did benefit. However, they often expressed the view that they would be happier if they would get power regularly even by paying for it rather than having it free but with the supply being very uncertain.

2. Given human nature as it is at present, anything supplied free-of-charge (with the exception of education) is likely to be misused. And there is no doubt that the facility of free electricity for agriculture during Badal's rule was grossly misused. For instance, through illegal connections it was used for non-agricultural vocations of various types. Also, for electric heater, air-conditioners and for electric cooking devices, etc. Of course, only the rich could do that but the resulting loss to the Punjab State Electricity Board (PSEB) was certainly quite big. With corruption in Punjab being sky-high, all this could be done without any difficulty.

3. While introducing free electricity for agriculture, Badal had said that the loss of the PSEB would be only Rs. 200 crores per annum and that the government would reimburse the loss suffered by the PSEB. This was a gross underestimate and a blatant lie. It was nailed down as such in the first session of the new Assembly itself by CPI MLA Hardev Arshi. Now everybody agrees that the loss was much bigger and not even any part of it was reimbursed.

4. Badal's claim that agricultural production in Punjab increased tremendously as a result of free power supply has not been substantiated convincingly.

5. The policy of free power supply for agriculture had two aims: (a) to increase the Akali vote-bank (b) to benefit the rich peasants and landlords groups which control the Akali Dal. It, however, had some negative social effects as well.

   Big sections of Hindu traders saw this measure as meant to help the ruralites as against the urbanites. Many saw it as a measure to help agriculture as against industry. Dalits in villages saw it as a measure which discriminated against them.

   The remedial measures taken by Badal were as follows: (a) Persons belonging to Scheduled Castes were assured free power supply for domestic purposes upto 50 units. But the conditions imposed were such that not many benefited. (b) On the eve of the February 2002 elections the Octroi levied by the urban local bodies in the State was abolished. This made the urban organs of local self-government virtually bankrupt because the step was taken without providing alternative sources of income.

6. The undeniable fact today is that this one measure (free power for agriculture) has done immense harm not only to the PSEB but to the entire economy of Punjab including its agricultural economy. This aspect deserves a separate article.

Place of English in Education System

During the British rule and for many years even after independence the progressive forces in the country demanded that mother tongue should be the medium of instruction up to the highest stage of education and in any case at least up to Matriculation to begin with. It was of course realized that there would be difficulties to achieve this at higher stages of education. Importance of English, as a language for international communication too was realized and concede. The truth that a child can learn and assimilate best in the mother tongue, however, was not thrown over board.

As years passed, thinking of many sections of people began undergoing a change. It was seen in the growing demand for English medium schools. In State after State so-called English medium public schools began coming up not only in towns but also in villages. Managements of even chains of DAV and Khalsa schools started good quality English medium public schools in towns. Fat donations at the time of admission were obligatory in such schools.

During the hey day of terrorism in Punjab, Punjab Istri Sabha and then the Punjab Istri Sabha Relief Trust raised funds to help children of victims of terrorism, to receive or to continue receiving education. At one time, more than 600 such children were being helped by the Trust with stipends. In the course of this work, it was noted that even mothers widowed by terrorists and belonging lower middle class and even semi-skilled and skilled worker's families wanted to send their children to English medium schools. And Punjab was no exception in this respect.

Soon after Badal led Akali-BJP Government came to power in Punjab in 1997, its Minister of Education Tota Singh, initiated a move to introduce English as medium from Ist primary class even in Government schools. As soon as the idea was floated, strong opposition was voiced by Punjabi Lekhak Sabha and a number of intellectuals and some parties. A partial retreat was made. Decision backed by Badal was announced that English from Ist Primary class in Government schools would not be medium of instruction but a compulsory subject. Argument put forward in support was: children of well off sections of people go to costly English-medium schools and therefore, in the job-market they will have an advantage over children of poor people. The argument was flawed. I asked some sensible primary teachers in some Government schools as to their opinions. They were unanimous in their opposition. They said: "Most of our students come from very poor families with illiterate parents living in houses in which there is no atmosphere for studying, etc. We find it very difficult even to teach them Punjabi—their mother tongue. The proposal to teach them English also will prove harmful for them". I was told that the teachers proved to be right. I have no doubt in my mind that a proper survey would bear this out.

What is surprising is that the Left Front Government of West Bengal almost at the same time re-introduced English as compulsory from Ist Primary class in government schools. It seemed that it was done under strong pressure of comparatively not-well-off sections of middle class not in a position to pay big amounts in private English medium schools. This is my impression from whatever news from West Bangal appear in Punjab papers. And now comes the news that the Government of Maharashtra too has decided to teach English as a compulsory subject from first primary class.

The argument about its necessity to help the poor to be able to complete in the job market is fallacious. The idea, that very many jobs will be created for those having mastery over English by the multinationals is not very correct. Notwithstanding all this, it is true that children of poorer sections are at disadvantage. Way out is not what State Governments are doing. Correct way out is make uniform curriculam/syllabus legally obligatory in all Government as well as private schools with compulsory inclusion of 3 languages formula of Jawahar Lal Nehru. This formula visualised that the first language to be learnt and the medium at the primary stage must be the mother-tongue/regional language. The second language to be learnt would be Hindi or one of the modern Indian languages in cases where Hindi is the mother tongue/regional language. English has to be the third language to be learnt at a proper stage after primary. (Sanskrit is not a modern Indian language and can be an optional subject at a higher stage but should not be smuggled into the three-language formula as has been done in U.P.

Be that as it may, it is high time that this whole matter is discussed by topmost educationists who have a scientific outlook and are free from bias in favour of everything foreign as well as from Hindutva bias. Such an exercise can help to evolve a national consensus (if necessary, through a national debate) about place of English in our educational system as a language and as medium of instruction. And this consensus can serve as a guideline for people, political parties and Governments.

Populism in Punjab

Populism has become a bane for the country and its economy. It did not require much intelligence to realize that free power for agriculture would do great-harm to Punjab's economy including agriculture. And yet Akalis made this promise at the time of elections to Punjab Assembly and implemented it very promptly when they came to power in February 1997. This was done for narrow electoral considerations. For the economy and the interests of the State as a whole, results as feared have been negative.

Another populist slogan put forward by Parkash Singh Badal related to old age pensions. He would say: "If we come to power, every man above 65 and every woman above 60, would get old age pension. Except age, there would be no other condition. Even I would be entitled to get an old age pension". What Badal promised also meant that Government employees would get two pensions—one as an employee (from the date of superanuation) and the old age pension after 65/60. This is the position in some highly developed countries. Badal's friends in the bureaucracy, if asked, would have told him that implementation of his slogan in Punjab would be well nigh impossible. Fortunately, good sense prevailed and Chief Minister Badal forgot what he had promised as would be Chief Minister. He did not even make any improvement in the scheme as it was before he took power. It would have been correct and reasonable if he had increased the rate of pension from Rs. 200/- to say Rs. 250/-. Instead, the Akali-BJP Government tried to increase his vote bank by allowing sanctioning of pensions to many not entitled while many eligible ones were not been able to get despite going from pillar to post.

Unfortunately populist slogans are not opposed even by Left parties for fear of losing votes. The above mentioned populist slogans of Badal were not opposed or even criticized sharply by any party in Punjab when they were advanced. Narrow electoral considerations have led to another evil. Most politicians don't say "No" to any thing if saying that is likely to lose some votes howsoever wrong the demand/request may be. My own experience is that a principled stand does not have a negative effect even from an electoral viewpoint.

A wrong request conceded may please the beneficiary but is likely to annoy some others.

In connection with the above, I may recall some incidents from my experience as President of erstwhile Municipal Committee Chheharta out of many having some relevance to the issue. At that time, President was also the Chief Executive Officer of the Committee.

1. Some new Sweepers were to be employed. A number of application had been received. Two or three days before the applicants were to be interviewed, one old man (a supporter of ours and known to me personally) met and told me : "My son has applied to be appointed as sweeper. Please ensure that he is appointed". I explained to him that we had been strong critics of favourtism, nepotism etc and hence appointments must be made strictly on merit. He told me "Please remember that you got eight votes of my family". This was somewhat unexpected. However, I took only a second to give my reply: "If you think that we should not go by merit, you may not vote for me/us during the next elections". He was taken aback and departed. Next day, he met and told me that he was wrong. He even apologized.

2. There were very few trained dais in the whole town. We started classes in the Municipal dispensary for training dais. Two/three trained dais were also engaged by the dispensary. They were to do delivery cases free of charge. Later they were allowed to accept sweets if offered voluntarily. Complaints began to be received about fees being charged illegally. Repeated oral warnings and persuasions produced no result. Minor punishments too failed. On the basis of some written complaints, an enquiry was ordered. One was dismissed. It was not expected that I being a trade union leader would do that. My own view was it would be totally wrong on the part of a trade union leader to tolerate corruption. The strong action taken did help and my rating as a trade union leader too did not suffer.

3. One sweeper while on duty having drunk heavily beat up one Sanitary Inspector. He was suspended. A big agitation was

built up by Congress with main mobalisation from outside Chheharta, i.e., from Amritsar. There was a firm refusal to drop the matter unless a written apology was submitted. A mass campaign was run by us to place true facts before the public. Finally, the offer was accepted.

It is not necessary to give more instances. The point sought to be made is that a principled stand does not necessarily lead to erosion of mass support if it does not smell of bureaucracy and vindictiveness.

Likewise, a principled stand against populism needs also be taken without fear of losing mass support. Sometimes that may give some temporary set-back. But then it is wrong to sacrifice long-term interests of the people for the sake of some immediate gains real or illusory. Just and correct demands which are also correct and reasonable under the given situation have to be raised and fought for. However, it would be wront to raise demands which will do more damage than benefit to the common people as distinguished from vested interests, economic or political.

Higher Education and Question of Fees

On 6th July 2003, the senate of the Punjab University discussed the directive of the Punjab government to introduce the detailed fee structure notified by it for higher education. In the interest of the country and the people, primary and even secondary education should be universal and compulsory. That however cannot be the case as far as higher education is concerned. Nevertheless, importance of higher education for the development of the country is indeed very great. It is therefore necessary that admission for higher education should be given only on merit and not for money at the cost of merit. In fact, money-giving capacity of an applicant should not count at all.

No one can claim that only students coming from rich families can be toppers. Toppers can come from lower middle classes also and even from poorer families. Policy in relation to admission and tuition fees, as well as funds, has to be such as will ensure that those deserving admission on merit are not denied the opportunity on account of inability to pay the required amounts. Such denials will not only be injustice to such meritorious candidates, it will be very much against the interests of the country and its future.

Since 1990 or so when a New Economic Policy of globalization, liberation and privatization was adopted it has been argued that even in case of such services as higher education full cost must be met by the beneficiaries. In other words, those who cannot afford to pay 'user charges' must go without it. March towards this goal started when Narasimha Rao was the Prime Minister. It has been speeded up by the present Government of India. Our Chief Minister also believes, in high speed in this matter. Exorbitant and shocking increases which are being forced upon on Universities and colleges including professional institution are a result this policy. It is already clear that many meritorious students who would have got admissions would not now even dare apply in view of the very high fees being forced by the Government. Some Principals-Senators narrated their experience of having to see many saddened parents and their wards going back when told the fees they would have to pay.

In every welfare State, Government has a responsibility in the matter of education. Our Governments in the centre and in the State want to give up the responsibility. The University has been told that if the proposed fees are not introduced, they will even then calculate the deficit of the University as if the same are in force. This will enable the Government to reduce its grant. Aim is to reduce it to zero ultimately. In case of colleges, threat is the same. Aim also is the same, i.e, to reduce grant equal to 95 per cent of deficit to zero. We can imagine the consequences of the policy, if the same is not resisted right now.

Guru Nanak and Punjabi Universities have loyally decided to introduce the exhorbitant fees because the Acts governing them are very undemocratic. Senates are only talking forums without any powers. Their Vice-Chancellors have more powers in relations to the Universities than the Chief Minister has in relation to the State. And a practice has developed to appoint such Vice-Chancellors who would loyally carry out the wishes of the Government. Punjab University fortunately is somewhat different. Its Senate is constituted much more democratically and also has real powers. It has therefore great responsibility too. And that is why it adopted a resolution which said that it would not implement the new fees structure notified by the Governmen. It also pointed out that the Government did not have the powers to give any such directive. During the debate, many pointed out that the Government did not even consult the Universities. I have no doubt in my mind that it did not because its decision was undefensible.

A few argued: From where can the Government get all the money needed? Look at the unthinkable and very exhorbitant increases in salaries, allowance, perks, etc given even by the present government itself to Ministers, MLAs, ex-MLAs, bureaucrats, police officers, etc. And look at the jumbo size Ministry as also an army of DGPs, ADGPs, IGPs, DIGPs and other high police officers, by no means needed now. And does not one read in newspapers every day about tons of crores of rupees out of the Government funds going down the drain in one scam after the other...No, it is not a question of lack of funds. It is the outlook that higher education must be the preserve of the exploiting classes and those who defend their interests.

Many Senators expressed the hope that the Govt. will change its outlook and not insist on its 'directive' being implemented. Punjab University Senate has acted wisely. It has asked the Vice-Chancellor to appoint a Committee to work out and recommend a reasonable fee structure and also to go into various funds being charged because, for the parents what matters is the total sum which they have to pay.

It is to be hoped that this committee will recommend to the Senate a fee structure which will provide freeships for all who need, half-freeships for those who cannot afford to pay full fees, etc and will also consider as to what increase if any should be there for the rest. Final decision of course will rest with the Senate, which was to be taken by the end of September. In the meanwhile there was to be no increase in fees in the University itself. It is hoped that managements of affiliated colleges will also act accordingly. It is also hoped that there will be adequate rethinking in the Government so that confrontation is avoided.

I was sorry to read the news report in the Chandigarh edition of national English daily describing as "populist" the dominant viewpoint in the Senate of the Punjab University. As far as I am concerned, I have always opposed populism. However, to defend the interests of the common people and of education and the country is not populism but a sacred duty. In any case, news should not contain the views of the reporter or the Sub-editor. To do that is not good journalism.

IV

Problems of Sikhs

Sikh Problems: Looking Back

When forced to quit India, the British imperialist rulers had succeeded in partitioning our country. They had been over a long period, pursuing a policy of 'divide and rule'. They had formed, fed and encouraged communalism. Certain vested interests for their narrow class aims had succeeded in rallying behind the cry for Pakistan, large sections of Muslims by misusing religion and its appeal. Various acts of omission and commission of the dominant leadership of our national movement and also mistakes made by its various components played into their hands.

Today once again a serious danger has arisen for the unity and integrity of our country. US imperialism is out to destabilise and even disintegrate India. As in the past, imperialism and its agencies are encouraging communal and divisive forces. They are also supporting the cry for 'Khalistan'. Vested interest wanting another partition of the country are once again misusing religion and its appeal. True, the big difference is that it is not Imperialism which today rules our country. That is one reason why the patriotic people—Hindus, Sikhs, Muslims and others alike—can feel confident of defeating the new imperialist conspiracy.

However, to be complacent will be quite dangerous. Once again acts of commission and omission of the erstwhile leaders of the national movement and our present rulers have helped the divisive forces. It is they who tried to use Bhindranwala card against the Akalis even though the Akali leadership too later used him against the Congress-I and its Government. Even now by first refusing and later by delaying a judicial enquiry into the violence that followed as well as the violence that preceded the assassination of late Prime Minister Indira Gandhi, the Government has only helped those who are interested in increasing the Hindu-Sikh divide instead of overcoming it.

The imperialist game unlike in 1947 will undoubtedly be defeated. What is needed is to defeat it without undue delay and without having to undergo needless sufferings and sacrifices. For that, it is necessary to recall some of the past mistakes and their lessons so that there is no danger of their being repeated now even in a modified form, And not for the Congress leadership alone. Let us first begin with the Left.

The British rulers sought to utilize every diversity of our great country to encourage divisions amongst our people with a view to weaken our common struggle for freedom. The duty of all patriotic forces was, to oppose the effort and not let it succeed. This required a serious study of India's complex reality in the light of laws of historical development. The Marxist definition of 'nation' given by Stalin led Indian Communists to grasp the reality of India being a multi-national country. This definition is as under:

> A nation is historically constituted, stable community of people, formed on the basis of a common language, territory, economic life, and psychological make-up manifested in a common culture. It is only when all these characteristics are present together that we have a nation.

Indian Communists noted that the Indian people spoke not one common language but consisted of many linguistic groups. Bengalis, Tamils, Telugus, Punjabis and others speaking different languages constituted stable communities with common territories etc. These were characterized as nationalities. The Communists also noted the fact that multilingual provinces were a British device and it was a part of their game of divide and rule. They (as all progressive forces all over the world) drew inspiration from the way the people of USSR had solved their national problem and built unbreakable unity of people of various nationalities in what before the October Revolution was rightly labelled 'a prison-house of nations'.

It is now no secret that in applying the Marxist theory and the experience of the Bolsheviks led by Lenin to the Indian reality, the Indian Communists fell into some errors. First, they perhaps tended to underestimate the fact of the growing common economy of India as well the growing consciousness of 'Indian-ness', of being Indian—consciousness which has roots in our long history and which was immensely strengthened by the need of the common fight against the British and the fight itself.

Secondly, in Czarist Russia, it was the Russians (exploiting classes) who oppressed all other nationalities inhabiting the Czarist Empire. This generated distrust of the Russians, to remove which Lenin assured these nationalities the right of self-determination including the right of secession. In actual practice this assurance helped to forge unity. In India no one nationality or linguistic group oppressed others. All were oppressed— economically as well as culturally—by the British. In the situation prevailing in India, to talk of the right of secession was not only uncalled for but was positively harmful because it could only play into the hands of those wanting partition on communal grounds.

Thirdly, Indian Communists came to believe that the demand for Pakistan was a distorted expression of the urges of those nationalities the majority of whose people were Muslim by religion. Likewise the demand for a Sikh homeland was considered to be distorted national expression of Punjabis a sizeable section of whom happened to be Sikhs by religion.

These serious errors misled Communists into taking wrong position with regard to these divisive and dangerous slogans. It did not take them long to realize their mistake, to own it and to correct it. In a futile attempt to embarrass and silence the Communists, Akali leader Sant Harchand Singh Longowal had been recalling this 38-year-old chapter in the history of the Communist movement. We recall it because of the danger of similar mistakes being made by some well-meaning progressives. That such a danger is there and needs to be guarded against would be clear, from the following instances.

By now it is well-established that the 1973 Anandpur Sahib Resolution of the Akali Party is permeated with the thinking contained in the thesis Sikhs-a-separate-nation. It explicity demands a Punjab in which Sikhs would politically dominate. And yet Inder Kumar Gujral has been repeatedly trying to create the impression that there is nothing wrong with this Resolution. Khushant Singh called it most dangerous.

In one of the 'Occasional papers for Private Circulation only', Balraj Puri of the 'Committee for Dialogue on Punjab', opined that in contemporary India, religion is one of the two 'most pronounced forms of sub-national identities'. He has in a way lent full support to the 1973 Anandpur Sahib Resolution. Here is what he says:

> Anandpur Sahib Resolution to which most of the Sikh leadership, including its extremist section, is formally committed does seem to accommodate the basic objectives of the community, preservation of the Punjabi community and the Sikh identity and maximum power for both.

There are some others too who have spoken and written about Sikh sub-nationalism. This cannot but feed the 'Sikhs-a-separate-nation' thesis. Many other have talked about separate Sikh political identity. Sikhism today undoubtedly is a separate and independent religion. It is so recognized by the Indian Constitution. Separate Sikh religious identity is a reality and it is the duty of all Indians to ensure Sikh religion its full and proper rights. All Sikhs in whatever nook or corner of the country they may be living (as all others), must feel secure and also free to believe in and practise their religion. Proper atmosphere for that, apart from constitutional and legal guarantees must be created. But to talk of an independent and separate political identity of Sikhs is not only wrong but dangerous.

Economic and political interests of Sikh workers are common with the workers of other religions and opposed to those of employers including Sikh employers. The same is the position of Sikh agricultural labourers, poor peasants, and others. To talk and to act on the basis of independent political identity on the strength of religion not only divides toilers and makes them line up behind their co-religion exploiters. It cannot but feed theocratic ideology and even separatism on communal basis.

Sometimes wrong and opportunist positions may help to mitigate some immediate difficulties but may prove quite harmful and dangerous in the long run. Jawaharlal Nehru very correctly talked about India's unity in diversity. Congress heading the freedom movement made a commitment to the Indian people that after India became free, provinces would be re-organised to form linguistic states. It was correctly understood that this would result not in weakening but in strengthening Indian unity. This commitment was sought to be thrown overboard after Congress came to power in free India. Powerful and united as also bitter struggles had to be waged before the States of Andhra, Kerala, Maharashtra, Gujarat, etc were formed.

The formation of Punjabi-speaking Punjab and Haryana got delayed because unfortunately the question of language in Punjab got mixed up with religion and communalism. Ultimately this too had to be done though some distortions remained. Those who propogated the merger of Punjab, Haryana and Himachal Pradesh and those at whose instance this may have been done, were wanting to repeat the mistake made in the past.

India's diversity cannot be wished away and its unity and integrity can be safeguarded and strengthened only by recognizing it. In fact, it must also be remembered that whatever development has taken place in India has strengthened self-awareness of various linguistic and cultural groups (nationalities, to use Marxist terminology). In the interest of a strong Centre itself, the Centre-State relations need to be adjusted keeping in view this fact. The proposal to merge Punjab, Haryana and Himachal Pradesh would a step in the wrong direction. If implemented, it will have serious negative consequences.

Some Akali leaders have been alleging that the Congress had gone back on some pledges given by it to the Sikh. They further allege that what they are asking for now is only the implementation of these pledges. The most often quoted and most relevant to the argument is the following utterance of Jawaharlal Nehru:

> The brave Sikhs of Punjab are entitled to special considerations. I see nothing wrong in providing an area and a set-up in the North wherein Sikhs may also experience the glow of freedom.

These words of Nehru are being interpreted to justify the demand for special rights for Sikhs, for a special status for Punjab and for pre-eminence of the Sikhs in Punjab. Nehru is reported to have made this statement in July 1946 at a press conference in Calcutta at the time of the All India Congress Committee session. By that time it had already become clear that India would be partitioned and besides a free India, there would come into existence also Pakistan. Akali leadership had entered into negotiations with the Muslim League leader Jinnah who was reported to have offered some sort of an autonomous region for Sikhs in Punjab. Akali leadership had also put forward the slogan of 'Azad Punjab' in which Sikhs would hold the balance and which could even be a buffer State between India and Pakistan. Overwhelming majority of patriotic Sikh masses were opposed to these anti-national positions of the Akali leadership and it was their opposition which made the Akali leaders retreat.

Jawaharlal Nehru, it seems, in his anxiety to minimize the damage did not place exclusive reliance on the patriotic Sikh masses. And he made the above statement to placate the Akali leadership—a statement which is capable of being interpreted, in a manner quite contrary to certain very basic ideas and principles propounded and/ or supported by Nehru. His ideas of secularism did require a firm assurance to all religious minorities that they would enjoy full freedom to practise and preach their religions; that all their religious right consistent with the rights of others would be fully protected while the State would have no religion of its own and would guarantee equality in different fields to all its citizens irrespective of their religious beliefs.

The statement Nehru made in July 1946 is ambigious, to say the least. It does appear that it was a short-sighted statement which the Akali leadership has been exploiting to the maximum. Perhaps some competent research scholars and historians could throw more and better light on it. One would only like to make the following observations with which this article will also conclude :

Punjab with Sikh pre-eminence and any special status or rights for Sikh will only benefit the exploiting classes amongst them. That will not benefits but will harm the Sikh toilers and common Sikh masses as it will harm the entire country including Punjab. The demand for *Khalsa ka bolbala* in Punjab is as wrong as the demand for Hindu Rashtra in India.

Notwithstanding the above-quoted utterances of Nehru, Sant Fateh Singh who successfully ousted Master Tara Singh from the leadership of the Akali party, made a categorical declaration that the Akali party while seeking more powers for the States would not demand more for Punjab than for other States. This had played a positive part in bringing about the linguistic re-organisation of the then Punjab. The demand for special rights and special status for Sikhs can only divide Punjab as the equally wrong demand for Maha-Punjab would do. Short-cuts in the political field even when sought to be adopted by giants can prove harmful and even dangerous in the long run.

Nanak Shahi Calendar

Before we discuss some of the controversial issues about the Nanak Shahi Calendar, taking note of some connected and not so controversial issues is necessary and will be helpful. All religions have much in common besides having many divergent and differing views. Hinduism and Sikhism (like Hinduism and Jainism as well as Hinduism and Buddhism) are nearer each other than any two other religions. It is in the interest of Hinduism and Sikhism as well as of Punjab and even India as a whole that this nearness continues. If Shiromoni Gurdwara Prabandhak Committee (SGPC) assuming it to be the Supreme body of Sikh religion were to demand and insist that holidays connected with Sikh religion would henceforth be observed as per Nanak Shahi calendar, normally others should have no objection.

Actually, however, big sections of Sikhs themselves pointed out that common holidays of Sikhs with Hindus, i.e, Diwali and Holi, should continue to be celebrated together. The sentiment was so strong both amongst Sikhs as well as Hindus that it had to be respected by champions of Nanak Shahi Calendar. They agreed. This was made easier because Vikrami Calendar admittedly is not a Hindu Calendar. "It has no source in any of the Hindu scriptures". It is so named only after the name of the king who introduced it. It is to be hoped that later on demand would not come up for having holidays for Diwali as well as for Holi-per Nanakshahi Calendar too.

When it was first demanded that Sikh religious holidays should be as per Nanak Shahi Calendar, Chief Minister Amrindar Singh took the position that he would go by the decision of the Government of India and in the meanwhile, he would go by the national Calendar (for the year 2003). He was sharply but wrongly criticized for this. In their zeal, champions of Nanak Shahi Calendar, forgot or chose to forget that Sikhs were living in many parts of India not only in Punjab and that any decision taken by the Government of Punjab alone would not be binding on other States, which too may be having some Sikh religious holidays.

The demand raised from certain quarters that Nanak Shahi Calendar should be made the official Calendar of Punjab has to be rejected outright on two grounds. Firstly, India has to have common Calendar. No doubt India is a federal country. It is also true that India needs to be more federal than it is today. At the same time India is one country and must not be allowed to be converted into a Federation of 28 or so countries. Any move in that direction will produce disasterous results for India and the Indian people.

Secondly, demand for a Calendar (openly claimed to be calendar of Sikh religious community) to be official Calendar of Punjab can have only one objective, i.e, Punjab to be made a theocratic state (within or outside Punjab) having Sikhism as its official religion. It is meant to subvert one of the basic features of our Constitution, i.e, secularism. If anything, secularism in India must mean one thing, i.e, while every citizen must have the right to profess any religion and worship according to its tenets, State must have no official religion and State and religion as also politics and religion must be separated. RSS denounces secularism as pseudo-secularism only because it stands for India becoming a Hindu theocratic State to be called Hindu Rashtra. Those who want a Sovereign Sikh State outside India call it Khalistan. Those who want a Sikh theocratic State within India with a very weak Central Anandpur Sahib resolution appear to have made a deal with RSS-led BJP that they will not object to India becoming a Hindu Rashtra in which non-Hindus will become second class citizens on the condition that BJP will allow Khalistan within India. Acceptance of this demand will inevitably lead not only to Sovereign Khalistan but also to total disintegration of India. Thus, it is not a coincidence that on the date (14-4-03) on which the first copy of the controversial Nanak Shahi Calendar was presented to Parkash Singh Badal, President of the Akali Dal (Badal) by Prof. Kirpal Singh Badungar, SGPC President, a UK-based leader of separatist Sikh outfit raised the demand for Khalistan at a Gurdwara in Pakistan. A report in *The Tribune* of 15-4-03 added : "Manmohan Singh Khalsa of the Dal Khalsa said implementation of a separate Nanak Shahi Calendar for Sikhs indicated that the Sikh community was moving towards achievement of Khalistan". Several Sikh personalities based in US and London and also some SGPC members from Amritsar were also reported to be present. While one can be certain that the patriotic Sikh community will oppose as it has done in the past, any move for another partition of India, some vested interests are determined to struggle for a Sikh theocratic State. Nanak Shahi Calendar, they believe, helps them.

It is also not an accident that the Nanak Shahi Calendar has declared Jarnail Singh Bhindranwala a 'martyr' and that too at a time when India is said to be fighting not only terrorism in India but also international terrorism and along with the 'international community'. Newspapers of 7th June, 2003 reported that on 6-6-2003 at a function organised at Dewan Manji Sahib (Amritsar) it was officially declared on behalf of the SGPC by its President (a Badal loyalist) that Bhindranwala had died in June 1984 and was a martyr. He could not have done this without the prior approval of Parkash Singh Badal.

Agreed that Badal is not an extremist but some other facts too have to be kept in mind. He had signed a Memo to UNO demanding Khalistan, may be out of fear of terrorists. But there are other facts: He has never repudiated the unanimous Akali resolution that Sikhs are a 'nation' nor the Anandpur Sahib resolution which demands a virtual Khalistan within India with a very weak Centre. We are aware of the fact that while hailing Nanak Shahi Calendar, he also said that it needed some changes which however, were not spelt out. Be that as it may, let us assume that Badal is playing a game to garner pro-extremist Sikh votes in the coming Lok-Sabha elections. No sane person can have any doubt that this is a dangerous game.

It needs to be noted that Congress too is playing this game. For instance, Congress President in Punjab, Hanspal said that Nanak Shahi Calendar should have been a Sikh Calendar and not an Akali Calendar. What for there should be religion based Calendars at all, unless they are to be used for political identities based on religion, which is a dangerous proposition.

Jantris can serve the purpose so far as religious identity is concerned. Amrinder Singh Government too does not seem to believe in separation of religion and State. We may deal with this topic some other time. Let us Tiger vs elephant end this article by reproducing a para from an article about the calendar by Gurcharan Singh Lamba, a Sikh scholar and Editor Sant Sipahi, a magazine founded by Master Tara Singh. It appeared in *The Tribune* of April 14, 2003.

It reads as under: "However, it is amusing that the Calendar which is being given the name of Nanak Shahi is rather a hybrid of Gregarian, Bikrami and a host of Sant Babas, Sadh mandlis, historians, politicians and whosoever wanted to be on the band wagon."

The Nirankaris

Many people ask such questions—who are Nirankaris? What role do they play? Are they against religion? Do they really make such attacks on the Sikh religion and Sikh Gurus and on other religions, attacks which are not consistent with morality and order and should therefore be banned by law? This is an attempt to answer these and other connected questions. It is mainly based on *My Voice*, a collection of articles and sayings of the Nirankari Baba, Gurbachan Singh, published by the Sant Nirankari Mandal, and on the book *Nirankari Baba* by Balwant Gargi. As narrated by Balwant Gargi in his book, the Nirankari Movement was founded by a tatto master—Boota Singh (1873-1943).

Boota Singh had a marvellous singing voice and would do *kirtans*, chanting the *baani* of the Sikh Gurus. He was, however, opposed to the rigid conventions and rituals of his religion, the Sikh religion. He was against all taboos and opposed divisions on the basis of external habits and appearances. In 1929, he was proclaimed the new Nirankari Guru by one of his followers, Kahn Singh, who carried him on his shoulders through the streets of Rawalpindi joyfully shouting his discovery. Before his death, Boota Singh told his followers that after him Avtar Singh would be their guru. Baba Avtar Singh (1899-1969) became the head of the Nirankari Mission in 1943. Years before, Avtar Singh had been a staunch Akali Sikh and had served three years in jail as a freedom fighter. After partition, he set up the Sant Nirankari Mandal as a registered body in Delhi in 1948. In December 1962, he nominated Gurbachan Singh, his son, as the new Baba and in 1963 a coronation ceremony was held.

The Nirankari Mission is run by a Committee of seven—President, Vice President, Secretary, Chief Editor of the monthly journal of the Mission (*Sant Nirankari*), Joint Secretary, Treasurer and one more who is in charge of Sammagams. They are called Seven Stars. Besides the Seven Stars, the Nirankari hierarchy has eight Zonal Chiefs under whom local branches function. All of them are nominees of the Baba. The choice of a new star or Zonal head lies entirely with Baba and his decisions are never questioned.

By 1973, the Mission had 354 branches—27 abroad and the rest in India. Today their number must be much larger.

The Nirankari Mission has a volunteer corps of its own. Known as Sant Nirankari Sewa Dal, it was set up in 1954 in view of the frequent attacks made on the Nirankaris. The controlling body is the Seva Dal Board. In 1973, they numbered 6,500.

For definite historical reasons, vast majority of the people have come to have a deep and firm belief in God and religion. At the same time, more and more persons revolt against rigid rituals which come to be associated with various religions. More and more people begin to disbelieve obviously unscientific dogmas and superstitions even though sanctified by religion. More and more people dislike many of the undesirable practices indulged in at least by a section of the priesthood and that too in places of worship.

Without in any way going against the essence of religion, the Nirankari movement came out against rituals and taboos of various types and denounced the established priesthood. Baba Gurbachan Singh found fault with 'such religious preachers who are themselves in the dark about the reality of God and the teachings of the spiritual Masters', but who 'have adopted religion based on certain signs, symbols, dress and dogmas'.

Baba considered it a misfortune that instead of understanding the scriptures and following the same, people have rather made them the symbols to be adored and worshipped; the holiest book cannot give us any spiritual benefit through mere reading; one can benefit only through practising what is written in the scriptures.

Also the following: "If we worship the scriptures or our hand-made.... idols, we will not get any benefit. Baba disapproves of people worshipping stones, books and animals (*Nirankari Baba* by Balwant Gargi, p.161). Baba "wonders at the people who worship God in a measured way. They have fixed timings for their worship. Some consider the mornings and the evenings as the appropriate timings for the purpose. There are others who do it, say, five times a day and there are still others who get religious satisfaction by telling the beads a hundred or two hundred times a day. Such devotees should realise that such calculation with God is only expressing one's thanklessness to the God Almighty who is beyond all such calculations and measurements."

According to Baba, "those who preach that God is confined to certain places of worship or the four walls of some holy places are guilty before the All-pervading Lord Master". Baba ridicules "the so-called religious leaders engaged in funny rites and rituals as part of worship of God". Gargi quotes Baba as follows on page 26 of his book: "Hindus and Muslims have fought over pork and beef as a religious crusade for centuries. Nirankaris do not ban any food: we only discourage immoderation". Nirankaris are against renunciation of the world. They believe that one should continue performing one's normal vocations and functions. According to Baba, "body, mind and wealth are a gift of God and their unattached use is the true renunciation". According to him, "We need not renounce these instincts (sex, anger, lust, attachment, etc)" but should rather rationalise them. "In fact, lust and not love is bad". Baba refers to Sadhus as 'the so-called saints', 'parasites on society', as 'runaways and social parasites'. Baba came out strongly against preaching of religious hatred. For him 'no particular scripture is better than the other, no particular prophet is lower than another and no particular religions is superior to others'. He had 'no plans to establish any new religion'. Besides coming out against many religious rituals and taboos, Nirankaris have also propagated certain measures of social reform.

Here are Baba's views on marriage: Members of the Mission should celebrate the marriages of their sons and daughters in a simple way without any conditions and demands whatsoever. They should totally do away with the customary marriage parties and dowries. They should avoid unnecessary burden on spending on decoration, fire-works, etc....It would be still better if the marriages are solemnised in the Sat Sang (congregation) itself in the company of the holy saints where the couple will get their blessings.

According to Gargi, 'as a social reformer, he (Baba) has brought about many inter-caste marriages, inter-caste get-togethers and community gatherings of people from all religions and castes sharing meals and problems with amazing harmony and freedom'. Also, he 'has blessed many weddings with the simple ceremony of garlanding and a few rupees, expense'.

A sort of equality even though superficial is also inculcated amongst the Nirankaris. For instance, Nirankaris greet fellow Nirankaris by touching each other's feet. A bejewelled Nirankari woman in silk will touch the feet of another Nirankari woman in a ragged sari, sweeping the floor. Likewise, when eating in Sangat, they share morsels of food with each other.

As already noted, Nirankaris are far from being irreligious or anti-religious. While they voice discontent with rituals and taboos and obvious evils of established priesthood, Nirankari teachings on God and religion seek to keep the common people away from the path of class struggle. While preaching a sort of superficial equality, they seek to justify exploitive society and glaring economic inequality. This will be clear from Baba's own concept, "A Nirankari is one who has been blessed with a lasting perception of the Nirankari—the Formless". Further, "Everything is pre-ordained by God and life travels invisibly....Some materialistic scientists claim that God is only a subjective reality, the figment of fearful or yearning human imaginations. But God is an objective entity. All matter, tangible and intangible, is swirling in the Formless, who is a Super-conscious Universal Spirit." (Baba quoted by Gargi, p. 98, emphasis added).

Also the following: "Everybody knows that right from the beginning, meeting and parting, riches and poverty, health and sickness, etc have been the cause of all pleasures and pains. Obviously, this is an eternal circle. Though equipped with all faculties man is helpless before Nature. How far is it correct or proper to be agitated for things and events which are beyond our control ...All the ups and downs of life should be taken as Divine Will... Today the religious preachers preach renunciation. In fact, they forget that body, mind and wealth are a gift of God and their unattached use is the true renunciation."

Nirankari Baba denounces the so-called sadhus as social parasites and gets many supporters for that. He tells his supporters that the wealth of the rich is a gift of God and thus objectively seeks to prevent them from seeing the truth that it is the result of the exploitation of the poor. A superficial equality is preached only to perpetuate real inequality and exploitation of man by man.

In view of the foregoing, it is not surprising that the Nirankaris' opposition even to rituals, etc is not quite consistent. "....these religious rituals may act as appetisers for God-realization", even though "by themselves no amount of such religious routines can bless us with God-realizations. Many people object to our indifference toward the conventional meditation, recitation, reading and repeating the scriptures. In fact, all religious routines are intended for God-realization after which these naturally lose their purpose and significance."

Nor is this all. The Nirankaris have developed their own rituals and even superstitions. For instance: "The ceremony of footwashing and drinking this water was started in 1945... Gradually it became a basic custom of the Brotherhood....The Nirankaris wash the feet of any apsotle...nominee or any fellow Nirankari who conducts their Sangats and drink this footwash...Baba Gurbachan Singh's footwash, the most holy, is stored in the Delhi Bhawan in a large drum with a tap so that devotees can come (and) fill their phials and glasses...They use footwash as the most effective medicine." (Gargi).

Let us now examine what is there in the Nirankari teachings which can be objected to by the high priests of Sikh religion. No evidence has been produced or cited except rumours to show that the Nirankaris insult the Sikh religion or the Sikh Gurus. Of course, there are certain things in their teachings, which are inconsistent with certain practices and beliefs of orthodox Sikhs. Orthodox Sikhs worship the Guru Granth-Sahib, their sacred scripture. The Nirankaris do not do so. They consider it as book which should be read, understood and acted upon. They do not worship it because they do not worship any book or idol. However, "All scriptures are true because in these have recorded prophets' personal experience in God-realization."

Secondly, Guru Gobind Singh, the tenth Guru of the Sikhs, had decreed that there would be no Guru after him. The Nirankaris hold just the opposite view. According to them there can be no God-realization without a living Guru. "For reaching Him you need no roads, but the knower who can reveal the All-pervading God. A cool contemplation of the problem in the light of the holy scriptures will reveal that for the realization of God, one does not need many lives but a true guide—a perfect master."

"We should therefore lose no time to find a spiritual master who could bless our soul with a holy union with the Over-Soul. This is exactly what my missions is. Neither these books can educate you nor can mere tools make you a technician. It could be possible only through a competent teacher or guide. So is God-realization which can be attained only through a man of divine vision or knowledge". "One cannot get Spiritual light through one's devotion to the prophets of the past. One will have to get the initiation through the master of the time."

There is no doubt that Baba is regarded as God's representative on earth, as a tangible form of Formless, not only by his followers but also by himself. This clearly goes against the orthodox Sikh belief. However, in this respect the Nirankaris are not the only sinners. Namdharis too believe in living Gurus. And some other sects too, with many Sikh followers. If Namdharis can continue to be regarded as Sikhs, there is no reason why Sikhs Nirankaris should not continue to be so regarded. It can also be argued that in the long run the Sikh religion itself will stand to lose if it tries to throw out of its fold all except the most orthodox. It may be in the interest of the Sikhs themselves, if some dissent were to be tolerated and allowed within the Sikh religion. It must however be conceded that it is a matter for the Sikhs to decide. But surely this is no ground to demand the banning of the Nirankari Mission or its teachings, much less to use force to prevent their Satsangs. Those who disagree with it are free to preach against it. There is no doubt that the overwhelming majority of the Sikhs, left to themselves, would accept this proposition. Not so the Sikh priesthood. The Nirankari Mission has been increasing its influence rather rapidly. In Punjab most of its followers have been from amongst the Sikhs. This cannot but the resented by the established Sikh priesthood. And that explains the attacks made on Nirankaris from time to time by a part of the Sikh priesthood, ever since the coming into existence of the Nirankari movement.There can be no doubt as to what must be the attitude of all democrats and all secular-minded people on the present Akali-Nirankari feud.

Firstly, the right of the Nirankaris to hold their Satsangs and to worship in the manner they like must be fully defended. Those who think that their preaching are harmful and wrong in one way or the other can so propagate in their own gatherings but must not be allowed to attack the Nirankaris with a view to prevent them from holding their Satsangs. Any concession in this respect will invite and encourage attacks on many others too. And all this cannot but weaken and disrupt the unity of toilers.

Secondly, there seems to be no justification for banning the books containing Nirankari teachings. No book can be banned merely because it says something which is not consistent with some belief, rule or dogma of some religion or the other. If the banning of books were to take place on such grounds, Hindus practising idol-worship could with equal justification demand the banning of literature of the Arya-Samajist Hindus who are strongly opposed to idol worship. In fact, this could lead to the demand for the banning of a number of books of various religions or religious groups. If any Nirankari book or any book of any other religion or mission or sect has to be banned, it must be shown that it contains matter which is really derogatory and insulting, which is not consistent with morality and order.

Thirdly, an edict or decree in the name of Sikh or any other religion to socially boycott Nirankaris or followers of any other Mission or Sect like that must be opposed firmly and strongly.

CPI in Punjab can be proud that it has, in this difficult matter, taken a very principled stand which has been appreciated not only by the Nirankaris and all non-Sikhs but also by big sections of the democratic minded Sikh masses. It is to be regretted that that CPM has been trying to do tight rope walking with the overriding consideration of not annoying the Akalis. It formally opposed the hukamnama. Once or twice it came out against some highly objectionable pronouncements of the Akali extremists. At the same time it has tried to provide alibis for the Akalis and has tried to confuse the real issue by making irrelevent and unsubstantiated allegations that the Nirankaris are linked with the CIA and are a semi-fascist organisation like the RSS. It openly supported the right of the Nirankaris to hold their Satsangs only after a section of the Akali leadership itself had been forced to take this stand.

The Akali-Nirankari controversy is still alive. As long as it is alive, it has dangerous potentialities. A common stand by the CPI and the CPM in Punjab on this issue will be a big weapon to resolve the controversy on a principled basis and in manner consistent with the principles of secularism. A common stand by the CPI and the CPM will also help democratic minded intellectuals including Sikh intellectuals to openly take a correct stand. A common stand by the CPI and the CPM will strengthen those in the Akali Parties who are trying to take a correct stand. And obviously it will help to rally still more all democratic Congressmen as well as democratic elements within other parties.

V

Society and People

Poverty and Population

Once again loud and shrill warnings are being heard from various quarters about the danger of doom which faces India unless the problem of population growth is tackled on a war footing. Many intellectuals in the country believe that the family planning programme of Sanjay Gandhi of Emergency days was a badly needed one for the good of the country. They only regret that it was made unpopular and was spoilt by the crudely coercive methods adopted to prevent 'population explosion'. They argue that in some form or other India must have a family planning programme on a massive scale.

Nor is this all. Voices have been raised in favour of legalised compulsory sterilisation instead of coercion without legal backing as during Emergency. For instance, Prof. Tarun Bannerjee out-going President of the All-India Obstetric and Gynaecological Congress, said in an interview that "legalised compulsory sterilisation is the only method of controlling India's rapidly growing population". (*Tribune*, December 30, 1980). Further, it is no secret that the World Bank has all along been pressing India to adopt effective planning measures to control population. In actual practice, too, we seem to be heading towards methods that were adopted during Emergency. In Punjab, for instance, this writer has reliable information that officials of some departments at some levels are being told to fufil sterilisation quotas or face the consequences. Only, this is not being said in writing.

My purpose is to warn that theories and methods which have been tried and failed miserably will not succeed one bit, if they are backed by force of law. Before explaining the serious objections and analysing past experience, it needs to be stated that the present writer is not a supporter of concept of 'one mouth but two hands' and that he is all for a small family.

What I object to, in the first place, is the ideology behind all this propaganda for population control. When it is sought to be made out that India is poor because of over-population and the rapid growth of the same, the conscious or unconscious aim is not to let the people know the real cause of their poverty even 55 years after the achievement of Independence—the capitalist path of development adopted by the ruling classes. When the need of the hour is to organise the toiling masses against the capitalist path, propaganda of the above type undermines this task by convincing the poor man that he himself is responsible for his lot; that he is poor because he is fast multiplying and that neither the ruling classes nor their policies are responsible for his poverty. The propaganda objectively serves the same purpose as is served by the theory that our sufferings in this life are the result of bad deeds done by ourselves in some earlier life.

No lengthy arguments are needed to prove that it is just not true that India is poor because of over-population. If that were so, Madhya Pradesh would be better off than Punjab because the density of population in Punjab is higher than in Madhya Pradesh. The reality however is very different. Punjab has the highest per capita income in the country, while Madhya Pradesh has one of the lowest. One may also point out that there are countries in Africa with much less density of population than India but which are much worse off than our country. Actually, it is not poverty which is the result of rapid growth of population. It is just the other way round. If the desirable objective of small family is to be achieved, poverty and its consequences of different types must be tackled effectively. India's own experience so far proves this to the hilt.

Crores of rupees have been spent year after year to propagate the benefits and advantages of a small family. Taking the country as a whole, most of these sums have gone waste. It is a pity that many politicians, intellectuals and professionals, instead of making a deep analysis of the whole matter, throw up their hands in despair and reach the conclusion that coercion or legal compulsion is the only way out. It is difficult to believe that anyone should propagate coercion and compulsion in such a delicate sphere of human relationship. And yet, those who do it are not few. A proper and detailed analysis of past experience will however make it clear that the desperate remedy suggested is not called for; in fact, it is no remedy and can only boomerang as it did during Emergency.

It is a fact that a small section of our population no longer favours big families and in actual practice too has small ones. These are the educated middle class people, especially when both husband and wife are working. There are many number of such couples who do not want and do not have more than two children. On the other hand, the norm among the poor remains the big family. The reasons for this contrast are obvious. In the case of the poor, children (male ones) are the only old-age security, and how many of the total will survive till then is uncertain. An educated middle class working couple on the other hand, have the means to ensure proper health for their children and are also likely to have such old-age securities as pension, provident fund, savings, etc. And educated working women do not like and cannot afford to be a breeding machine.

The point sought to be made out here is also borne out by the experience of Kerala. As noted by Pran Chopra in an article in the *Indian Express* (November 6 and 7, 1980), "The birth rate (in Kerala) is significantly lower (than the all-India one), and that despite the fact the Kerala has never practised high-gear family planning, let alone punitive or even coercive measures for enforcing birth control." The birth rate in Kerala has been falling at the rate of one point per year, from 39 in 1961 to 26.5 in 1974. "As against the country's birth rate of 31 per thousand, Kerala has already brought it down to 24.2. In a couple of years the target of 21 suggested by WHO for India as a whole by 2000 AD may be attained". (*Indian Express* editorial, July 10, 1980).

Thomas Mathai in an article (*Indian Express*, September, 9 1980) has noted that the population growth rate for Kerala has been the lowest in India. The reasons for this are not far to seek. There is general agreement that these are as follows: Literacy in Kerala is the highest in India, 69 per cent against the national average of 34 per cent (1971 census). Kerala is also on top where women's education is concerned. "The Keralites, native sense of cleanliness and hygiene has also made its significant contribution to the standard of health. The State Government for its part has covered every panchayat with a dispensary (at least one) which again is a record for the country" (*Indian Express*, July 10, 1980). Infant mortality in Kerala is only 56 against 129 for all India as of 1976 and expectation of life at birth has improved to 61 for men and 64 for women, again a record for the country.

"The per capita consumption of calories in rural Kerala is almost half that in Punjab. Yet the rural infant mortality rate and rural death rate is 50 per cent lower. The key to the riddle is also the same old one: a more equal distribution of what nourishment there is, which is ensured by a double method....". One, the system of well composed free meal at school for children in the age group of 6 to 10, second, a public distribution system of fair-price shops which covers practically every household, rural or urban. The example of Kerala thus disproves the theory that coercive methods of birth prevention are needed for controlling the growth of population. It also proves that development and higher educational level, particularly of women and better healthcare are the best contraceptives.

Experience of many a country outside India too can prove instructive. Take Bulgaria. Before the building of socialism, families in that country were generally quite big ones. Socialism did away with poverty. It made education universal and free. It provided a very sound system of health care accessible to all, not on paper but in practice. It gave women real equality. It provided a system of old-age pension for all. What has been the result? Without any propaganda for family planning, the birth rate has fallen steeply. When I visited Bulgaria in 1974, found people unwilling to have more than two children despite Government propaganda in favour of having at least three children and despite the many incentives and benefits given by the state to encourage the same.

What has been stated above leads to certain clear and definite conclusions. No amount of propaganda in a poverty-ridden society (with a high rate of illiteracy; with no proper and adequate health system; with no social security for old age; with women confined to the kitchen, etc) can lead to a small family. Futile attempts in this sphere can lead to the desperate but disastrous conclusion that coercion is necessary. On the other hand, basic socio-economic transformation resulting in lessening of poverty, better literacy and education rates, better healthcare system, genuine equality for women and adequate social security for old age, etc, will almost automatically lead to a smaller family. There is no objection to reasonable publicity or propaganda for making known birth control methods. However, the propaganda that fast breeding by the poor is the cause of their poverty, must be exposed.

It is a matter of regret that many Left-minded intellectuals too fall victim to World Bank and Government of India propaganda in this respect. That in turn is a result of the failure of the Left parties on the ideological front. The sooner the Left parties overcome this weakness, the better for the cause they hold dear, the cause of the toilers, the cause of taking India away from the capitalist path.

Some Stray Thoughts on Relief Work

Natural calamities like earthquake, flood, etc. causing large scale loss of life and destruction of property evoke tremendous sympathy for the victims. Bigger the tragedy greater is keenness to contribute towards helping the victims. No one says: It is the duty of the Government. While there has been no dilution in the keenness to help, concern as to whether what all is contributed will really reach those for whom it is given, has been increasing.

Before India achieved independence, a tradition had developed in our country concerning relief. Political parties would come together for collecting as well as for distributing relief. And none out of those donating whether in cash or kind would have any doubt about relief being distributed properly. For some time after Independence too, this tradition continued. Gradually corruption as well as efforts to make partisan political capital out of relief work increased. Common people did not like it but they continued to contribute. Some would even say openly: we are contributing because atleast part of it will reach those who need help most. At the same time, it needs to be emphasised that many NGOs do remarkably good work. Not unoften media reports that non-official organisations have been more prompt than the Government in providing relief and have done much more and much better than the official agencies. It is a clear that non-official relief must continue to play an important part in providing relief to victims of natural as well as man-made disasters. It is therefore necessary to take steps to ensure that corruption in non-official relief and also its partisan politicisation is reduced to the minimum. Out of political formations, Left seems to enjoy best reputations. It is time that the Left takes initiative to revive the tradition of united and non-partisan relief committees. After independence, it was but natural that providing relief would be considered also the duty of the state Governments as well as the central Government.

They have now regular Relief and Resettlement Departments. Unfortunately, they are as corruption-ridden as other departments of the Government. Not unoften, a great part of Government relief is cornered by those who did not suffer even a bit while many of those who suffered most, don't get anything. Allegations of discrimination too have been there and not without foundation. Such allegations have been most serious as well as most, widespread in relation to relief in Gujarat and even in relation to non-official relief. The fact that Prime Minister Atal Bihar Vajpayee himself felt compelled to appeal for non-discrimination would go to show that allegations were not baseless. Strong public opinion demanding no discrimination in relief on political, religious or caste basis must be built up.

Apart from departmental official relief, there are Relief funds of Chief Ministers and 'Prime Minister's Relief Fund' also. Punjab has two such funds: 'Chief Minister's Relief Fund' and Chief Minister's Flood Relief Fund.

These are supposed to be entirely voluntary but in reality they are not. A good part of the funds raised are from public undertakings. For instance, for relief for victims of Gujarat earthquake 41.41 crores were given to PM's Relief Fund by oil PSUs alone. Often PSUs contribute funds on oral orders of the Chief Minister or because the bosses of the undertakings want to be in their good books. That may be excusable if these funds were to be used properly. Experience in Punjab at least is that Chief Minister's Relief Funds are mostly misused.

During the Punjab Vidhan Sabha (1992-97), there were two unstarred Assembly Question seeking information as to how funds raised were spent. Given notice of by Vimala Dang and Hardev Arshi—both of the CPI—the questions were admitted by the Speaker. In case of the Chief Minister's Flood Relief Funds, only a small part had been spent to give relief to the victims of floods. These funds had been spent largely for purposes which could not be considered even remotely connected with relief, e.g, donations given to Bar Associations, Press, Clubs, etc. This was one donation even to a political party. This scandal was widely reported by the media. Chief Ministers involved belonged to the Congress. I have no doubt in my mind that things have been no better after Akali leader Parkash Singh Badal became a Chief Minister. My conviction stands corraborated by the refusal of the Speaker to admit two similar Assembly Questions of Hardev Arshi for the Budget Session beginning 1-3-2001 relating to the period 1997-98 to 2000-01. In violation of the Rules governing the functioning of the Assembly, Speaker has not given any reason for this refusal. One cannot help drawing the conclusion that Speaker was told that information asked for, if supplied would be very embarassing for the Government.

It is not without significance that accounts of neither of the two funds are audited by A.G. They are audited by internal auditors who would not dare to find any fault. Possibility of such funds in other states and even the Prime Minister's Relief Fund being similarly audited is very much there. All these funds must be audited by the AG and Audit reports must be made public.

Last but not the least, one must take note of the big role which media has begun playing in relation to relief. Generally speaking they collect fund for relief funds of Chief Ministers or Prime Ministers Relief Funds. People would not even come to know whether all funds collected say for Kargil were actually disbursed to families of Kargil martyrs. However, funds collected by the Shaheed Pariwar Fund started by Hind Samachar Group of papers (Jalandhar) for victims of terrorism were disbursed at Jalandhar, by a non-official committee set up for purpose in full glare of the media. Disbursements were published. And this fact was a big factor in making this project perhaps the biggest non-official Relief project of Independent India. With cooperation of media of states from which relief is collected and media of States in which the same is disbursed, the entire work of media may be done in the glare of publicity.

Secularism and Official Functions

At a meeting of the Indian Congress, one of the Young Turks flayed the leaders for associating religion (Hindu) with many of the things they did as ministers. He gave a number of instances. The fact was not challenged by anyone; but Jagjivan Ram, the Congress President, sought to prove that the criticism was misplaced. It is a pity that the voice of the Young Turks proved to be a voice in the wilderness. The point he sought to make was (and is) not only very correct but was also of considerable importance for the cause of national integration and national unity.

Past Practice

During the freedom struggle many of the Congress leaders used to import Hindu religion in various functions of the Congress. This no doubt was one of the factors exploited by those who were against a powerful national movement. It cannot be denied that the failure of many of the Congress leaders (honourable exceptions apart) to act in a completely secular manner from the political and public platforms did do some harm. Continuation of the same mistake cannot but cause harm even now. Interests of progress and of the common people demand that religion must be kept completely divorced from state as well as from education. This wholesome principle does not mean any disrespect to religion in general or to any particular religion.

To follow this principle, one does not necessarily have to believe that religion is 'the opium of the masses' nor has one necessarily to be an atheist. All that this principle means is that religion is and should be a private affair of the individual and all politics as well as education should be secular.

Emotional Integration

No one who does not believe in this principle can claim to be a consistent progressive. Even in a country in which all the people might belong to one and the same religion, progressives are duty bound to stand and work for this principle. For a country like India which is inhabited by people of many religions, this principle is of especially great importance. Not only the state and education must be secular but all public acts of ministers performed by them as such must be performed in a completely secular manner. Non-observance of this principle will not, of course, rouse any communal passion or create any communal tension, but will certainly be a hindrance in the way of the fullest emotional integration of Indians as Indians irrespective of their religious affiliations.

Suppose, a minister inaugurate a new school, a swimming pool, or a road, accompanised by singing of Vedic hymns or performs other Hindu religious ceremonies. Will it be conducive to make non-Hindus—Muslims, Christians, Sikhs, and others—feel that in India people have equal rights and opportunities irrespective of their religious persuasion? The answer is obvious.

It is unfortunate that Jagjivan Ram refused to see the correctness and validity of the criticism made by the younger Congress leaders. It is also a pity that the Left and progressive forces in the country have not been vocally critical of this wrong practice on the part of many ministers. All of us need to be as fearless and forthright even in relation to such questions, as we used to be during the days of freedom struggle and the youth need to be even more fearless and forthright in this matter. Apart from the responsibility of the progressive parties and organisations in this respect, individuals too can play their role in such matters. Taken the country as a whole, responsibility of progressive individuals who belong to or come from Hindu religion is greater than that of others for obvious reasons.

Negative Reaction

In respect of the tendency criticized by one of the Young Turk leaders, the Akali-led Punjab Ministry is quite a few steps ahead. Here are a few instances.

The State Government and its entire machinery was directly and fully involved in organizing the celebrations of the 500th birth anniversary of Guru Nanak—the founder of Sikh religion. Guru Nanak is much respected by the non-Sikhs too, especially by the Hindus. There was no opposition from any quarter to the State Government organizing large-scale celebrations of his 500th birthday. However, it is a fact that the way the State Government went about it, did create the impression that it was boosting up one particular religion. This was not only not appreciated but also invited critical and negative comments from not a few in the State—may be in informal discussions.

During these celebrations, a very large number of Government schools in the State organized *Akhandpaths*—continuous reading of the *Guru Granth Sahib*, the holy scripture of the Sikhs—during school hours and all the students—Sikhs or non-Sikhs—were presumably expected to attend the service. Generally speaking, this too did not invite large-scale vocal criticism from the platform or through the Press except some by the Communist Party of India. There is, however, no doubt that the fact of *Akhandpaths* in Government schools did contribute to the growing feeling amongst large sections of non-Sikhs in the State that the Punjabi Suba is being gradually but steadily converted into a Sikh Suba—a feeling which obviously is not conducive to unity of common people and to national integration.

Government Schools

The prevailing atmosphere at that time would be clear from one example. In one particular school, the headmistress turned down the request of some (Sikh) teachers to organize *Akhandpath* on the ground that a Government institution must not associate itself with religious ceremonies of one community or another. There was agitation against the headmistress and the matter went to the Deputy Commissioner, a Sikh gentleman. He fully upheld the viewpoint of the headmistress. Now the agitation turned against him and, ultimately, the Deputy Commissioner was forced to beat a retreat and to ask the headmistress to permit the *Akhandpath* in the Government school.

Another example concerns a rural development conference, held from September 5 to 7, 1959, at village Bhail (Behla) Chola Sahib Block in Amritsar district. An Assistant Professor of Extension Education of the Punjab Agricultural University (Ludhiana) was reported to have arranged the conference in collaboration with the residents of the local area and the Panchayat Samiti Chola Sahib. The Samiti contributed a sum of Rs.685 for the conference. The District Agriculture Officer, District Education Officer and the Development and Panchayat officers of the Block took part in the conference. The announced programme of the conference included *Akhand Kirtan* by Akhand Kirtan Jatha, Lundhiana (led by Dr B.S. Bains, Punjab Agricultural University), and *Dharmik Vichar* by Dr. B.S. Bains, Dr Bhagat Singh, Minister for Social Welfare, Punjab, Sant Chanan Singh and Sant Fateh Singh.

oral instructions are reported to have been issued to Government schools to have *Akhandpaths*, etc. during school hours.

From many of the Government offices—including the Chief Minister's office—pictures of Jawaharalal Nehru, Dr. Radha Krishnan and other have disappeared while pictures of Guru Nanak have appeared to the exclusion of any other.

A crude example was provided by Atma Singh, a Minister in the Gurnam Singh Cabinet. He went about preaching Sikhism everywhere even when on official tours. He would refuse to take *salam* from any Sikh constable who had his beard trimmed. He would distribute

Karas (iron bangle which every Sikh is supposed to have as a part of his religion). Activities of Sri Atma Singh were too brazen to be ignored. They were criticized and even the Chief Minister had to advise him—though in private—to stop all this. The Minister, however, would not yield though he slowed down a little.

Unfortunate Tendency

There is no doubt that the Akali-led Ministries in Punjab slowly but surely undermined the secular character of the State's administration. It is a pity that except for the CPI, no other secular party or group or individual has seriously protested against it. As far as progressive Sikh intellectuals are concerned, there is quite a strong tendency among many of them even to justify all this except for the most crude behaviour. This is rather unfortunate and needs to be seriously pondered over by all who claim to be progressive.

The tendency does not, of course, lead to any immediate trouble like a riot or even tension. It, however, hinders the process of emotional integration of Indians as Indians, irrespective of religion and creates a situation which can and will be exploited by the communalists when it suits them. That is why it is a matter of considerable importance that the secular character of the State, the Government and the administration is fully preserved, safeguarded and strengthened and that ministers and officers in all their public activities are completely secular.

UN Year for the Elderly

Problems of Senior/Old citizen deserve serious attention. No doubt our country is a developing country and lot of resources are needed for its development. That, however, cannot and must not mean that the state in India can evade its responsibility towards those who worked throughout their lives but now are too old to earn their living. Any attempt to shift the responsibility to private sector/ private initiatives will mean leaving them in the lurch and to their own fate. This would be the position as a whole though it does not mean that there can be no good private initiatives.

Of course, the fact of India being a developing country and the needs of its economy have to be kept in view. For instance, in highly developed countries every old person is entitled to old age pension. As a result, a large number get two pensions—one as a retired employee and the other as an old person. I donot think India should follow them. Punjab's Chief Minister Parkash Singh Badal during Assembly election in February 1997 promised old age pension to every man above 65 and every women above 60. This was a wrong promise and the Government had to go back on it. What was decided by late S. Beant Singh remains valid—old age pension for every old person whose personal income is below a particular level.

Pension for any old person is perhaps the most important thing for him/her. I dilate upon it to some extent. Central as well as State Government employees have been getting pensions since long. Employees of Semi-Government bodies too should get the pensions. Pension scheme introduced by Employees Provident Fund Organisation—thanks to the pioneering efforts of Comrade Parduman Singh representative of AITUC on the Central Board of Trustees—is a very big step in the field of Social Security. It has proved to be a big boon for workers and employees in industries, especially small and medium units. Efforts must be made to remove some of its weaknesses. Resistance of the Government of India has to be overcome.

Immediate aim, should be to have a suitable scheme to cover landless agricultural labourers. Another important and immediate task in my opinion is to pay serious attention to the working of old age pension (subsistance allowance) schemes of Social Welfare Departments of various State Governments. I illustrate my contention by pointing out some aspects of the Punjab Scheme.

1. Rate is Rs. 200/- per month. Obviously, it is inadequate. Even this does not get paid for months together. Rate needs to be higher and regular payment of pensions must be guaranteed.

2. Thanks to widespread corruption in the department as everywhere else, applications remain pending for long and often get lost. Often those deserving most get rejected while those not eligible and quite well off get pensions sanctioned. There are shocking

instances of hundreds of application getting lost, after having been diarised. This state of affairs has to change. Forms and procedures must be simplified. Unnecessary attestations should be done away with because wrong attestations having become very easy to get as a result of downhill journey of moral values. I have a suggestion to make. Affidavits of applicants and verifications by local body members should be relied upon. However, 10 out of 100 affidavits and verifications taken out at random should be got checked up by officers having undoubted integrity and capable of withstanding pressures of all types. Relevant laws should be amended so that those found to have given wrong affidavits, etc are prosecuted and get deterrent punishment on conviction. I am sure that this will go a long way to eliminate giving pensions to those who are not entitled to get it. Deterrent punishment for proved corruption on the part of officials has to be provided for and made obligatory.

One more suggestions. Some Government employee pensioners are demanding increase in the rate of pensions after the age of 75 because of increase in expenditure on health etc. The demand is just and reasonable and should be accepted in case of all pensions including those given by the Social Welfare Department of State Governments. This brings me to the question of health facilities for the old. We cannot look to hospitals in the private sector as far as the poor are concerned. We have to struggle to improve the functioning of Government hospitals, to ensure that the charges are not high and beyond the reach of the poor.

The issue of 'Homes for the Old' is rather complicated. However, private sector can play some role in relation to the old of middle and upper classes. Political parties and mass organisations too can play a role. I am happy to state that such a Home for Aged built by C. Rajeshwar Rao Foundation for Social Progress was being inaugurated in a village in Andhra by the Chief Minister of Andhra. Late C. Rajeshwar Rao was the General Secretary of the C.P.I and C. Rajeshwar Rao Foundation was sponsored by the C.P.I to perpetuate his memory. A former Governor of the State and a former Home Minister of India also attended function. I do hope that this Home for the old will be successful and others also will emulate the example.

Last but not the least, people of all ideological and political views agree that family is the basic unit of our society. No state measures of Social Security can replace the need of family. Children have a duty towards the old parents. They must discharge it. They should also realise that their old parents may not be able to earn but can give very useful and wise guidance to them and to their children and it would be unwise to dispense with that. Old persons needs the warmth and affection of family while it is well known that often grand parents love their grand children even more than their parents.

Struggle to End Caste and the Fight for a Just Society

The caste system is a unique feature of Indian society. No other country in the world has such a system. Marx referred to Indian castes as 'these decisive impediments to Indian progress and Indian power'. A fairly large number of outstanding social reformers starting from Gautam Buddha in ancient India to Kabir, Nanak Gandhi and Ambedkar fought in their own ways against the inherent and inbuilt inequalities of this system. Notwithstanding this, the caste system of the Hindu society infected considerably the Muslims and Christians in India. Even Sikhs are a victim of it even though Sikhism began with the fight waged by Guru Nanak against it. No doubt, faster development of industry, commerce, trade, transport, education, etc, etc in post-independence India have to some extent alleviated caste sentiments and distinction, in social life. The deep roots of the system, however, remain. Even today the upper castes will not tolerate a girl of theirs marrying a boy belonging to the Scheduled Castes, however highly qualified and better placed. Both or one of them may even face death. The situation has been further complicated and aggravated by a contradictory process. As pointed out by S.G. Sardesai:

> The root of that contradictory process lies in this, that in a bourgeois-feudal society, whose culture is more feudal than

> bourgeois, the introduction of parliamentary democracy and adult franchise is exploited by the upper class combination in society for grabbing politics power and the loaves and fishes so easily amassed by the abuse of political power. Caste affinity and appeal have turned castes into vote-banks—casteism as a weapon of political and economic aggrandizement has assumed the magnitude of a Frankenstein.

It is an unfortunate fact that there has been a virtual absence of any conscious struggle against the pernicious caste system in post-independence India. There has been a total failure in this respect at least on the part of the Left. In this background, the decision of the Philosophy Department of the Punjab University Chandigarh to hold a seminar regarding 'Elimination of Inequalities with reference to the Caste System in India' on March 9-10, 1998 was indeed a welcome one. I was happy to be given an opportunity to participate in it. The seminar was attended by a good number of intellectuals, some social workers and activists.

Some participants even while conceding that the caste system had strong negative features tried to argue that it has positive aspects too. For instance, it was said that it has provided identity and security without explaining what good caste identities did for society and what security it provided to the lower castes. According to one participant, the caste system helped the spread of education as various castes tended to start their own educational institutions. It was also claimed that the higher percentage of voting in rural areas was because the ruralites tended to vote on caste basis (and it was thus a good thing). It was surprising that some intellectuals should have put forward such spurious arguments. More surprising and even shocking, however, was the all-out defence of the caste system put forward by one participant. The argument ran as follows:

> Minus the role of politicians, the caste system was growing naturally. Shudras never revolted because they had no reason to revolt. They were getting equal treatment...They were an integrated part of society...They were satisfied because they knew that whatever disabilities they suffered, were the result

of their own wrong deeds in their previous lives. Except in the case of Vaishyas and Shudras, the Shastras allow others to have more than one wife. One is allowed to marry a girl of a lower caste except a Shudra. Where the woman had the right to be the legal wife of a higher caste person, there is no torture etc.

Another gentleman who seemed to agree with this atrocious defence of the caste system also made some suggestions for softening any hardships involved in it. For instance, it was suggested that Brahmins might be offered five times the wages given to Shudras for doing the work which the latter do. Other suggestions were not only even more impracticable but also ridiculous on the fact of it.

I could not help remarking to the participant sitting next to me: "The way the caste system is being defended by the university people is shocking". She said: "They are from Delhi". My spontaneous reaction was: "They are nearer the BJP-in-power". I also wondered what effect the BJP heading the Government of India would have on our intellectuals. This reaction of mine soon got vindicated when another participant put forward a strange thesis. He enumerated almost all the ills from which India is suffering today including poverty, illiteracy, criminalisation of politics, etc. His conclusion was that India was much worse off than under the British and that all these ills were the result of appeasement of some (minority) communities and of some castes (Scheduled Castes, etc). And his remedy was very simple: "The office of the Prime Minister as well as of the Chief Minister should have an irreducible term of five years". I felt thankful to him for not suggesting that the British should be requested to return to India to rule us. All these, however, were the sidelights. There was a good deal of informed, interesting and useful discussion.

There was the view that the Chaturvarnya system was formed at the end of Rigvedic period. Some considered that the seeds of the caste system based on hereditary division of labour and endogamy, lay in the Chaturvarnya. They conceded that originally the Chaturvarnya was quite fluid but it developed into a system with inbuilt inequalities condemning large sections to the most miserable life and the most gruesome violation of their basic human rights. Some, however, thought that India could go back to the original Chaturvarnya system while others argued that India must look ahead and that the caste system must go lock, stock and barrel as it was doing only harm and no good to Indian society.

One participant made an interesting and important point. She argued that the caste system tended to perpetuate gender inequality. In support of her contention, she cited the upper caste viewpoint that a "Chamar woman can be enjoyed any time". She also argued that the caste system by restricting marriages within the castes encouraged the dowry system. Surprisingly the same lady almost justified child marriages. According to her, this institution originated from the need to preserving the chastity of young girls. She even said that *gauna* before maturity should be made illegal but not the marriage as such. The right of young people to choose their own life-partners did not seem to be of much importance to the lady.

There was an interesting exchange of views regarding reservation of jobs. Some said that no reservations should have been there from the very beginning. Some were of the view that these should have been there only on the economic basis. Others recognised and defended the need for reservations for the Scheduled Castes. They argued that these had helped. However, even they pointed out that reservations should have become unnecessary by now. This had not happened because necessary steps like radical agrarian reforms, universal literacy and education, etc which would have enabled all to compete on an equal footing had not been achieved. Some have their vested interests in ensuring that such steps are not taken while others are interested in using the slogan of reservations as a weapon to form vote-banks. No one seemed willing to propagate the truth that reservations are like crutches and their perpetual use can only be as a result of perpetuating inequalities of the caste system. As regards reservations for OBCs, V.P. Singh came in for criticism for coming out with the Mandal Commission report all of a sudden for political ends. The exclusion of the creamy layers of the OBCs as well as of the Scheduled Castes was suggested by some.

The question as to how to fight the system and its inequalities had been posed sharply. This was discussed inadequately though. It was emphasised by some that the caste oppression of every type must be opposed and fought by mobilising the people of all castes, all decent human beings and not by counter-casteism, that is, by treating all belonging to the so-called upper castes as enemies. This is easier said than done because it can cost votes in the short run. The Left at least must be guided by the long-term interests of the society and not by the desire to have more seats in legislatures any how. The Left must lead the fight against every caste atrocity and also the ideological fight against the caste system. Neglect of this job and pandering to casteism and to counterism for the sake of short term gains has cost it heavily in Bihar as well as in UP and perhaps elsewhere too. It is high time to draw the necessary lessons.

All progressives must realise that besides seminars on the caste system, there is an urgent need for workshops of Left-minded intellectuals and activists to discuss ways and means for getting rid of the curse of the caste system. As pointed out above, the capitalist system creates objective conditions for that but cannot automatically lead to its disappearance. On the other hand, as also noted above, there are strong vested interests whom the caste system helps economically or/as well as politically. An organised struggle against the inequalities of the caste system as well as the system itself both on the mass and ideological levels is a must. The struggle, of course, will be very prolonged and its final victory will be achieved when India has a just society but it has to be waged continuously. That indeed is necessary to achieve the just society.

Populism

We find these days a large and intellectuals criticizing populist measures and populism. However, one does not come across any precise definition of populism. Nor can it be said that there is a common understanding of the meaning of this term. A discussion about it will thus be useful. Here are some instances of populism in our opinion. Bank loans for weaker sections was a correct idea. Loan

Melas which Congress (I) activists organised and the propoganda which preceded and accompanied them was sheer populism. People were told that though called loans these amounts were gifts from Indira Gandhi and therefore need not be returned. People were also told that they could use the loans for any purpose not withstanding the fact that purpose for which given was entirely different. Damage done to the banking system of our country and to our economy by such loan melas needs to be assessed as also whether these did any substantial good to the loanees.

Writing off of loans or converting short-term loans into medium term ones and converting medium-term loans into long-term loans in case of people affected by natural calamities cannot be taken exception to. However, writing off of loans upto a particular amount even in normal times and off and on especially during the years preceding elections is clearly a populist measure. It cannot only do damage to economy. It also encourages a wrong type of mental outlook which can prove harmful in the long run.

Old age and widow pension schemes for persons in these categories with no one to support them and with no or very little earning of their own is an essential measure of social security. However, it was sheer populism when a few years ago Congress (I) Government of Haryana announced an old-age pension scheme for every old person above a particular age irrespective of their own incomes or the incomes of their sons. Hard realities of life forced the Haryana Government to retreat and to amend the scheme to exclude some categories.

Immediately after Beant Singh Government came to power it announced that it would give pensions to every old person. This was sheer populism. This decision announced in the Assembly has remained unimplemented. On the other hand, outdated conditions for entitlement to such pensions have not been amended. Even the most deserving persons would not be entitled if they were to fill the application forms truthfully. Government announcement of 'pension for every old person and every widow' accompanied by 'pension camps' and 'loan melas' on the one hand and refusal to change outdated conditions for entitlement produced some very negative results. Very undeserving persons easily got pensions by making blatantly false declarations and by bribing the officials. On the other hand, often even the most deserving ones failed to get just because they didn't have the money to bribe.

Another obvious example of populism is the demand of peasant organisations to further increase procurement prices decided upon by the Government even though the latter are already more than remunerative. Some peasant organisations keep on demanding still higher procurement prices even when ordinary peasants are more than satisfied and are anxious only that they should actually get the announced prices.

Another populist measure which is destroying work-culture in our country is the continuous increase in the number of holidays in Government offices. Government employees these days see nothing wrong in demanding even a substitute or compensatory holiday if and when a festival or national holidays falls on a weekly holiday.

One however cannot agree if a decision to supply foodgrains to the poor at prices within their reach even by subsidizing is dubbed as populist. After all, growth and development must not only be for the rich and at the cost of the poor, making them poorer. Such a decision becomes a populist one if it is impracticable or has the potential of damaging the economy. Together with the policy of liberalisation and globalization, new slogan emerged from certain quarters. It was "For a number of years poverty has to increase if the country is to develop". To reject this slogan is not populism but sounds economic as well as real commitment to democracy. At the same time, slogans if implemented, will land the economy in a mess; harm even sections of people supposed to benefit from them, should be rejected as populist and dangerous.

What then is populism? Do the above instances help to define this very much popular term? Perhaps they do. Populist measures are those which are not necessary for meeting the minimum essential needs of the poor; which put unjustified burden on economy; and/ or undermine work culture and which are motivated by short-term and temporary political gain.

Tributes to the Founder of Pingalwara

Bhagat Puran Singh, the founder of Pingalwara (Home of the incapacitated), is no more. He passed away at the age of 87 on August 5, 1992 in the PGI Chandigarh. He had been shifted there for treatment from Amritsar. Very rightly, most glowing tributes have been paid to him by the press and by publicmen belonging to different and even opposing schools of thought and political parties. Many have called him Mother Teresa of North India.

He served and looked after almost with motherly affection the handicapped, the incapacitated, the mentally retarted and the sick whom no hospital would admit. Those admitted to Pingalwara included not a few near whom most would not like to stand because of foul smell from their wounds or some such other reason. These deserving most human sympathy and help were his only love. Bhagat Puran Singh remained bachelor throughout his long life. Passing away of such a personality was bound to cause deep sadness all round. The same was rendered deeper because his death put a question mark before the future of Pingalwara in Amritsar.

I came into contact with Bhagat Ji more than once. Both my wife Vimla Dang and myself had requested him to admit some deserving persons in Pingalwara. He never refused any. As president of the erstwhile Municipal Committee Chheharta, Ms Vimla Dang was keen to help Pingalwara. This was unanimously agreed upon by the committee and its annual contribution continued till Chheharta was merged into Municipal Committee Amritsar, which later became Municipal Corporation. Once some other institution was trying to misuse the name of Pingalwara to raise funds for itself. I remember having tried to help Bhagat Ji to the best of my capacity. Both of us had advised some friends that they should give their donations to Pingalwara. These friends wanted to donate some amounts for a good humanitarian and non-partisan cause. To the best of our knowledge, only one of them did not heed our advice. He said: "Bhagat Puran Singh has a press in the premises of Pingalwara and a part of the money that pours in for the destitutes goes towards printing a lot of literature consisting of articles and essays written by himself. And these he distributes free."

Bhagat Ji as is quite well known by now, was a vociferous reader. He also wrote a lot and wrote well. His favourite subjects from the very beginning were environment, pollution, deforestation, population, etc. It may not be an exaggeration to say that in some of these matters of vital importance to mankind, he was perhaps one of the pioneers in Punjab. This however, was not appreciated by those who wanted their money exclusively to be used for the maintenance and looking after of the destitutes.

When I was a member of the Punjab Legislative Assembly, I had pressed the Government of Punjab to give (to resume giving) regular financial help to Pingalwara. I did not succeed. I was told: "Bhagat Ji should agree to have a Government representative to look into his accounts which should be regularly audited". Bhagat Puran Singh was not prepared to brook any Government interference. Totally selfless, he believed that all his staff members, those who collected money in buses and trains in the well known locked black boxes with 'Pingalwara' written on them and slot in the lids for pushing in money; those who worked in the Pingalwara premises and wards and others, were also selfless like him. On the other hand, some believed that some unscrupulous persons had crept in. There were complaints about handling of money. Once it was alleged that the press was being misused to print Naxalite pamphlets, etc. Later on it was alleged that some Khalistanis had penetrated and were misusing the press and the institution. Bhagat Puran Singh had at the time of the Blue Star operations returned his Padam Shri to the President as a mark of protest. A section of the people liked it. Another section did not like but understood it. Yet another disapproved of it.

On a much earlier occasion, I had gone to Pingalwara. I noticed that there were many slogans written on the walls condemning 'the atrocities of Communist regime in Cambodia', I did not like that. Much later, it was proved that my views in the matter were wrong and those of Bhagat Puran Singh were correct. The Communist regime in question was that of the notorious Pol Pot. Even then one can have the view that institutions like Pingalwara are better kept away from all controversial politics and may be of all politics.

I last saw Bhagat Ji alive when he was in a private nursing home in Amritsar before being shifted to the PGI. Of course, I along with Ripudaman Singh, Secretary Amritsar city Committee, CPI, attended his cremation in Amritsar and we paid our homage to the remarkable man who was no more. A very big crowd had gathered. I felt very sad to note that overwhelmingly it belonged to one community. May be the absent community was at fault to some extent. However, those who have taken the charge of Pingalwara, would do well to ponder over the matter.

How Secular is Our Secularism?

India can be proud of the fact that it is a secular country; that the state in India has no religion. The fact that India opted for a secular state structure is all the more creditable, because the British who ruled India before 1947 succeeded in their game of weakening our country through partition and formation of Pakistan as a theocratic Muslim State. If the back-lash of the 'Muslims-a-separate nations' theory was not much and if India refused to become a Hindu theocractic state 'in retaliation', credit goes to our people, our national movement and also to the Left on the one hand and leaders like Jawaharlal Nehru and Maulana Azad on the other. At the same time it is high time that we take note of weaknesses in our practice and even concept of secularism. We should also take note of the concessions, which even the most secular leaders of the freedom struggle and those who claim to be carrying forward their policies, have been giving to the anti-secular forces. This is necessary if our secularism is not to get subverted. Here are some examples:

1. The Indian National Congress (INC) which led the freedom struggle was undoubtedly a secular party and was pledged to secularism. Despite that, sometimes it acted in a manner contrary to its professions of secularism. For instance, not unoften

during the days of freedom struggle and also after independence, Congress functions were accompanied by Hindu rituals. This could not but help those who wanted Muslims and other minorities to keep off the freedom struggle. This helped such forces by enabling them to paint the INC as a Hindu body. It is our opinion that this kind of departure from secularism took place because the nationalist thought of the leadership of the INC taken as a whole, did have a 'tinge of Hinduism'—to use the words of the well known historian Bipin Chandra.

Here is an instance of the practice noted in this para: "A hymn from upnishads was recited by choir singers while Indira Gandhi was escorted to the dias of the plenary session of the Congress-I held at Calcutta towards the end of December 1983.

Tribune of 30-12-83

Use of Hindu symbols by almost all the (Hindu) leaders of the INC to rouse national consciousness also weakened forces of secularism.

2. Principles of secularism, besides other things, in our opinion, would also require that taboos of one religion should not be forced on followers of other religions— while sentiments of all should be respected by all. This would apply to beef-eating as well as smoking. Beef-eating is said to be a taboo as per Hindu religion—religion of the majority in India, while smoking is a taboo as per religion of majority of the population of Punjab, namely the Sikh religion.

The Constitution of India desires ban on cow-slaughter throughout the country even though in a round-about manner. It needs to be considered as to whether or not, the relevant provision in the Constitution was the result of the 'Hindu tinge' in the nationalist thought. Perhaps it was. Similarly, the provision in the Constitution that the minorities including religious minorities would have an absolutely unfettered right to run their educational institutions without even any reasonable restrictions was, perhaps a concession to anti-secularism in another (non-Hindu) direction.

Anti-secular forces of different hues can and do exploit these provisions of the Constitution, not only to strengthen religiosity but even communalism directly. This happens particularly on the eve of general elections.

3. After independence, many official State functions have been accompanied by Hindu rituals.

4. Prime Minister Indira Gandhi herself and also some other State leaders have been going to temples offering Puja, etc and the mass media has been giving it massive publicity. This is done with a view to increase the vote-bank. There can be no objection to any state leader professing any religion and worshipping in accordance with its tenants. But that must remain a strictly personal matter. When it is publicized on the mass media, it cannot but weaken secularism. And that would remain the position, if the State leaders were to visit places of worship of other religions too and even though these visits too were to be publicized in the same manner.

   Let it not be thought that only the VIPs belonging to the ruling party at the Centre have the temptation to use religion for electoral purposes or that they alone have 'Hindu tinge' in their thought. Some of the stalwarts of the bourgeois opposition parties may even be far ahead of the ruling party VIPs in this respect. NT Rama Rao of the Telegu Desham won laurels in this field when he declared his intention to make Tirupati into a Hindu Vatican.

5. Unlike Jawaharlal Nehru, many Congress leaders these days think that secularism means that state must promote all religions equally and not that state should not promote any religion.

   And some hold the belief quite strongly and refuse to give it up.

   When late Rashtrapati Giani Zail Singh was the Chief Minister of Punjab, he got the Punjab government to construct the 'historic Guru Gobind Singh Marg' with great religious fervour and with many religious rituals. There was no objections from Hindus as such. Only the Left forces warned that this was an attempt to fight the Akalis on their own ground and would prove counter-productive.

Even though the Chief Minister did something similar for the Hindus too, the warning which the Left had given proved correct. Gianiji, however, thought otherwise. He had even supported the incorrect Akali allegation that Hindus had from a communal angle opposed the Marg being named after Guru Gobind Singh, which in fact was not the issue at all.

The false allegation as well as its corraboration by the Giani Ji is contained in a booklet entitled: 'Hindu-Sikh Conflict in Punjab—Causes and Cure' brought out by '*Transatlantick India Times*', London. Here it is:

"Replying to my question of present day Hindu-Sikh relationship, Sant Longowal explained that when Zail Singh, as Punjab Chief Minister, named a secondary road as Guru Gobind Singh Marg, he was strongly criticized by Punjabi Hindus inspite of their knowledge that Guru Gobind Singh (and also his four children and his father) was born, lived and died for the protection of Hindus.

"Four days later, I had the privilege of meeting President Zail Singh in Rashtrapati Bhawan who confirmed that there indeed was unfortunate opposition to his naming of Guru Gobind Singh Marg." (p. 5)

6. Some cities in our country are considered holy by followers of one religion while some others may be holy for other religions. One would have thought that a secular state and a Government professing secularism would not think of officially declaring any such city as holy and of using that device to force taboos of one religion on followers of other religions. But what is the reality?

Even when Akalis were demanding that Amritsar be declared a holy city with tobacco shops banned therein, the Congress-

I Government of Bhajan Lal in Haryana declared Kurukshetra as a holy city with liquor and meat shops banned. We have already referred to the TD Government of Andhra Pradesh wanting to make Tirupati into a Hindu Vatican. Towards that end, Lord Venketeshwara himself had been made the Chairman of the Board set up to manage its affairs while the Chief Minister was made its Vice-Chairman.

The historian Bipin Chandra has pointed out the 'Hindu tinge' in the nationalist thought of pre-independence India and the harm it did. Researchers into the political developments in the post-independence India can point out instances not only of continued presence of this Hindu tinge in more than one political formation but also of other tinges in some other formations. What is worse is that these when sought to be used for winning votes do much greater harm.

7. A good part of our Army continues to be organized into communally named units in which persons belonging to a particular community pre-dominate. Not is this all. They go into action shouting 'Jai Bajrang Bali' or 'Jo Bole So Nihal—Sat Sri Akal', etc depending upon the predominant composition—whether it is Hindu or Sikh. What is wrong with this might not be quite clear when our Jawans went into action against Pakistan—though even then it should not have been difficult to see it. When those who risked their lives during the Blue Star Operation in the Golden Temple did so shouting, 'Jai Bajrang Bali', 'Har Har Mahadev'. The harmful effect of introducing religions into the State organs should have been obvious to anyone who is genuinely committed to national unity and national integration on the basis of secularism. On no other basis the same would be possible.

8. In December 1983 this writer happened to visit one big Public Sector Unit—in Bangalore—perhaps it was HMT. Big majority of the workers were Hindu though workers belonging to other religions were also there. In at least one shop—we came across a virtual temple right in its middle. (This shop too had workers

professing Islam and other religions). To permit a Hindu temple in a Public Sector Establishment with workers of different religions, in our opinion, is a clear violation of principles of secularism. And in fact it reflects the 'Hindu tinge' in the thought of the management which should be thoroughly secular. It would not become right even if a mosque were also be allowed.

9. I received an invitation card in December 1983. It was from The Municipal Labour Union (Regd) Amritsar —a Congress(I) led trade union. The invitation was to attend a programme of *Akhand Path* of Sri Guru Granth Sahib, Bhog of the same and of *Kirtan* and *Jagran.* The writer is also aware of such programmes having been organized also by some Left-led unions even in case of Mills having a complement of Muslim workers too.

Above instances are more than enough to prove our contention that there is great and urgent need to work for clarity about what secularism really means and to strengthen genuine secularism. In my opinion, at least the following are essential ingredients of secularism:

(a) State must have no religion and it must keep aloof from all religious activities. Political parties and trade unions and other organizations of this type too must try to keep aloof from religious practices. Members of these organizations must be educated as to why it is necessary and also in their own interest.

(b) Everyone must be free to profess and practice any religion.

(c) Freedom to preach has also to be there but that must not allowed to be exploited to throw mud on other religions. Those who wish to preach atheism should also be free to do so. Each other's sentiments should be respected.

(d) Taboos of one religion should not be sought to be forced on followers of other religions—either by force or by law.

(e) Religion and politics must be separated.

(f) Religious places must be used only for religious purposes and their income should be used only for welfare purposes besides propogation of the concerned religions. They should not go into the coffers of any political party.

(g) No place of worship etc must be allowed to become an arsenal and to harbour criminals.

Open Letter to an IAS Officer

Dear Officer,

If I mistake not it was only once that I met you during the last five years. After you were finished with the matter regarding which I had called on you, we drifted into some general discussion. I had said: "It is a tragedy that the IAS too has been very much affected by the virus of corruption. In view of the eminent place the IAS has in it, it is bad for the entire administration and hence for the state" I had gone on to ask: "Am I correct when I say that now only a minority of the IAS officers are uprights and honest?" Your reply was: "No, you are wrong. It is only a microscopic minority which remains honest."

As a result of observation over a number of years. I had come to the conclusion that there were more upright persons amongst the direct recruits to this prestigious service while amongst the promoted ones, the proportion of dishonest officers was greatest with outstanding exceptions in both categories. It was also my observation that the upright direct recruits too tended to become corrupt with the passage of time. Out of those who would not be corrupt, only a minority would be willing to fight the corruption. The rest of the upright lot while not themselves indulging in corruption would turn a Nelson's eye to the rampant corruption both above and below them.

Despite all this, your aforementioned observation made me realise that things were worse than what I had thought. Even then, a glimmer of hope about the IAS remained in my heart. One reason was my belief that the honest politicians were even a smaller minority of their tribe. Another was the fact that some very bright and upright officers had been in the Punjab cadre of the IAS like N.N. Vohra, Prem Kathpalia, P.H. Vaishnav and K.D. Vasudevan. They were the seniors who have retired. I can name other IAS officers who would not carry out wrong and illegal oral orders of their Ministers and who would even risk displeasure of the latter by telling them: "I have given my opinion in writing. Sir, you give your orders on the file and I would carry them out faithfully". I also know of a few upright young IAS officers ready to be penalised but not willing to compromise their conscience. I felt vindicated when some young IAS officers of UP organised a secret ballot to name the three most corrupt in the service.

I was looking forward to something happening in Punjab. Nothing happened for long and when something did happen, soon after Prakash Singh Badal took over as the Chief Minister. It was in the reverse gear, demoralising even those who had been fighting corruption in their own ways at the individual level.

In relation to the controversy about two cases referred to the CBI under orders of the previous Chief Minister, I hope you will agree with me that the informed public view has been by and large sound. Even while criticising the effort of the present Chief Minister to prevent the CBI from investigating the two cases, various quarters have not hesitated to talk about the good reputation enjoyed by R.S. Mann. The vocal section of the IAS in Punjab, however, has not added to the prestige of the service.

Your Association became suddenly very active but with the sole objective of targetting one of your fellow-officers for the role he allegedly played in getting the cases referred to the CBI. It is not my duty to defend him. May be some internal rivalries of your service also played a part. But whatever the motives of the former Chief Secretary and the former Chief Minister, no sacrilege had been committed. In any case, the IAS was no longer a holy cow which had only to be worshipped. It is only a degree or two less profane than the politicians.

Why should not intelligent officers like those in the IAS realise that their pretending to be shocked at the case of any IAS officer being referred to the CBI can only evoke derisive laughter? Please tell me why no one in the General Body meeting of your Association talked about the need for fighting corruption in the service, of setting your own house in order *first* or at least *also?*

I don't think anyone will disagree with me that a *prime facie* case of corruption exists against the new Principal Secretary. Even after the conditions attached with the anticipatory bail granted to him, he did not quit his present office—which under a popular government is much more important than that of even the Chief Secretary. Is his refusal consistent with IAS ethics? And when Badal too wants him to stick on to the post, was it not the duty of your Association to ask him to quit? And what is one to say of the manner in which the meeting of the GB of the Association was conducted? Is the IAS adopting the new Congress culture in its entirety?

I am convinced that there were officers in the meeting whose voice would have been the voice of sanity? Why was this voice not heard?

And why did many good officers keep away?

It is time for every upright IAS officer to realise that if the service has to be saved for its own sake and for sake of the country, the fight has to be joined. The minimum which seniors like you are expected to do is to inspire the younger lot to put up a fight; I know quite a few want to but don't know how to. They rightly feel that individually they can do nothing. They have to be guided as to how to join hands and wage a struggle. Once the fight for uprightness starts, many who are themselves upright but have chosen to sit on the fence will pick up courage and join the ranks. In this noble cause, I am sure all of you will have the good wishes and blessings of your retired seniors, some of whom have been named above by me.

It should not be difficult to imagine the impact, the fight for moral values and uprightness in the IAS will have on other services. And that alone can help the IAS to regain its proper place.

With regards, Yours sincerely,

April 17, 1997, Ekta Bhawan,

Chheharta (Amritsar) PIN-143105

Satyapal Dang

Delink Quota from Vote-Bank Politics

It is time to examine where we stand in the matter of caste-based reservations in the services, legislatures, education, etc, after more than half a century of Independence. Such reservations in favour of the Scheduled Castes were justified when they were introduced. The Scheduled Castes had been kept suppressed socially as well as economically and educationally for centuries. They were in no position to compete with the upper castes. Thanks to Gandhiji and others, the country accepted the need for such reservations. There was little opposition to them.

However, it should have been clear from the very beginning that reservations could be aptly compared with crutches provided to a victim of some accident or disease to be used by him till he is cured. Efforts thus should have been to ensure development in society in such a manner that it would become possible to do away with the reservation crutches at an early date. This unfortunately has not happened.

Reservations no doubt have helped, but even today the Scheduled Castes as a whole are not in a position to compete on an equal footing with the upper castes. This is because measures like radical agrarian reforms have not taken place; and education for all has not been given the priority it deserves. Such policies and measures would hit the ruling classes. It suited them more to convert reservations into a weapon for procuring votes. What is tragic is that those provided the reservation-crutches want to have them for all time to come instead of fighting for policies that would make these crutches unnecessary. The Left in the country too needs to make a self-critical review.

Even with the reservation for the Scheduled Castes continuing for the time being, change of policies in some respects need to be considered seriously. There is no doubt that a creamy layer has developed among the Scheduled Castes—among land-owners, in the bureaucracy, (the IAS and the IPS), etc. When brighter children coming from the so-called upper castes but belonging to much poorer families are kept out because of reservation, no amount of arguing convinces them that what has happened is correct. And that encourages casteism in reverse.

Reservation in promotions too needs to reconsidered. In any case, the seniormost should get promotions and not made junior to their juniors. Reservation in promotions can be given ex-cadre.

In Punjab, reservation for Scheduled Caste students in medical colleges was first introduced when a minister wanted his son to get admission. With experience, it was decided to continue such reservations but also providing some essential minimum standard at a lower level than for the open category. In many parts of India, students belonging to the Scheduled Castes can get admissions even in medical and engineering colleges with zero marks in entrance tests. This has to go and radical steps have to be taken to help Scheduled Caste students to overcome this situation.

A few words about the reservation for the OBCs, a la Mandal Commission. V.P. Singh dug up the report of this Commision, which lay buried in the files for quite a long time for political reasons. Be that as it may, let it be conceded that the OBCs too needed reservation. Should we have not excluded such OBCs as had ceased to be backward? Should not the creamy and exploiting layers among the OBCs be kept out? A section of the Left even opposed the Supreme Court judgement directing the keeping out of the creamy layer. In some states like Punjab, 27 per cent reservation being demanded for the OBCs even in the State services, though they are not even 10 per cent of the population. If this demand is accepted, casteism will increase tremendously. And is it not a fact that tailing behind the Janata Dal of V.P.Singh, the Left too equated social justice with reservation (and hardly anything more)?

There is a race in the country to exploit not only the slogan of caste-based reservation but also caste-based benefits without paying any attention to the long-term negative effects. Let me give one instance from Punjab. During the elections to the Punjab Assembly in 1997, the Akali-BJP combine promised Rs. 5000 as 'shagun' on the marriage of every Scheduled Caste girl. No land for Scheduled Caste agricultural labourers but 'shagun' for every SC girl on the occasion of her marriage. After coming to power, it was decided to limit the benefit to such families as had an income below Rs. 10,000 per annum. The benefit was later extended to Christians on the same income condition. It is obvious that if any such benefit is to be given, it must be related only to income so that all poor families benefit. Not to do that is to widen caste divisions instead of narrowing them.

When caste-based reservation becomes a principle for every party, who will fight for the abolition of the caste system which Marx described as a big hindrance in the way of India's progress? There are also reservations which are not caste-based. Unfortunately, these too are becoming popular with votes in view. I am all for honouring freedom fighters and even providing adequate benefits to them. However, it should not lead to garnering benefits in a manner that will lead to a loss of respect for them in the community as a whole. There is no doubt that reservation cannot be dispensed with altogether just now. But it is high time to delink the questions of reservation from vote-bank politics and populism.

Conversions—A Case Study

Asha (35) was working under a contractor in a Mill about 12/15 kilometres from Chheharta along with her brother and another girl of Chheharta (Amritsar). While returning home on 10-3-99, they were involved in an accident. Asha received serious injuries and died on 13-3-99 leaving behind her husband Hem Raj (40) and three children. When I learnt that Asha was a Christian but was not buried but cremated, I became curious and decided to interview some members of the family.

I began with Rakesh (29) one of Asha's brothers. I give below my questions and his answers :

Q. Were you born in a Christian family or you changed your religion?

A. Both my parents are Christians and as such I have been a Christian since my birth. I don't know whether my father too is a Christian since birth or is a convert from Hinduism.

Q. Why was Asha cremated and not buried?

A. Like me, Asha was a Christian. However, her husband Hem Raj came from a Hindu Family. My sister's in-laws told us that as Asha had married a Hindu, she should be cremated and not buried. My brother-in-law had no objection either way, so we agreed to cremation.

Rakesh who had studied upto 10+1, and was till recently a worker in the O.C.M. Mills Chheharta, wanted to tell me as why some people change their religion and become Christians. He told me of a case (a Hindu) who was suffering from some serious disease, which neither medicines nor Jadoo-toona could cure. Some Christian advised him to go to Church and pray as advised. According to Rakesh, the patient recovered as a result of his prayers. Later on he became a Christians. I asked him :

"It Christians prayers without any medicines can cure, why are there doctors in countries having predominately and even 100 per cent Christian population?

Rakesh had no satisfactory reply but insisted that what he had said was true.

After Rakesh, I interviewed Asha's husband, Hem Raj. He is a worker in a small factory in Amritsar having a few twisting machines.

Q. What was your religions when you married Asha?

A. I was born in a Hindu family. Our caste was Choudhry. I was a Hindu when I married Asha.

Q. Was the marriage as per Hindu religion or Christian religion?

A. Ours was a court marriage because I and Asha belonged to two different religions.

Q. When and why did you become a Christian?

A. I became a Christian sometime after my marriage. No one canvassed me. No, not even my wife. Yes, on her request I would sometime accompany her to the Church.

Q. *Your marriage was a love marriage?*

A. Yes, our families are neighbours. My parents were opposed to the marriage but became reconciled to the fact later on. My family was not happy when I became a Christian. No one else in the family changed his religion. My children have been brought up as Christians.

Finally, I interviewed Jagan Nath, father of late Asha. Here is what he said in reply to my questions.

"I am not sure but I may be about 62. I was born in a Hindu family at Muktsar. I must have been 8/10 years old when my father became a Christian. He was a labourer. He was the only earning hand in the family. I don't know what was the family's caste before my father became a Christian. I started working as labourer when I was only about 12 years old, while my brothers remained at Muktsar I migrated to Chheharta in 1957 or so. Here I got a job in the OCM Mills and became a member of the Union.

"I got married two or three years after I came to Chheharta. I must have been 18/19 years old then. My wife Sheela Devi belonged to a poor Christian family like ours in Gurdaspur district. There was no Church in her village as is generally the case as far as small villages are concerned. Nikah was performed by a Padri in the house of the bride. My wife delivered 2 sons and 5 daughters, out of whom two sons and three daughters are alive. My younger son Rakesh got a job in the OCM Mills but resigned recently. He is at present unemployed.

"Asha's body was cremated and not buried because her in-laws had so desired. We did not like Asha having married a Hindu but as parents, we had no alternative but to reconcile ourselves with the fact. If in-laws of Asha had not insisted on Asha being cremated, we would have to take her body to the Christian burial ground in Putlighar area as there is none in Chheharta. There is a Church in Chheharta. We go to the Church only occasionally. No one there has ever asked us to try to influence Hindus to become Christians. No missionary has ever contacted us. Padri of the local church, however, does visit us, sometimes. He only enquires about our well-being.....only from T.V. I have learnt that Christians are being attacked in some parts of India...I have a black-and-white TV which we purchased about 15 years ago. I don't find any change in the attitude of people towards us in Chheharta. In the area in which I live, there are only 4 or 5 Christian families. There is no fear in any one's mind. All my children studied in the Government School in Chheharta. I never thought of sending them to any Christian Missionary school. These schools charge fees which we cannot afford. Also, they are far off. It is absolutely false to say that Christians are not loyal to India. We are as good Indians as any one else. And when needed, we will make sacrifices for the sake of our country. There are many Christians in the Indian Army and they have always carried out their duties loyally."

Talhan and its Fallout

Talhan, a village less than 15 kilometres from Jalandhar has been in news for about 6 months in 2002. Overwhelming majority of the population are Sikhs. Sikhism was born in the struggle launched by Guru Nanak against casteism of the Hindu society. All the 10 Gurus of the Sikhs firmly stood against casteism and preached against it. And this did contribute to caste system in Punjab becoming less ugly and ferocious as compared with some other parts of India. However, it is also a fact that casteism is very much there and quite strong even amongst Sikhs. Exploiting sections have a vested interest in ensuring that it continues. For instance, it helps capitalist landlords (mostly Sikh Jats) to keep divided agricultural labourers mostly Dalits, e.g, Mazhabi Sikhs and poor peasants mostly Jats. This and nothing else explains the refusal of the Akali leadership to come out against many villages in Punjab having separate caste-based Gurdwaras and also cremation grounds. Even today, if a Sikh Jat girl were to marry a Scheduled Caste boy (a handsome one, having fairly good income, etc), chances of one or both of them getting murdered would be there. More chances would be that, Jat Akali leaders would not denounce the murder.

Talhan has about 7000 Dalits out of its total population of 9070 or so. Jats are a small minority. The village is a prosperous one. Many of residents or their relatives live abroad as N.R.Is. And lot of money from them flows to the village. There are caste based Gurdwaras in the village. There is also one Mazar of a Muslim Pir who is very much respected both by Jats and by Dalits. Once in a year there used to be a function at the Mazaar. All would go there to make offerings and to give 'Deg'.

Offerings at the Gurdwara controlled by the Jats are massive. NRIs generally have deep faith in the Gurdwara named after a martyr and having nearby a Samadh too. They make big offerings there when they visit the village. The same are estimated to be about Rs. 4-5 crores every year. The Jat Managing Committee has been using these funds as per its discretion resulting in comparative neglect of the Dalit parts of the village. Panchayat has very little funds and NRIs would not give it any grants. It has also been alleged that Jats pay their electricity and water bills not out of their own pockets but out of the Gurdwara funds. It is the uneven development of the village that seems to be the root cause of the social tensions.

Demand had come up for Dalit representation in the managing committee of the cash-rich Gurdwara. This was sought to be resisted on one ground/pretext or the other. Tension increased. Jats declared a social boycott of Dalits. There was no intervention by the administration or the Government despite intelligence reports. Caste clashes and even wars had begun taking place. Also there had been no move to enforce the law relating to social boycott of Dalits nor any political move to resolve the dispute on a just basis. Dalits went to Commission for Scheduled Castes and Scheduled Tribes. If I mistake not, some instructions to the Government were issued but this too had not effect.

Complete passivity on the part of the district administration can be explained only by political leadership not wanting to intervene and to let matters drift. Possibly, administration was also asked to wait and watch. First it was thought that it might be some Congress game of vote-bank politics. On deeper study, it became clear that the game was likely to cost heavily to the Congress as Dalits of the village had been mainly with it but now they were being badly let down. A leading Delhi based journalist has argued that it happened because Principal Secretary to the Chief Minister is also the Home Secretary. It is a fact that CM's Principal Secretary has so much work that he would hardly have the time for the Home Department. As far as my memory goes, never earlier a Principal Secretary to a C.M had also been made incharge of the Home Department. However, this blunder cannot explain the complete non-intervention by district level as also state level leaders of the Congress unless all of them had stopped reading even daily papers. I am therefore inclined to think that some financial links between the Congress leadership and the powerful Jats and NRIs of the village can be the possible reason. If that is ruled out, only other possible reason would be total political bankruptcy, which does not seem to be the case as yet.

On 15-6-2003, there was annual function at the Mazaar. It witnessed the first-ever communal clash in the village. And then came the curfew. There were Dalit demonstrations in Jalandhar and clashes with the police. A Dalit youth was killed as a result of police firing. For a number of days, no Congress leader or officer visited the familty even for condolences though financial help of 2 lac, a job, etc were announced. Village was visited by the Chief Minister accompanied by Manmohan Singh, one of the top Congress leaders in India and some others only when told by Congress President Sonia Gandhi to do that. Chief Minister was greeted with black flags by a number of Dalit youths.

Sensing that the Government would now move strongly, the managing committee passed/made public a resolution inviting Damdami Taksal of Bhindranwala to take over the Gurdwara and a Taksal force had already reached the village. At this stage, Congress leadership decided to keep off in view of the hostility it was facing and entrusted the job to the top police officers in and some other officers to bring about a settlement. It goes to their credit that they succeeded. BSP and some other non-Congress leaders boasted that they had not allowed the Congress anywhere near the negotiations.

Campaign against the Congress which was then run by BSP and Badal Akalis, clearly showed that earlier they had only been watching to let the Government drift as ultimately that would help them to denounce it as anti-Dalit. No non-Congress party really criticised sharply the Congress Government for its non-intervention. Neither did any other party took any concrete steps to defuse the situation nor suggested any steps to be taken by the Government. Failure of the Left in this respect is to be regretted most. Not having a mass base in this village is no alibi for completely shutting the eyes in the face of very serious and dangerous developments taking place in Talhan. Question of Dalit representation has been resolved in principle at least. Danger of Damdami Taksal taking over the Gurdwara seems to be over. But tensions persist and much more needs to be done. New problems have also arisen. And let it be noted that in many parts of Punjab, Dalit-Jat tensions have been increasing. It seems to me that Left must wage a continuous and consistent struggle against casteism and the caste system, which has penetrated even amongst Muslims and Christians. It helps only the vested interests.

Non-Congress and non-Left parties, particularly the BSP and the Akalis are now making all out efforts to make political capital out of what all happened in Talhan. BSP which had lost its mass base in Punjab hopes to regain it. Akalis led by Badal himself are trying to lend a helping hand besides hoping that Akali Party too would make some gain. First shot was fired when Mayawati was invited to Talhan/Jalandhar promising her a massive rally. It was openly declared that the main aim would be to expose alleged anti-Dalit character of the Congress. Chief Minister decided not to allow it. Fortunately, a way out was found. BSP rally was shifted to Chandigarh. Confrontation that took place, has raised an important question. It is the same as arose when Chief Minister Chautala of Haryana and his police gave all the help Badal wanted, when Punjab police/V.B men went to Haryana to search Badal's palace in the State.

It is bad enough that all political leaders with exceptions here and there don't hesitate to use all means including very foul ones to achieve their ignoble ends. It would be much worse if even Chief Ministers behave in the same manner. The question is: Should not some norms be there to be followed when a Chief Minister wants to go to another State to address a rally declared purpose of which is to denounce the political party to which the Chief Minister of the host state belongs, in an already very surcharged situation? Similarly, should not there be norms for police of two States when police of one goes to the other for search etc of properties, assets, bank accounts etc of some former ruler of the former State, who allegedly owns properties and assets in the other state built, acquired or created by massive corruption? Should it not be ensured that raiding police must act in accordance with law and also that the police of the other state does not non-cooperate or hinder? In relation to many other issues too, similar questions would arise. It is time that the matter is debated and some guidelines are agreed upon.

Views on Aruna Asaf Ali

A friend has written to me: "You write a lot. Why have you not written anything by way of your tribute to Aruna Asaf Ali even though you know fully well that she was not only very fond of your wife but you too got plenty of affection from this great daughter of India." I plead guilty to the charge and wish to make amends.

Aruna Asaf Ali, when I was young, was perhaps the most popular heroine of the youth, especially of male species. The youth of those days felt proud of her immense contribution to India's struggle for freedom. Her capacity to make sacrifices for the cause won her tremendous respect mixed with awe. What she did in the Gwalior Tank Bombay in 1942 and her role in 1942 movement made India's womanhood proud. Innumerable young men and women throughout the length and breadth of India, went wild with joy when she hailed the Naval Revolt which proved the last blow against British rule in India, even when some topmost Congress leaders were denouncing it. She was Mayor of Delhi for some years and proved herself to be incorruptible. She was there with every good cause. She did a lot in the fight for equality of two sexes. In order to inspire the fight against terrorism, she visited even rural areas of Punjab more than once when terrorists ruled the roost in the border state of Punjab. To the end of her conscious life, she fought for the poor and the downtrodden.

Young men of my age when I was a student first in Lahore and then in Bombay, were also proud that this elder sister of theirs and also one of the leaders who were also heroic fighters, was one of the most beautiful women in India. Her beauty was the gift of nature. To the best of my knowledge she never tried to make herself more beautiful with devices like lipstick and what not. She was known for utmost simplicity too. Aurna Ji was no Beauty Queen. In fact there were no Beauty contests in those days. Many of the girl students who became activists and leaders of the All India Students Federation too were beautiful. We admired the work as well as the natural beauty of these collegeues, friends and sisters of ours. They too did not seeks to make themselves more (?) beautiful by artificial means.

There are many Beauty Queens these days—Miss Universe one for every year, Miss World, Miss India, etc. Soon we will have Miss Punjab. I think we already have a Miss Moga. Most Beauty Queens who win their titles after parading their real as well as so-called beauty declare after being selected as Beauty Queens that henceforth they would serve the poor. In fact most of them serve only themselves and those who sponsor these Beauty contests to boost up their commercial ends. These Beauty Queens and those who aspire to be so, undermine the fight of their sisters for equal status with men in society. They strengthen the extremely harmful idea that women need to look as beautiful as possible to please men. It is not my intention to run down female beauty. I admire it. My own wife was beautiful girl in her younger days. And a sister of hers (ours, I can say) was even more beautiful. Beauty needs to be admired. But someone has rightly said: "Beauty lies in the eyes of beholders."

Let young girls of today follow the example of Aruna Ji. Let them be satisfied whatever beauty nature has bestowed on them. Let them remember that the secret of beauty does not lie in beauty contests. It lies in the once very popular piece from poetry of Urdu Poet Majaz. It runs like this:

"Tere chehre pe yeh anchal bahout hee khoob hai lakin

"Too is anachal se ik parcham bana leti to achha thah."

(The veil on your face is wonderful. However, it would be excellent if you were to make a banner out of it.)

And let me tell, young women of today young women and girls of my youth days (such as knew Urdu) would read poetry of (Faiz) and Majaz when lying in beds to sleep and when sleep was about to overpower them, they would put the poetry-book below their pillows. During day time they were busy studying, working and fighting for some good cause. Woman of India is known not only for gentleness but also for being more upright, more honest, and less prone to crime and corruption than the male. Beauty contests and craze for them is a danger signal. If it is not heeded, women will became victims of all those evils of which male society has already become one. We will soon be having female Sukhrams. To end, I for one will till the end of my life feel proud of the fact that Aruna Ji considered me worthy of her affection.

Beauty Market

Women organizations are mobilizing and organizing women to fight for equal rights for both the sexes, against various types of injustices being done and atrocities being committed against women, etc. These include neglect of the girl child, dowry deaths, wife beating and rape. Even minor children are being raped. In their noble fight, women organizations are being supported by all progressive forces. This is as it should be because the women's struggle for gender equality is in vital interests of society as a whole.

Young educated women coming from middle classes should be in the forefront of this struggle. Unfortunately, there are forces which are seeking to divert their energies and time to look beautiful, to take part in beauty contests which are now taking place from town to international levels. It may not be long before rural women too are persuaded to take this path. Beauty contest now go by different names. I received an expensively brought out multi-coloured invitation card to attend Rhythm Saturday Nite and Miss Punjab – A Charity Show on 2-5-1998 at Guru Nanak Bhawan, Amritsar, 6-30 PM onwards.

At the function, young women suitably dressed would parade to be selected as Miss Punjab, 98, Ist Runner Up 98, IInd Runner Up 98, Miss Beautiful Hair, 98, Miss Beautiful Eyes 98 and Miss Pretty 98. I am not against beauty; I like it. Natural beauty is the best beauty in nature as well as in human beings. In any case, the so called beauty contests in different forms at which young women are paraded are generally organized by commercial concerns as a part of their strategies to popularize themselves and their goods/ services to earn more profits.

The Invitation Card in question informs: The Rhythm Saturday Nite is presented by Lazziza Restaurant. The names which appear on the Card (as sponsors) are Dance and Modelling Institute, Lawrence Road, Amritsar with collaboration (of) Show Time (Regd.), School of Fashion and Modelling, Near Jagat Cinema Chandigarh. The name of Satkar Properties also appears on the Card. It goes without saying that higher we go, bigger are the business concerns which sponsor and organize such shows. Even multi-nationals are involved in the game.

It should be obvious even to the blind that these contests are a means being used by profit seekers to exploit beauty—natural or otherwise – for marketing their goods/services. If in the process, young women get diverted to concentrate their energies to beautify them instead of using them for the good of society and their own gender community—all the better.

Let young women ponder over it. Let their role models be women like Rani Jhansi, Mai Bhago, Sarojini Naidu, Preeti Vadhedar, Mother Teresa, Aruna Asaf Ali, Captain Lakshmi Shegal and others like them.

Let us get back to the invitation card. According to it a top officer of the Government of Punjab was the Chief Guest at the function. Top personalities announced included one ex-Minister of Punjab (Congress), President of Youth Akali Dal (B) Amritsar and two gazetted officers of the Government of Punjab. Some however did not come. Right of such VIPs to patronize such functions may not be disputed. However, their association with exploiters of beauty for their marketing, need not be considered desirable.

Tail-a-piece. One of my friends is a friend of the organizers of show which is an annual affair. Last year, I was approached for help. A BJP leader had threatened to lead a demonstration of women against their show and this had made the organizers panicky. As I did not favour the show, I said I would not intervene. They were advised by a friend to seek posting of police pickets at the gate and nearby as a precaution against any violence. The organisers rejected this suggestion for obvious reasons and thought of a method of their own. And this worked. The BJP leader who had threatened to lead a demonstration of women against the show was invited to agree to be honoured at the function. He readily agreed. Perhaps he had himself sent a feeler. My friend told me that show went off very well and the BJP leader was very happy. One wonders why no BJP leader was invited this time.

Letter to an IAS Officer's Daughter

My dear granddaughter,

I would have liked to address you as my daughter. However, in view of my age (75), grand daughter seems more appropriate. And please don't forget that often grandparents give greater love to grandchildren than even their parents. I know you are in distress because your dream of becoming a doctor has been shattered. It is for this very reason that I am writing to you. I fully share your agony and all my sympathies are with you. There is nothing wrong in wanting to become a doctor. That is a very legitimate desire. And if the same is frustrated by blind justice, pain is natural.

Being very fond of you, your parents were keen to help you. They did everything possible. Highly placed in the system of governance, they searched for a way out when they found you left out because of a demon called merit. Others even more highly placed and their political masters had faced a similar problem. Among them were some for whom what worried your parents was no problem at all. A system of nominations had been devised. Children of officers and unscrupulous politicians, who did not merit admissions, had at least one merit–of having enough money to buy seats in some other States – but they would lack security there and would run the risk of being shot by terrorists because their parents had fought terrorism by virtue of being a member of Punjab's bureaucracy even though they might not have lifted even their little finger against terrorists. A neat scheme indeed! Some tried to point out that it was nothing but a crude scheme to befool people at large. Theirs was a cry in wilderness.

You were nominated and all in the family felt happy. As bad luck would have it, the applecart was upset by those who had the power to do that and who had different ideas.

What and why went wrong when only a very legitimate desire was sought to be fulfilled? To aim high is not at all bad, but to use wrong methods to reach the goal is bad, very bad, because it does injustice to others who may be more deserving and who have an equal right to aim high.

When I was a student of your age, there was no IAS. But there was the ICS—the steel-frame of British rule in India. Certain sons and daughters of ICS men and the likes of them even while loving their parents from the core of their hearts, did not like their parents helping the British, who were doing great injustice to India. They decided to fight the British and for the downtrodden people of India. Their parents did not like it, but sooner or later they got reconciled to it.

Theirs is a good example to follow. If one does not have the desire or the will to fight injustice in society, at least one should not try to climb over the back of others. Parents may want their children to do that out of love. They should be thanked and given greater love in return, but this type of help should be rejected—firmly even though politely.

I can anticipate your reply: "There is a rat-race in society for top posts, for admissions, for more and more money—by means fair or foul. The honest are not even tolerated; gone are the days when the educated middle class and students were motivated by idealism. Unless you act as others do, you go under."

You are right, but not fully. In any case, if all begin to think this manner and no one reacts against injustice, it will not be long before our country goes under and collapses. And that will be the doomsday for all of us. Surely, you don't want that. Who will react against injustice if not educated young men and women like you? Aim as high as you like but try to reach it by means everyone should concede as honest and fair. You will be more at ease with your conscience and happier even if you reach one step or two lower on the ladder than the one aimed at. Let the youth be a source of inspiration for the old like me.

Love

Yours affectionately,

Satyapal Dang

July 1995

Procurement Prices, Producers and Consumers

For some years before 1995, the Indian politico-economic scene has been witnessing at regular intervals a familiar drama. It takes place on the eve of the harvesting of each of the two major food crops – wheat and paddy.

The Agricultural Prices Commission (APC) makes its recommendations on the procurement prices for the coming crop. A hue and cry goes up against these recommendations. The landlord and the kulak lobby is invariably most vocal. The APC recommendations are characterized as anti-producer and anti-farmer. Much higher prices are demanded which are described as remunerative. Some economists and intellectuals write articles in defence of prices recommended by the APC and oppose any increase in them. They do so in the name of consumers and on the ground that higher prices would add to the inflationary pressures.

The Chief Ministers meet in conference convened by the Union Food Minister. Often they speak in different voices and fail to reach a unanimous conclusion. Decision as to what is to be the procurement price is left to the Government of India and its decision is invariably an ad hoc political decision. In this whole process, the landlord and the kulak are able to a considerable extent to rally behind them the middle and even the poor peasants. The cause of the worker-peasant alliance suffers.

It is necessary that the Left and democratic forces pay much greater attention to this problem than hitherto, if the game of the reactionary forces to make use of the issue to rally the peasantry behind them is to be successfully countered and defeated. Not that the Left parties have been without any policy in this respect. The Communist Party of India, for instance, has been rightly demanding remunerative prices for peasants for their agricultural products (including food-grains), take-over of the wholesale trade in food grains, and efficient public distribution system functioning under the control of popular committees. This policy is generally considered correct by other Left parties and groups too, notwithstanding sharp differences among them on other issues.

Obviously, this policy seeks to ensure remunerative prices to the peasants and to reduce the difference between these prices and the purchase prices to be paid by the consumers (bulk of them belongs to the labouring and middle classes) at the cost of the wholesale trader-turned-hoarder and by trying to ensure that the small shopkeeper gets a reasonable but not undue and black market profit. This, obviously, is correct and unexceptionable. Such a policy, if accepted and implemented sincerely, will go a long way to serve the genuine interests of the producers as well as consumers. However, the possibility will still be there that what may be regarded as remunerative price for the peasants; may be too high for the bulk of the consumers and what may be considered reasonable for the latter, may be less than remunerative price for the peasants. The gap may be too big to be met by subsidy, to keep low the issue price.

The Left and democratic forces have not been unaware of this problem either. They have offered a solution on the following lines:

1. The working class, agricultural labourers and the urban middle classes must be educated about the necessity of the peasants getting remunerative prices; about the negative effects which would otherwise follow for the national economy and themselves. Simultaneously, peasants must also be educated about the negative consequences that would follow exorbitant prices for food grains for themselves and for the national economy.
2. Workers, peasants, agricultural labourers, middle classes, etc all must be explained as to how the problem can be solved in the interest of all the toilers and the common people if they together fight against the monopolists and the pro-monopoly policies of the Government, for securing cheaper fertilizers and other agricultural inputs and for cheaper cloth, etc. Success in this, together with state trading in food grains at the wholesale level, etc would make possible a price which the common people can afford and which at the same time is based on remunerative procurement price for the peasants.

This obviously is very correct and has to be fought for. However, it represents a long-term solution. The question as to what attitude should be adopted in the meanwhile at a given particular time regarding procurement prices, etc remains. For instance, now a controversy is raging as to the procurement price for wheat to be fixed by the Government of India. In connection with such controversies, the following must be kept in mind:

1. It is essential to ensure remunerative price for the peasant. Amongst the progressive intellectuals, there are not a few who underestimate this aspect of the question. They tend to overlook or minimize the problems and risks which peasants have to face.

2. With the growth of capitalism in agriculture, powerful elements have arisen which, in fact, want maximum possible profits but put forward demand for the same in the name of remunerative price.

   The capitalist landlords and kulaks who want the right to indulge in profiteering as is enjoyed by industrial big capitalists, are politically quite powerful. They have a strong lobby in the ruling party itself, though they carry on their campaigns mainly through the Rightist parties. They are not without their representatives in the intellectual world either. Here is, for instance, what B.R Shenoy wrote in an article in the *Illustrated Weekly* (November 10, 1974):

   "Our food grains price policy rests on the theory that farmers should have no reason to complain if procurement prices covered costs and brought reasonable profits. But what farmers seek for their produce, is the best price that the market will permit….." And in case this is sought to be prevented, what will Shenoy's farmer do? Here is answer by Shenoy: "The only escape open to farmers and traders from this price riddle is hoarding, smuggling and black marketing."

   The Left and democratic forces must take into account, this lust of the kulaks and the landlords for exorbitant profits and oppose it.

3. The common and especially the poor peasants do not stand to gain by exorbitant procurement prices. Soon after the sale of their produce, they have themselves to make purchases. Even at the time of the sale, quite a number of them do not get even the officially fixed procurement prices. They have to sell at lower prices to the local trader or the kulak because they do not have the means to transport their produce to the markets.

4. With a view to rally all the peasants behind them and to confuse public opinion in general, the kulak and the landlord lobbies use all types of arguments.

   Often it is argued that procurement price of wheat must be raised in proportion to the rise in the prices of agricultural inputs instead of arguing on the basis of the cost of production per quintal. This is important because the production cost per quintal of wheat does not rise in the same proportion to, for instance, the price of fertilizers per bag.

Similarly, for a long time, the procurement prices fixed for wheat in 1967 in Punjab were taken as correct and increase in them demanded proportionate to the rise in prices of agricultural inputs. This deliberately overlooked the fact that the 1967 procurement prices were, in fact, higher than what would be described as remunerative.

Now an exorbitant wheat procurement price of Rs.150 per quintal is being demanded on the ground that "the average price last year was about 120". (*Tribune*, March 14, 1975)

This does not take into account at all the fact that even the landlords were more than satisfied last year with Rs.105 as the procurement prices that dissatisfaction grew when the Government announced that traders could sell at Rs.150 and that the rise in prices much above Rs. 105 was the result of the Government surrender before the big traders.

The aim of all such propaganda is to create a strong psychological feeling of injustice being done to them, even amongst those peasants who have very little to sell and who have to make purchases within a few months after the harvesting. Without exposing and countering the real aims of the landlord and the kulak lobby, while demanding and fighting for justice for the peasant too, the Left and progressive forces cannot win over the poor and middle peasants.

5. Note must also be taken of the fact that the landlord and kulak lobbies want state intervention only when and where free play of the market forces does not favour them. Where the market forces enable them to get exorbitant prices, they favour the same and oppose state intervention in the form of state trading.

6. The available data as regards cost of production per quintal is generally not reliable. Even some of the Agricultural Universities

in the States doctor the data for the benefit of the so-called progressive farmers because of their bias in favour of capitalist landlords and kulaks. This bias as far as the Ludhiana University is concerned, could be seen by all when it openly opposed the lowering of the land ceilings.

7. The cost of production per quintal is not the same for all producers. It is less in case of landlords and rich peasants who use a lot of agricultural machinery. It is more in case of the small peasants.

Keeping in view the above relevant factors, the Left and democratic forces should adopt the following line of action:

(a) They should consistently and persistently fight for the lowering of prices of agricultural inputs as also of manufactured goods at the cost of exhorbitant profits of the monopolists; for state trading in all food grains at the wholesale level, including single-State food zones and procurement of all marketable surplus and for an efficient distribution system; as well as for prices which are remunerative for the peasants and fair for the consumers.

(b) In relation to every crop, they must themselves work out the cost of production per quintal. In doing this, they will naturally take into consideration all the relevant factors such as prices of agricultural inputs, likely or actual average yield per acre, etc. Further on this basis, they should demand procurement prices which would be remunerative but not exorbitant.

They must also suggest issue prices, taking into account absolutely essential overhead charges and when necessary, based on an element of subsidy to a reasonable and practicable extent.

(c) Any procurement price, if it has to be remunerative for the middle and the poor peasant as well, cannot but leave a considerable higher margin of profit for the landlord and the rich peasant. Ways and means of mopping up this excessive profit by the state and utilizing that for subsiding the issue price when necessary, must be considered seriously.

(d) The Left and democratic forces must expose and isolate the capitalist landlords and the kulaks on the question of procurement price as also their spokesmen and must not keep quiet and trail behind them.

VI

Communist Unity

Open Letter to H.K.S. Surjeet and A.B. Bardhan

Dear Comrades,

I hope you will not grudge me the right to address this open letter to you.

As good patriots, all genuine Communists cannot but be extremely worried about what the future holds for our great country, India and her people. For many years after independence the percentage of our people below poverty line was getting reduced even though at an extremely slow speed. Since 1991 or so, this has been again going up. In relation to illiteracy too, reverse process may start soon. Already medical treatment expenses are beyond the capacity of the poor.

At the other end, thanks to the major sections of even the middle classes going consumerist, corruption has been increasing by leaps and bounds. It has a negative effect on development. Also moral values are degenerating fast. Very soon whatever can fetch more money will be considered moral and whatever slows down the Get Rich Quick process will be considered immoral.

Commercialisation of politics has been followed by its criminalisation. The same process is now on in relation to some professions. No wonder our newspapers carry day after day stories of crime, land grabbing, murders, deaths in police custody and ever increasing number of women including female children being raped.

The non-Left parties are clearly not in a position to stem the rot. The Left alone can save India. But can it? –that is the million dollar question. It is too weak and is growing weaker. To me it seems that the main concern of Communists today should not be to somehow get some more seats in Parliament/Assemblies. It should be to ensure that this process is reversed and the Communists begin to grow stronger and become a strong national force as early as possible. The Communists owe this not only to themselves but also to the country and its common people.

There are more than one reason for the present state of affairs. The division in the communist movement is one. I see no reason as to why this cannot be overcome. The situation has been ripe for that for quite sometime.

When the CPI split in 1964, the CPI characterized the CPI-M as Trotskyite while the latter characterised the former as revisionist. And they would not touch each other even with a pair of tongs. They even went at each other's throat. The bitter experience of life brought about a change. The need for joint actions was recognized. And many joint campaigns and joint struggles did take place.

The process of unity-in-action needed to be taken further. United actions were good, but within the united actions the effort to grow at each other's cost could be felt together with its negative fallout. I can recall instances when the CPI-M-led trade unions denounced the CPI-led unions for having allegedly betrayed the struggling workers by signing agreements with employers, when they themselves would have felt greatly relieved to sign if placed in similar circumstances. I believe this has been happening in reverse to. I can recall strike struggles led by united action committees of the AITUC and CITU during which the CITU leaders carried on a campaign against the "reformists" of AITUC and the latter against the former as "adventurists".

The CPI took a big step forward long ago. It recognized the two parties as Communist Parties and called for "communist unity on a principled basis". The CPI-M, however, would take no such step. It recognized the CPI only as a Left party with which the "real" Communist Party, that is, the CPI-M, could have at best only joint actions.

The CPI-M leaders justify their refusal to unite on the ground that there are still "fundamental" differences between the two main segments of the communist movement in India. They point to programmatic differences. The truth is that neither of the two parties have today any programme. The CPI discarded its programme and adopted an interim programmatic statement. It has failed to hammer out a new programme—over the years. The CPI-M some years ago came to the conclusion that their programme had become outdated but it too failed to agree on a new programme. Why then talk of fundamental differences? Differences within each of the two parties are perhaps more than the ones between the two.

A belief is growing that the unification of the Communists in India in one party is not being realized because of subjective considerations.

Once there was a proposal put forward perhaps by the CPI-M that mass organizations led by them should unite first, instead of trying to unite the two parties. I was a member of the National Council of the CPI when it discussed this. Two middle-level leaders of AIKS (CPI) warned that the united Kisan Sabha would be completely in the hands of the CPI-M.

The ranks of both the parties want the two to unite. If that happens many other segments too would march in sooner rather than later. As far as the CPI-M is concerned, I was pleasantly surprised when I once discovered that they were as keen for unity as the CPI ranks. The occasion was a seminar at Amritsar organized by the CPI-M some years ago. The audience almost entirely belonged to the CPI-M. The applause I got when I emphasized the need for the two parties to unite was loud and heart-warming. Comrade Surjeet as the main speaker spoke last. He referred to the issue but said only this: "Dang is a free man but I am bound by the party discipline. So I cannot say anything."

Dogmatic understanding of "democratic centralism" prevents the ranks from taking steps to force the leaders to agree to unite and to work out modalities for the same.

I am writing this open letter to appeal to both of you to take steps to achieve communist unity in India before it is too late.

Whether one thinks of the danger of Indian society going barbaric or of the danger of India's disintegration as a result of the activities of terrorists of different hues or as a result of forces wanting a Hindu theocratic state in India becoming strong, the challenges can be met only if the Left becomes a strong force in India. Communist unity is one of the preconditions for that.

With fraternal greetings and respectful regards.

Yours sincerely

Satyapal Dang

Need for Struggle to Realise CPI-CPM Unity

Communist unity, desired very much not only by Communists of various hues but also by many upright non-communist patriots, has as yet remained a dream. However, two positive developments of considerable significance in this respect have taken place. One was the reunion of the UCPI in Tamil Nadu with the CPI which took place on April 8, 2000. Prior to this, as in the case of many non-Left parties, a process of splitting had been going on in the communist movement also. The CPI split into the CPI and the CPI-M followed by more than one split in each of the two over a number of years. The UCPI-CPI merger in Tamil Nadu is the first reversal of this trend and it can be the beginning of reversal of the process of splitism and of a new process of reunification. After all, what has helped the UCPI-CPI merger in a big way in Tamil Nadu is not State-specific.

The serous danger of the semi-fascist RSS taking over the country is a nationwide threat. Communist unity is one of the essential conditions to make certain that this threat is defeated and overcome decisively. The second was the electoral alliance in Bihar between the CPI and the CPI-ML (Liberation) which opposed both the BJP-led NDA as well as the RJD of Laloo Prasad Yadav and won 12 seats in the Bihar Assembly losing quite a few very marginally. Earlier there had been cooperation among the two in relation to mass movements and struggles. This was the first important electoral agreement between the CPI and CPI-ML.

Till recently the CPI was of the view that the CPI and CPI-M must unite and that would be followed by many other communist group joining the united Communist Party. Life has shown that the road to communist unity may not be exactly as visualized by the CPI. A comprehensive strategy must now be worked out learning from the two positive developments referred to above. Of course, this must not mean giving up the slogan of CPI-CPI-M unity. In fact, it needs to be reviewed as to why no headway has been made towards realization of this slogan.

It is no secret that the CPI-M has never recognized the CPI as a Communist Party. Further, it has been of the view that the CPI is only a Left party. Further, it has been of the view that the CPI is destined to disintegrate with a section of it seeking to join the CPI-M and another joining the Congress. Even when talking of greater cooperation, united actions etc the CPI-M has been consistently working for the CPI's disintegration. For long, it opposed unification of the two parties initially pointing out "basic differences" in general between the two and subsequently on the ground of programmatic differences. It does not answer the argument that differences within the CPI as well as in the CPI-M are greater than between the official political lines of the two parties; that there can be no Communist Party in which basic, even programmatic, differences can be ruled out, etc. For quite sometime now, neither the CPI-M nor the CPI has any programme. Both have been striving to evolve new programmes. Why cannot they merge and evolve a programme for the united party, if necessary by majority?

From the above, it does not follow that the CPI-M alone is responsible for the continuation of disunity. The CPI too has to bear its own share of responsibility. There was a time when this question used to be discussed in the National Council of the CPI. A small minority would argue as follows:

The ranks of the CPI-M like the ranks of the CPI want the two parties to unite. The leadership of the CPI stands for unity on a principled basis but refuses to struggle and fight for it. Unity will come only if the CPI takes the issues to the ranks of both the parties so that they debate and discuss the obstacles in the path and work to remove them. Towards this end, the CPI comrades must answer the CPI-M's arguments against merger, about basic differences continuing, etc etc.

The view of the minority would be opposed by the leadership by asserting that this would annoy the CPI-M leadership and make even joint work, etc impossible. This was a false argument but unfortunately the majority invariably supported it. It is high time to realize that the CPI-CPI-M unity will not come without struggle, and debates, and joining issues, etc, of course, in a fraternal way. To give just one example: why should the CPI-M ranks not be told that the CPI-M has invariably been rejecting the CPI's proposition that in relation to any election the CPI and CPI-M should first agree upon a joint strategy and then jointly negotiate with other non-Left parties with whom they wish to seek adjustment or agreement? Also, why should not the CPI-M and CPI both agree that during joint campaigns as well as struggles neither party should try to gain at the cost of the other, etc etc? If issues are taken to the ranks, discussed and debated in a comradely manner, the desire for unity will become an irresistible force. Persistent refusal of the CPI's leadership to adopt this course has given rise to a doubt in the minds of many that it too does not really want CPI-CPI-M merger.

It is high time to confront this issue and evolve a correct strategy for CPI-CPI-M unity.

Some comrades may ask: what about the negative development in Bihar, that is, the CPI and CPI-M not being in the same electoral camp but in opposing ones? Suppression of honestly-held opposing views on important questions in the name of Left unity or cooperation cannot help the cause of communist unity. This can only harm it, notwithstanding some immediate electoral gains. I for one felt happy and relieved when the CPI refused to line up behind Laloo, just because the CPI-M wanted it to do that.

VII

Fight against Corruption and Kidney Scam

How to Fight Corruption ?

Notwithstanding his and oft-repeated declaration of determination to root out corruption, Prime Minister Gujral was not able to carry much conviction. There were many things which created doubts.

He called far a mass movement against corruption. He, however, did not even pose the question: "who will lead the movement?" No political party could do that. Leaders of non-Left parties (with exceptions which prove the rule) were upto their necks in the cesspool of corruption. They all talked of "fighting corruption" of others but not their own and of their own parties! Left leaders are not involved in any scam (at least not as yet) and this goes to their credit. However, it is doubtful if even the Left can wage an uncompromising fight against this evil. They seem to have their own compulsions arising out of short term electoral considerations.

May be Prime Minister had in mind NGOs. He perhaps was not aware that many of the NGOs were there only for their own good with the help of money doled out to them by government and some international agencies. Not long ago I observed an interesting phenomenon-Beant Singh won Laurels for his contribution towards restoration of peace in Punjab. However, his name was in mud for unprecedented corruption under him. Anti-corruption Forums came up at many places. The one at Amritsar launched itself by inviting as chief guest a person who had become notorious for his money-collection for his political bosses. If he had in mind Forums to be formed by persons of undoubted integrity, he could make an appeal for that. Forums consisting of such persons against "corruption, communalism and criminalisation" are badly needed.

Parliament in its special Session to observe the Golden Jubilee of India's independence adopted an Agenda for India which contained only generalities. Why did not the Prime Minister ask the MPs to pledge to enact some special laws which would help fight corruption, for example:

1. a law to make obligatory for all MPs and class I officers to lay on the table of the house annual statements of their assets and liabilities as well as of members of their families;
2. a law to make obligatory confiscation of properties found by appropriate authorities to be the result of corruption, nepotism and misuse of powers beside providing for terms in jails;
3. a law to declare anyone who draws salary or allowances of any type from state exchequer as a public servant so that all from MPs to Sarpanches are definitely covered by the prevention of corruption Act; and
4. obligatory establishment of Lok Pals at all levels to which citizens can go with their complaints without being required to pay heavy fees and without fear of being sent to jail if they are not able to prove their complaint. There are other methods to discourage and keep out frivolous complaints. Proceedings of all Lok Pals to be open.

Such proposals have been made from time to time by many but they have not been getting the attention they deserve. If the Prime Minster had at least called for such laws during the special session of the Parliament, his credibility would have been high.

There is much talk about corruption at the top level. That is as it should be. Corruption at the lower levels however hits the common man immediately and very hard. And yet no attention is being paid to the latter. To justify that, a thesis is put forward: "If corruption is eliminated at the top levels, it will automatically become a thing of the past at lower levels too". That may seem to be an obvious truth but it means telling the common man that he is condemned to suffer for an indefinite period.

Another wrong thesis is in circulation. Badal says "If corruption is to end, people must stop giving bribes". So the people are responsible for corruption. Those who give bribes to get undue favours need to be treated at par with bribe-takers but not those who have to give bribes to get what is their right and what they need badly and urgently—may be a power-connection, a water connection, etc. And there must be no justification for bribe-takers at lower levels on the ground that their salaries are low, etc. Law should be enacted to make deterrent punishment obligatory once corruption or nepotism or misuse of power is proved.

It does not happen at present. I may give an instance or two. A Government doctor incharge of an ESI dispensary used to steal dispensary medicines on a large scale. Despite documentary evidence it took an MLA one year to force the government to order an enquiry and to accept that allegations have been found to be correct. Yet, the doctor was not dismissed and no criminal case was registered against him. He was only censured.

In another similar case, the culprit was transferred after a year's struggle but has not joined duty on the strength of false medical certificates although another year has passed since his transfer orders. And he has not given charge as yet with all the relevant records remaining in his custody.

The two examples are from Amritsar but they are typical. Some serious thought on the part of any Prime Minister/Chief Minister is necessary about such cases too, if he really wants to fight corruption.

There has been much talk of transparent government but no one seems to be willing to ensure every citizen a legal right to get copies of documents including muster rolls, etc, if he thinks corruption has taken place in some project or works—at least at the local level.

Last but not the least, there must be laws—Central as well as State, declaring corrupt all those whose duty is, to punish the corrupt but who save them by hushing up complaints. Prime Minister and Chief Minister should act in this respect also.

The State may fund all elections. No one need object but it is an illusion that it will end corruption. It may make more funds available to buy votes. For ending corruption, amending suitably existing laws and having laws to deal effectively with economic offences should be one of the first priorities.

Apex Court and Jain Diaries

I, like innumerable other laymen, have been a great admirer of the system of Public Interest Litigation (PIL) introduced by the Apex Court and of judicial activism notwithstanding the reasonable limits being transgressed here and there. At the same time I, like many others, have felt much disappointed at the actual results in some very crucial cases. Take the case of *hawala kand*, the mother of scams. Even very careful readers of newspapers had forgotten almost entirely the infamous Jain Diaries when they hogged the headlines as a result of a PIL case and the orders passed by the Supreme Court. Many Ministers had to resign. Some having saint-like reputations stood unmasked. No due on ever had any doubt in his mind about the correctness of the Jain Diaries.

When some of those named in them admitted having received the amounts mentioned against their names, the issue was finally clinched for everyone except the judiciary, which it is understood, must go by law— statutory or laid by itself. A court held that the diaries needed to be corroborated by some independent evidence which the CBI had not cared to collect. It also ruled that diaries were not account books, which baffled many ordinary men like myself. The saint-like reputation of some was restored when they were acquitted and finally when the order of acquittal and the reasoning that led to it were upheld by the Apex Court. We had no alternative but to reconcile ourselves to it. The view began to grow that in the end all would be let off the hook. This view tends to stand confirmed by the judgement given by a Delhi Court in the case relating to Devi Lal, a former Deputy Prime Minister.

As per the Jain Diaries, Devi Lal had received Rs.51 lakhs out of Rs.65 crores involved in the Jain *hawala* cases. The CBI proved that the Deputy Prime Minister took with him the alleged *hawala* dealer, S.K. Jain, to Norway in an official delegation for the funeral of its King. Special Judge V.B Gupta said the inclusion of Jain in the official delegation was an act of "gross abuse of official position."

The judge said:

> By this act, Mr Devi Lal had taken for granted the high office of the Deputy Prime Minister of India to be his personal empire..;. He had squandered the taxpayers' and public money without just and sufficient cause.

Hards words no doubt, but they break no stones. The important question is: For what purpose did Jain go to Norway? Surely, no to express his condolences for the family of the deceased King! It would seem obvious that it was a business trip—*hawala* or otherwise. Devi Lal was only helping his benefactor. We don't have the full text of the judgement and we don't know whether such questions have been posed and discussed. But it does seem to us that such circumstantial evidence can lead criminals to gallows. But on this occasion obviously it was considered inadequate to hold it as case of proven corruption. Aded to if was the ground that there was no prima facie other evidence than the two Jain Dairies, Devi Lal and all other accused, including Jain and two very near relatives of Devi Lal, were discharged.

One wondered whether the CBI would in for appeal. Even if it did, one was not sure that the Delhi High Court or the Supreme Court will upset it. After all, later the Apex Court had ruled that even if it is proven that an MP voted for money to prevent the fall of a government, he cannot be proceeded against because the Constitution protects him. This interpretation of the relevant Article of the Indian Constitution shocked not only many laymen but also many learned editors and other intellectuals.

Some of our judges often display gender bias. It seems that class and even political bias are having their way, though the Hon'ble Judges may not be conscious or aware of it.

Corruption and Trade Unions

India undoubtedly has become one of the most corrupt countries in the world. Stinking corruption at the top level has been attracting great attention. This is as it should be, because *Hawala* type scams can do immense damage to the economy of the country and that in the long run will hit hard all sections of common people, including workers and employees.

The fact that most of the leaders of all major non-Left parties have become corrupt to the core constitutes a very serious danger to our polity. Politicians becoming criminals and criminals becoming politicians is one outstanding result of this. Many bureaucrats and police officers have taken the same road. And this has led to increase in crime in the country to an alarming extent. This is epecially so in the matter of crime against women.

Lower Level Corruption

Another result is that in fact only an extremely insignificant part of huge amounts, which are allocated for development get so used. It is only right, that the whole country should be worried about this phenomenon. However, it is unfortunate that widespread corruption at the lower levels is not getting the attention it deserves.

It is corruption at ground levels which makes the day-to-day lives of common people miserable. One has to pay bribes even for most essential as well as small needs of the family. Life cannot but become miserable! Bribes have been given new respectable names but their essential nature remains the same. Your telephone may remain out of order for many days despite repeated requests unless you pay up. Same is the position in relation to power supply. Poor may have to pay bribes to get old age and widow pensions sanctioned and then to get them regularly. Someone's palms may have to be greased a lot, if one wants his plan for building a small house sanctioned. So on and so forth.

False Theories

Some false theories contribute towards neglect of corruption at ground levels. One is that, this corruption is because of low salaries/incomes. If that was really the main cause, there should be no corruption amongst top level police officers, bureaucrats and politicians. Reality however is just the opposite.

Even if some corruption is because of inadequate salary/income, condoning it is very wrong. It will become a habit and appetite for, it will increase with the increase in salary/income. Another false theory is that bribe givers and bribe-takers are to blame equally. Bribe-giver cannot be so blamed if he is forced to give bribe to get what is his due. He is the victim. Taker and giver can be treated as equally at fault if the bribe has been given to get something which is wrongful. For instance, when bribe is given to grab someone else's land or property.

Trade unions also often don't fight corruption on the ground that it will weaken their support. The fact is that, in the long run corruption cannot but greatly undermine the vitality and strength of the trade union movement. Also, one should not forget that in today's World, public opinion counts a lot. Support and at least sympathy of the public is vital for the success of trade union struggles. Corruption cannot but undermine this sympathy and may even contribute towards making the public at large hostile.

Teachers

In all schools, colleges, and universities, teachers preach honesty, integrity and high moral values. There are teachers who in practice themselves act otherwise. In not a few cases even students' funds are embezzled. Obviously such teachers don't help in bringing up a new generation of upright and honest citizens. Signals they send is that, practice may be quite opposite of what one preaches. Not to fight corruption at ground level in educational institutes is harmful right now as well as for the future of the country.

TUs

From the above it follows that it should be one of the duties of trade unions especially of employees in the service sector to fight corruption at the ground level. Corrupt political leaders fight corruption of others but not their own. Some trade union leaders have followed them. They expose and even fight the corruption of such officers as don't oblige them in the matter of transfers, appointments, etc. But not of those who oblige them. That is no real fight against corruption.

No trade union should try to hush up corruption of any of its members or leaders. Of course, extreme punishment may not be just in every case. There should also be an attitude of reforming. But to overlook corruption in the name of reforming or avoiding alienation, can only encourage corruption. Obviously, a trade union whose key leaders are corrupt cannot fight corruption. It is therefore a matter of utmost importance to try to ensure that no corrupt person is in the leadership at least. Whenever a corrupt officer or employee gets caught, he will invariably be able to find out persons who can put pressure on those who can help him to go scot-free. It is, therefore necessary that trade union leaders should not only have a will to fight corruption but should be strong enough to withstand all pressures.

Trade unions of government employees should educate their members about the need of attending to the grievances of the public and individuals promptly and efficiently. It needs to be remembered that delays breed corruption. Changes which are necessary in existing laws and rules to minimize corruption should be demanded and campaigned for. Perks which are liable to breed corruption, should be replaced by cash allowances. For instances, reimbursement of medical bills for outdoor treatment should go. Instead fixed medical allowance may be given. Unions should not put under the carpet complaints which they may get alleging corruption against any of their members. Unions should do all they can to ensure transparency in the administration.

Public Sector

Let it not be considered that trade unions of industrial workers of public sector or of private sector have no tasks in relation to corruption. There is plenty of corruption in public sector units. It should be the job of unions to bring about a situation so that workers are ready to fight against it unitedly. That is necessary to save the public sector itself. As far as trade unions in the private sector are concerned, they have to be vigilant against corrupt elements acquiring positions of responsibility in the factory or any higher level leadership, which they may misuse to sell interests of workers for their own selfish ends. More over these unions should also ensure that their members get their non-economic and non-trade union rights not by paying bribes but by fighting corruption with the help of the Unions.

Obligatory

Last but not the least, working class has to be in the forefront to defend national interests and the interests of the common people. This task demands that all the trade unions should join hands with all other healthy forces to fight corruption at all levels including at the highest levels. They should lend strong support to such general demands as the following:

1. All candidates for being elected as MPs and MLAs should be required by law to file along with their nomination papers statements of their assets and of assets of their family members. Subsequently, such statements must be placed on tables of their respective houses every year.
2. All elected persons right from the MPs up to the members of local bodies, who draw any amount in any form from public exchequer must be declared as public servants for the purposes of Prevention of Corruption Act.
3. CBI must be made into an autonomous body. It must be ensured that it is manned by persons of undoubted integrity and high character.
4. Effective Lok Pals with sharp teeths must be set up at all levels.
5. No complaint about corruption including nepotism, favouritism, land grabbing, etc. must be hushed up. Hushing up of such a

complaint by any authority should itself be declared a corrupt practice.

6. Every act of proved corruption must invite appropriate punishment. In case of high level corruption, imprisonment as also confiscation of all ill-gotten wealth and properties must be provided for in law.

Fight against corruption is not going to be either easy to short. It has to be fought and fought continuously if the future of the country is to be safeguarded. The trade unions have a responsibility to discharge in this task.

Fighting Corruption

Majority of politicians in our country are undoubtedly corrupt—perhaps corrupt to the core. The pity however is that even the upright politicians who are in a minority don't give priority to the job of fighting corruption at all levels. In fact, conscience remains fully satisfied as a result of the fact that they themselves don't indulge in corruption. Position in the bureaucracy is more or less the same. Once a totally honest serving IAS officer told me: "Only a microscopic minority of the IAS officers are upright. However, even they too don't fight corruption despite seeing it day after day both above them as well as below them." As long as the honest amongst politicians and bureaucrats don't consider it their duty to fight corruption tooth and nail, future of the country is going to become more and more bleak.

Tonnes of money meant for poverty-alleviation schemes have gone down the drain. Percentage of people below the poverty line instead of going down, has gone up not mainly because of wrong economic policies but also due to corruption. In Bihar sixty per cent of people are now reported to be below the poverty line. As regards economy, black money in circulation is much more than the white one and there is a regular parallel economy in the country. While this is recognized by most and will be admitted by almost all, not many realize the damage which corruption in the field of education does to our future generation.

Imagine a school in which the Head Teacher makes one teacher known to be corrupt incharge of all the funds. The Head signs blank cheques and gives them to this teacher. Huge amounts get embezzled. Part is kept by the in-charge and such teachers as collude with him. The rest goes to the Block Education officer upwards to the highest level. Such teachers preach honesty in their class rooms. As every one knows, pupils learn much more from the practice of their teachers and parents than from what they hear from both. Not to fight corruption at all levels and everywhere is to be a party to ensure that next generation will also be corrupt.

Here is another instance from Amritsar district. Government announced a scheme for Urban areas under which, it would open new primary schools if desired by Municipal Committees, provided built up of accommodation for the same was provided by the local bodies. Municipal Committee Chheharta requested 4 more new Government primary schools so that pupils would not have to cross main road to reach their schools and run the risk of being run over by some bus or truck in view of the heavy traffic. One of these was to be in locality Kartar Nagar. The ground floor of a building was taken on rent, which was decided through mutual negotiations. This was in the beginning of 1972 or 1973. Rent fixed was Rs. 339 p.m. Landlord was fully satisfied. Accommodation was reasonably good. Electricity and water supply were also there. On the first floor, a son of the landlord was living. However, the portion occupied by him was entirely independent. Many students got admitted. People of the area were very happy. Not long after, Municipal Committee Chheharta was merged with Municipal Committee Amritsar, which later became Municipal Corporation.

Six/Seven years after the then BEO Verka gave oral as well as written orders to the then Head Teacher to vacate the building for repairs "temporarly" as it was dilapidated and shift to another building owned by the same family. The teachers objected but were over-ruled. In fact, the building was not at all dilapidated. It was said that the building had been declared "unsafe" by the XEN, P.W.D.

The new building lacked adequate accommodation. Very unsatisfactory water-supply and electricity arrangement were cut off as bills were not paid. The school was never shifted back to the original building. Nor was the same ever repaired as no repairs were infact required. On the first floor, one family had continued to live even though the portion below it with the school therein had been declared as "unsafe" by PWD (B&R).

In 1998 NGO, the landlady of the new building, daughter-in-law of the landlord of the first building, filed a suit in the court of Ms. Manjot Kaur Sub-judge, Amritsar claiming Rs. 2,50,000/- or so as rent at the rate of Rs. 2760/- p.m. Market rent at the time when the school was shifted there would not exceed Rs.1,000/- p.m. The department it has been revealed, had agreed to keep the new building instead of shifting the school to the original one. How much bribe was given is anyone's guess. Rent of the building was got assessed from the PWD at an exhorbitant level obviously in the same way.

1. Mrs. Vimla Dang, then an MLA, in her letter dated 15-10-93 had written to the then D.C. as under:

   "It seems to me that the certificate given by the XEN, PWD is not correct. The school is situated in a part of a big building. I am told that in the same building the landlord, his sons and their families and perhaps some others too are living. The building is such that only the portion in which the school is there cannot be unsafe while remaining building remains safe". Mrs Vimla Dang had requested re-inspection.

2. The clever landlord and the corrupt officials had got drafted a memorandum which said that the new building was very good. The landlord managed to get it signed by many people including some Councilors. Requested to sign, Mrs Dang refused but made an endorsement to the effect that she would have no objection to the school being shifted to a new building if the department was satisfied that it was suitable and better than the original one.

3. As early as 1981, the landlord had tried to throw the school out of the original building on the basis of a false plan of the entire

building showing the school portion as occupied by the landlord. The plan had been got prepared by the PWD construction Division No. 2. The attempt to physically throw out the school on the basis of this plan was foiled by public intervention. The matter was brought to the notice of Mr. B.A. Willian, the then DEO (Primary) by me vide a letter written in August 1981.

Coming back to the suit filed by the landlady claiming rent to the extent of Rs. 2,50,000/- or so, Education department of the Government of Punjab told the their DEO that it had no money to make this payment alongwith interest and fine which Sub-judge might impose. This would mean that the building would be ordered to be vacated. This would not hurt the landlady much as she would proceed to recover the rent due through a civil court. Sufferer would be about 150 pupils and their very poor parents who would not be in position to send them to other (private) schools in the locality being unable to afford their high fees.

This writer advised the DEO that the department should disown the rent-deed as having been executed as a result of a big bribe to some in the department at the relevant time. The department would not agree. Instead, it reached a settlement with the landlady to continue to pay the exhorbitant rent and to pay arrears by instalments. No doubt neither the corrupt officers of the PWD (B&R) and of the education department nor the bribes givers have suffered in any way. However, the school has been saved. The department has now been requested to acquire land in the same locality to have its own building for the school. It is doubtful whether it would adopt this sensible course because even primary education for the poor is not on its priority lists.

Medical Ethics

Lack of medical ethics amongst a big section of doctors, if not a majority, is an extremely serious matter. This has not only sullied the Next-to-God-reputation of the medical profession. It has very negative consequences for the society as a whole. No doubt, some fight is being waged for medical ethics in some parts of India, for instance by the journal. ***"Issues in Medical Ethics"*** and the medicos behind it. Considering the seriousness and the extent of the problem, the same is far from adequate. It needs to be strengthened and spread.

Briefly, I wish to point out the very widespread practice of many doctors issuing altogether false medical certificates and how difficult it is to fight this practice. I shall give some experiences of ours. During eighties as a legislator, I was also a member of the Amritsar District Grievances (Removal) Committee. In connection with the discussion on a specific item, I had said: "I can give different rates at which money is charged for issuing false medical certificates in medico-legal cases under different sections of IPC, e.g., 324, 325, 326, etc". I then quoted the rates. The then Civil Surgeon when asked by the Chairman confirmed my assertion. When I asked what he was doing about it, he expressed his helplessness. There was some uproar but ultimately the matter was talked out.

It was perhaps in 1994 that Amritsar correspondents of *Times of India* and *Nawan Zamana*, a Punjabi Daily published from Jalandhar, did some investigative journalism and carried a long report alleging that issuing of false medical certificates was a normal practice in the Civil Hospital Amritsar. They cited about 10 cases giving full details and also the names of the doctors responsible for issuing these false certificates. Mrs Vimla Dang, an MLA at the relevant time, gave notice of an Assembly question and carried on prolonged correspondence with the Minister and the Secretary. The matter was agitated in the Assembly at least twice. After more than a year two doctors were transferred. Punishment given was like sending a cold blooded murderer to jail for 6 months only.

During made 1998, one retired LIC officer and his sons from his second wife attacked his son from his first wife and his daughter-in-law to throw them out of a shop-cum-residence which they were occupying lawfully. The daughter-in-law was attacked on her head with a big iron lock. It resulted in bleeding. The retired officer and one of his sons inflicted on themselves one injury each. All went to the police. The police asked both the parties to go to the Civil

Hospital and get medical certificates. The retired LIC officer and his son were admitted. The daughter-in-law was threatened by a goonda gang outside the Hospital. She was forced to go back to Chheharta. On the intervention of the public local police first sent an unarmed Home Guard and then an armed policeman. She too was then admitted.

One member of the aggressor party got a medical certificate for Section 326 for a small injury on the finger next to the thumb. The other got certificate for Section 324, while the other party (the daughter-in-law) was given a certificate u/s 323 IPC, which is non-cognisable. SP incharge of the area ordered registration of criminal cases u/s 326 and 324 IPC, etc against the aggrieved son and his wife who had received a head injury and two neighbours who had tried to save them. Only agitation saved them from arrests. A proper investigation by the ASP was ordered by the SSP. He held the finger injury as self-inflicted. The case was then represented to the I.G Police who ordered an enquiry by one SP. The SP came to the conclusion that the second injury too was self-inflicted. He also ordered registration of cases against those who had got a false FIRs registered at the police station. This, however, has not been done as yet.

The point to be noted is that, the injured young woman, her husband and two others would have been sent to jail and possibly convicted by the court on the basis of the false medical certificates but for public agitation. Such public intervention does not take place everywhere. I have no doubt in my mind that many suffer imprisonment because of false medical certificates. The entire matter was brought to the notice of the Health Minister and a thorough enquiry was demanded. After two reminders, a reply was received that the Secretary was being asked to get the matter enquired into. In turn, the Secretary/the Director has asked the Civil Surgeon who deputed his Deputy to hold the enquiry. No one expected any worthwhile result because the large scale issuing of false medical certificates over a long period could not have taken place without their connivance, and possibly more.

Originally not many doctors indulged in the malpractice of issuing false medical certificates. They did so for money. With the growth of corruption, number of such doctors has been increasing. With the rapid growth of consumerism in the middle class after the New Economic Policy of Narasimha Rao, this number has reached alarming proportions. Nor is that all.

A nexus has developed between criminals and a section of doctors. The criminals are helped by such doctors by issuing them false certificates, of course, for consideration. There is much and very justified talk about politicians-police-criminals nexus. It is time to take note of nexus between criminals and some professions including those of lawyers and doctors. It is indeed gratifying that an article by Dr. Sanjay Nagral in ***"Issues in Medical Ethics"*** had took note of this nexus as far as medical profession is concerned. Steps necessary to put an end to it need to be debated and discussed. Immediately, a widespread discussion is needed as to the concrete steps which will at least minimize the malpractice of issuing false medical certificates by the black sheep in the profession, which are by no means few.

The Ugly Aspects of Our Health System

The great kidney scandal of Amritsar was in headlines of the print media of Punjab for some months. That has exposed the fact that a section of even doctors gone consumerist are ready to commit crimes against the poor and the society as a whole in the name of saving lives of such rich patients as need kidney transplants. It also stands exposed that in actual practice they are not concerned even about the lives of the rich patients, making money being their only Dharma. For instance, it has become widely known that for long in the private hospital in which kidney transplants were being done, donors were not being tested for AIDS, etc. Also, for the sake of making tons of money in the shortest possible time, two, three and even more operations were being done in a day when it is not considered safe to do more than one. However, some other ugly aspects of kidney transplant business have yet to be exposed. For instance, how the society, the government and the medical profession have not felt concerned at all by the fact that the poor needing kidney transplants have to resign themselves to death, not being able to raise the money needed for medical expenses before and after the transplant poor are discarded even if a relative with matching blood group is willing to donate his/her kidney. This is also a fact that no police officer except one Inspector (a small fry) politician or any magistrate involved in the racket has been booked as yet when some at the top are believed to have been fully involved. Sooner or later, therefore, the kidney scam may hit the headlines once again. In the meanwhile, let us draw the attention of the powers-that-be to some other ugly aspects of our health system.

1. Long ago it was made obligatory to print the maximum retail price of every medicine being sold, on the bottle or the packet, as the case may be. Declared objective was to prevent the customer from being looted and to ensure that prices were within the reach of the poor. What actually has been happening is just the opposite and the culprits are generally reputed companies. Here are three instances from our own experience, i.e. of myself and my wife.

    (a) Cetirizine is effective against incurable bad cold due to some allergy. Dose is one or two tablets a day (10 mg.). Retail price for one tablet in case of Glaxo is Rs.3 per capsule and in case of Ranbaxy, it is Rs.2,60. Recently the latter was purchased for me from a wholesaler by a friend of his at the rate of 50 paisa per unit. I did not find it less effective in any way. In fact it has proved to be more effective. My own chemist told me a "secret" when I asked him about such a big difference. He said Ranbaxy gets it prepared/manufactured from others and only markets it just as Bata Shoe company gets shoes made by good cobblers and the same with necessary polish are then marketed by it while Glaxo does the whole job itself. Actual cost, I have been told, per capsule comes to 10 paisa only.

    (b) For Typhoid, Ranbaxy product is Zanocin (Salt-Ofloxacin). Another company Cadila sells Oflin based on the same salt. Yet another product in the market based on the same salt is Zenoflox-200 of a company called Mankind Farma. More than a year ago, I purchased for my wife Zanocin tablets at the rate of Rs. 31/- per tablet. Rate of Oflin then was Rs. 10/- per tab. And in case of Zenoflox it was Rs. 3/- only. Our chemist had told me that the rate of Zanocin would come down because its sale was going down though it might take some time. He suggested that I might consider saing in for Oflin or Zenoflox since salt in all three was the same. I preferred to go by the doctor's prescription. Rates in the market now are Rs. 7.70; Rs. Five and Rs. 3.25. One can imagine the loot indulged in by Ranbaxy over years before it was forced to reduce its price from Rs. 31/- to Rs. 7.70 and also by Cadila which had to reduce its rate from Rs. 10/- to Rs. 5/-.

(c) Blood pressure is another common disease, which like typhoid, does not spare the poor either. In February 2001, my wife was prescribed Amlopin (5 mg). She had taken it for full two years. It would cost about Rs. 3/- per tab. After she had taken it for full two years, one day when I went to buy, our chemist's shop was closed. I went to another and asked for 26 tablets of Amlopin. He gave me Amlodac. When I pointed out that it was not what I had asked for, he said: "Salt is the same and you can believe me that it would be equally effective". I was sure that he would not cheat me. I went in for what he gave me. It cost us only Rs.1/- per tab. My wife's doctor, a topmost and very upright doctor confirmed what the chemist had told me. And it has been so in actual practice.

It is obvious that my competent doctor would be able to give many more examples of the above type. Medical salesmen canvass medicines prepared and sold by different companies. Upright doctors would prescribe medicines, which they consider quite OK. However, there are doctors also who will prescribe medicines of only such companies as give them benefits of different types. If the system of brand names were to be abolished, then salesmen on behalf of companies would start canvassing chemists. On the whole however, it seems that consumers would benefit. Be that as it may, why cannot upright NGOs including trade unions, our MPs and MLAs (at least of the Left) agitate for a system of all medicines carrying either reasonable "maximum retail price" or fixed retail price and for a system that would ensure that retail price charged from all customers are really reasonable, providing only for reasonable ads and reasonable publicity, besides reasonable profits?

Why should not Associations of doctors, nurses and para-medical employees too, raise this demand instead of being concerned only with incomes/salaries of doctors? Let them be fighters not only for justice for themselves but also for patients and hence for medical ethics too.

Here is something else which too should worry all. It is a news which appeared in a leading English daily of North India on 19-1-2003. It is as under:

"The kidney scam it seems has opened the Pandora's box for the medical profession. Eye surgeons who supposedly have the gift of restoring sight are under cloud now.

"Though the corneal transplantation trade is not associated with huge amounts of money and a vast net work, the medical fraternity has been aware of this (eye) racket since long, but they chose to keep mum. Probably, because the donors in this case were dead and not living persons. Doctors on condition of anonymity, alleged that Forensic Science departments of various medical colleges in Punjab were involved in corneal thefts......

"Doctors said that in this racket, eyes were removed from a corpse (mostly accident victims, medico-legal cases and unidentified bodies in Punjab) sent to Delhi, where surgeons earned millions from corneal transplants. A forensic science surgeon of Punjab was caught twice for removing eyes.....

"In some cases, where the relatives found out and protested, payments were made to settle the matter.... Human rights organizations also feel that there is need to create awareness about eye donation.

Doctors also say that legal action would not help as much as promoting the cause of eye donations.... Besides awareness, social activists are unanimous that profession needs cleansing, as many surgeons have been cheating patients...."

Moral of this news report is obvious: "Let no doctor become a trader in human organs—may it be kidneys or corneas or any other organs". And let this become the battle-cry of all such doctors as wish to remain loyal to their oath.

Illegal Kidney Trade

Common people have more or less same views about the illegal kidney trade that has been going on in Amritsar and about all that has been taking place in this connection. A small section of people have quite different views and some questions are being raised by it. Here is an attempt to answer those questions, at least some of them.

Q. Why doctors alone are being arrested? Why not others? Should not donors, recipients and dalals have been arrested first?

A. It is not correct that only doctors-at-fault are being arrested. Before any doctor was arrested, a number of donors, some *dalals* and even two lawyers were arrested. Some poor labourers too had been arrested who were said to have had (only) intention to sell one kidney each for money. Arrest of two doctors came much later followed by one mores. Some more are absconding.

It is true that not one of the Magistrates who had attested altogether and clearly false affidavits has been even questioned, not to speak of being booked. In fact, a senior member of the Special Investigating Team (SIT) has said that they do not intend to do anything in this regard because that will divert attention. I am in total disagreement with this view. No one should be considered above law howsoever high he may be. It is also my opinion that it is the duty of the Chief of S.I.T to inform the Hon'ble Chief Justice of Punjab and Haryana High Court through proper channel about the role played by some Magistrates as also about names of Magistrates who clearly and knowingly attested false affidavits.

It is also true that all that has been happening could not have happened without the connivance and participation of some policemen including some top police officers on the one hand and some influential politicians on the other. It is good that the Chief Minister has assured that not even IPS officer(s) involved would be spared. People want this assurance to be implemented at the earliest. There are strong reasons to suspect involvement of one former Chief Minister, one MLA and one Minister. There may be others. Public must be told clearly what exactly is the position regarding these and other politicians who may be involved or suspected to be involved.

Some supporters of doctors who have been arrested seem to be of the view that no doctor should be arrested unless all suspects from other categories are also arrested first or simultaneously.

It is unfortunate that more than once contradictory statements have been made on behalf of S.I.T. For instance, it was first stated that 3 journalists had been paid Rs. 5 lacs (by those running the (kidney trade). Their names were even given. After three days, it was said that there was no evidence about it. Here is another instance. After having been briefed, the Chief Minister himself declared that Badal had received Rs. 50 lac from Dr Sareen and that he would not be spared. Later, a member of S.I.T. announced that as yet there was no evidence. Some assert that one MLA and one senior police officer were present when Rs 50 lac were paid to Badal. System of keeping the people informed needs to be improved considerably.

Q. When a poor person sells his one kidney, he violates the law. Should not he be proceeded against in accordance with law, just because he is poor as it is being suggested by some. What about the patient who has been transplanted such a kidney purchased by or on his behalf?

A. Any person even if he is poor who sells his kidney for money really voluntarily as also one who buys it by paying the price decided can be arrested and proceeded against.

What is happening in actual practice is very different. Generally, people are not willing to part with one of their two kidneys. It requires an operation which is not very minor. After one kidney is given, 3 months medical supervision is essential. Patient can be allowed to go for some days and even more than once during this period, depending upon his condition. If necessary, he should be given medical care, etc even beyond 3 months. Moreover, one who gives one kidney runs the risk of losing his life if it so happens that, his other kidney gets damaged and becomes useless. The risks involved will specially be greater in case of the poor. Those who have enough money, don't want that any of their near relatives or even close friends should run the risk. Palients from this class would like to buy kidney from some one else, even though it is illegal. The patient has to find some one who is prepared to give kidney for money and also that this person's kidney will suit his body. This can be decided only by surgeons who have to operate to take out a kidney after various tests.

It is in this background that illegal trade has developed. Unscruplous surgeons and allied doctors charge huge amounts; *dalals* find out suitable poor persons who are made to agree by promising some amounts, by pressurizing and even beating etc, by kidnapping them and forcing them to "agree". Some die because of lack of post-operation-care. There are some in the illegal trade whose duty is to get the dead bodies cremated as unidentified and unclaimed. In many cases full amount promised is not given to the donors but only a much smaller amount or none at all. Not long ago, *Times of India* reported that if some big amount had been promised and the donor was likely to insist on getting the same, he would be got murdered.

Obviously donors whose kidney is taken by pressure, threats, etc etc cannot be considered guilty even if some money is given. Not they but those who got removed kidneys by above methods, are the real culprits and they need to be proceeded against in accordance with law and above all, those who head the mafia or have set up the organisation and share the loot with various types of actors in this trade.

As regards recipients, even those of the family who went about the job of getting a suitable kidney may also be liable to be prosecuted.

Q. Who else are liable to be arrested and prosecuted?

A. (a) If donor is made to give a false affidavit that he is giving his kidney out of attachment or affection and not for money, an Magistrate who attests such an affidavit even when it is clearly false.

(b) Lawyers who help prepare false affidavits.

(c) Police officials of different ranks and politicians helping the illegal kidney trade.

Q. What has been public reaction to the arrest of some doctors and what has been the reaction of doctors?

A. Public at large welcomed it. As far as doctors are concerned, opinion has been divided. An organization of PCMS doctors welcomed the action while another strongly opposed it. Some other organizations too condemned the arrests. It was even alleged that arrests were the result of some conspiracy and the accused doctors were totally innocent. In view of strong public opinion and also the view of the silent majority in the profession, the tone had to be changed.

Now it began to be asked: "Why only doctors are being arrested" (though it was factually not correct).

Calls for strike and Dharnas did not evoke much response and petered out. Whatever support the mafia had was for the following reasons:

1. A section of doctors (as most politicians) consider making money by any means justified. There has been erosion of medical ethics as of moral values in general.
2. Generally the idea of their Associations (as of many others) is that their only purpose is to fight for higher and higher salaries and other facilities, etc and that they must defend their collegues right or wrong. Interests of public, especially the poor, are not their concern.

This and this alone can explain the fact that while in the leadership of doctors' agitation there were some quite well respected doctors, there were also some with very shady past. One doctor during nineties had been caught regularly stealing medicines from the dispensary under him—day after day. After much agitation in and outside the Assembly an enquiry was ordered. He was held guilty and instead of taking steps to dismiss him and to register a criminal case against him, he was only censured. Soon after, he committed another serious misconduct but managed to escape any punishment. In due course, he got promotion and was transferred but continued to occupy a quarter in Amritsar illegally without paying even penal rent. Against another leader, someone once went to District Forum for removal of grievances of consumers. He earned the remark that he deserved to be thrown out of the profession. Both these doctors are office bearer of one or the other organization of doctors. Doctors rightly blame politicians for most of the ills from which the country suffers. But instead of fighting for correct policies, a good section of those in profession have been following in the foot-steps of politicians of the type they condemn. A radical change is called for here too.

Last but not the least, an influential organization of Nurses which demanded cancellation of licenses of doctors running the kidney mafia to do medical practice deserves to be congratulated.

Anu's Questions Regarding (Industry) and Kidney Transplatation Answered

About 4 Weeks ago, I received a letter purporting to be from Anu Gupta, Chheharta, Amritsar through Vijay Kumar Chopra, Editor *Punjab Kesari*. The letter wanted answers from me to some questions. The Editor did not think it proper to print the letter though she requested him to do that. I am now requesting Vijay ji to print the letter and also my replies as these are issues of general interest too.

1. Letter says: "You destroyed industries of Punjab through repeated *dharnas* and have made all the youths of the State unemployed.

A. No individual can be strong enough to do this even if he wants to, much less this writer. I have been living in Amritsar since

1952. Not one mill or factory has closed down because of any *dharna* or even strike. As far as I know, same can be said about Punjab as a whole.

Some industries have closed down for various reasons. For instance, entire small scale washing soap industry in Amritsar closed down because it could not compete with Sunlight, Nirma, etc. "Big fish eat the small ones" is the law of capitalism.

Some big textile mills closed down. In place of each, two or three or even four apparently new factories appeared on the scene and started working. On paper, these were independent units but in fact real owner(s) was/were the same. This happened because of two reasons. Excise duties were levied only on units having more than a fixed number of workers. A mill would split into 2, 3 or 4 units (sometimes under the same roof) to escape paying excise duty. There was also such splitting to escape legislation beneficial to workers of units having more than a particular number.

Some industries/units shifted to other centres and even States because of two Indo-Pak wars. A decade of terrorism also resulted in such shifting. Proprietors and top managerial officers of one big mill left Amritsar and even Punjab leaving some inexperienced person(s) to run the Mill. It had to close down because of this inexperience.

Some Mills/factories closed down (and can close down in future also) because of quarrels between partners, mismanagement resulting in losses, etc.

Workers would never want an industry to close down because that would render them unemployed. Many a time they even agree to compromise on their very just demands to ensure that the industrial unit in which they are working does not close down.

As a result of the policy of so called globalisation, liberalization and privatisation, more than 6 lac units all over India including Punjab had closed down. All know that Governments of Narasimha

Rao and Vajpayee are responsible for this. We have been strongly opposing these wrong policies and have been seeking the cooperation of industrialists. Unfortunately, these days many of industrialists prefer to become traders rather than join hands with workers to save industries.

Many years ago, Amritsar silk weaving industry was in danger of closing down because Amritsar was getting yarn produced by some monopolist at much higher price than the industry at Surat and therefore could not compete in the market. It was at our initiative that trade unions and associations of employers came together and launched a joint struggle for yarn at a reasonable price and for a spinning mill in Amritsar.

Anu Gupta is a victim of false propaganda of those who don't want strong trade unions so that they can maintain and increase their profits at the cost of workers and so that workers are not in a position to fight for justice.

2. "You (Dang) want to be in the headlines of newspapers (but) people do not like you during elections".

A. I can only say that I have never sought publicity for the sake of publicity. Media has great power and it should be used to get justice, to fight oppression, etc. I go to the press only for a cause, which in my opinion is just. As regards elections, I was never fond of fighting elections. I had to do as my party ordered me to do that. I lost in 1957 and 1962. Constituency then was such that CPI could not have won. Party decided to contest to take its policies to the people on a big scale.

I won in 1967, 1969, 1972 and 1977. I lost in the next election. Last time I contested, I did so after it was decided that I would not be asked to contest in future. After a spell of Presidents rule, elections were held in 1992. My wife Vimla Dang was asked to contest. She agreed because her refusal might have led some to think that she was afraid of being killed by terrorists. (A number of candidates were killed). C.P.I won the seat again.

3. Letter adds:- "Since you have not got any other work, you along with some others are determined to bring bad name to the profession of famous doctors of our Punjab. You should first find out the truth. You don't want any surgeon to remain in Punjab and if some do remain, they should flatter you. You have already your one foot in grave. Why do you want to harm the people before leaving this World?"

A. Yes, I am 82 Plus. Before I leave this World, I want to do whatever I can to fight against injustice, oppression and exploitation of man by man. Common people appreciate this.

4. Intelligence can be used for good of common people as well as for doing much harm to them. Those who come in the first category will become famous and those of the second category will become not famous but notorious. In case of surgeons too, some are famous, some are notorious. And this applies to kidney surgeons too.

A. Moral values of a section of our people are no longer what they should be. For them everything is justified if it gets then more money. Rot started with the politicians and bureaucracy but has spread to most of professions too. Speaking generally, doctors are no longer regarded as gods next only to God. A section of doctors including a section of kidney surgeons and their accomplices too are prepared to do anything to mint money. An axis has come into existence of corrupt amongst doctors and corrupt amongst politicians, bureaucrats, police officers, Advocates and even Magistrates—all determined to make maximum money. Such kidney surgeons are not at all concerned with the health and even lives of donors, who are poor and are offered money for their kidneys and/or even coerced and forced to part with them and who are often not paid even the promised amounts. They are not concerned much even about health and lives of recipients as has been shown by cases in which donors were not subjected to tests for AIDS, etc.

This is also a fact that when with difficulty only one kidney transplant can be done on one day, some surgeons do 2, 3 and even more. Dangerous consequences can be imagined.

It is such doctors who are bringing bad name to the medical profession. I believe that majority of doctors are human and try to be loyal to their oath. Unfortunately, they constitute silent majority. We feel sure that sooner or later they will speak up. I know of some doctors who were saying more or less what the writer of this letter has said about my stand, but already they have understood the truth. Common people from the very beginning were happy that the kidney market scandal was being exposed. They hope that culprits would get the punishment they deserve. If they do not, they will become so daring that even during broad daylight they will get picked up persons from amongst the hapless poor to remove their kidneys for the rich patients.

5. The letter asks: "If tomorrow one of your blood relations needs a kidney, how much will you be willing to pay to purchase one or will you let him die.

A. If a blood relation of mine needs a kidney, I will not be able even to think of purchasing a kidney, because I am not a rich man. Even if I were to have the needed amount, I will not entertain the idea as this practice is highly immoral and wrong.

Any amongst our near relatives having matching kidneys will donate one. If there is none, we will try to get kidney of a brain-dead person. If by then, registers are being maintained of persons willing to donate one kidney, we will try from that source. While searching for a kidney, we will try to keep alive the patient with the help of dialysis.

People should be willing to make sacrifices for others. In any case, no decent person will want to try to save the life of a relative by forcing a poor person to risk his life.

Last but not the least, Anu Gupta in her letter, appealed to the Chief Minister to ensure starting of industries in Punjab "so that the poor youths can earn to live". I hope Chief Minister (and the Government of India) listen to this appeal. We fully support it. But should not the writer of the letter think of the poor also when she pleads for the right of the rich to purchase kidneys of the poor endangering their lives and without realizing that they may also be endangering the lives of the recipients too because of malpractices of money hungry surgeons and their accomplices?

Let us together worship really God like doctors but let us expose and fight those who are worse than devils. And let us work for the needed changes in the law.

Amrinder's Fight against Badal's Corruption

It would be an interesting and useful exercise to examine the strategy and tactics being adopted by Badal to defeat the offensive launched by Captain Amrinder Singh to prove his and his family's allegedly massive corruption as the third-time Chief Minister of Punjab.

In the first instance, he asserted again and again that he would fully cooperate with the investigations and would quit politics if proved that he has ever committed even a minor act of corruptin. As the later developments proved conclusively, it was only a public-relation exercise to make, at least, a section of the public believe that he was innocent and was only being harassed.

When Vigilance Bureau teams went to search Badal and family's palaces and Farm Houses at different places on dates announced previously, they were "greeted" by hostile crowds (big or small) of loyalists. Teams legally authorised to search were themselves searched first to make sure that they were not carrying anything objectionable with the intention of planting the same in the premises to be searched. In Haryana, the police of that State instead of cooperating with the Punjab police, as required by law and the Constitution, appared to be helping their own Chief Minister's friend-in-trouble to the extent of hindering the work of the raiding parties from Punjab.

Many people in Punjab were asking one queston: "What purpose would searches with advance notices, serve? Obviously, all objectionable documents, etc would have been removed before the arrival of the search parties of Punjab police". Would the morale of the Badal camp not go up when it is declared that "nothing incriminating was found". It was not long before the real purpose of these "Searches" began to become clear. Badal's men would object to measurements of the buildings and rooms, etc. They would also object to videography, etc. Even Advocates brought for the purpose told the Punjab Vigilance Bureau officers that the court had allowed only searches and they would not allow anything else. Operation had to be stopped and clarificaton was sought from the court. View point of Vigilance Bureau was upheld. The court ruled that what was sought to be done was implied in the orders allowing search. People then realized that one of the common methods of enjoying corruption and even black money is to utilise it to build luxurious houses with even marble etc. imported from other countries.

If corruption money is to be estimated or unearthed or exposed, much more comprehensive searches of buildings are necessary than was done by the Punjab Police even after the clarification given by the court referred to above.

Fearing Badal family getting cornered and trapped, loyalists led by Dhindsa, Union Minister in the Vajpayee's Cabinet, accused the Central Government for not coming to the aid of its ally. Principle of collective responsibility was thrown over board by the Akali Minister. When there was no response even after this, withdrawal of Akali support to the Vajpayee government was openly threatened. This seemed to work. The Deputy Prime Minister told the Government of Punjab that the Government of India had the power to act if it did not stop "harassment" ofAkalis. Advani even misquoted some Articles of the Constitution of India. Captain Amrinder Singh did not give in. In fact, he called off the bluff. Instead of forcing Amrinder Singh to retreat Mr Advani himself had to beat a hasty retreat.

It was after this that Badal decided to play the communal card. Equating himself with the Panth, he charged that Amrinder Singh by attacking him was attacking the Panth, i.e entire Sikh community. Unfortunately for him, this too did not get any response. Badal's argument was so fallacious and so wrong that even his most loyal followers would not repeat it.

Badal is now playing his trump card and that is not altogether without effect. He has leveled serious allegations of corruption against Amrinder Singh himself and also against many of his ministers. He has denied allegations against himself, has got rid of one Minister and given clean chits to others. All this may convince some but not many. There are questions that need to be answered by the Chief Minister.

1. Why is he not appointing a Lok Pal? Institution is already there. The post of the Presiding officer is vacant. A high Judicial officer of undoubted integrity and known to be incorruptible must be appointed to fill the vacancy.The present Lok Pal Act is defective in many respects. Let steps be taken to get it amended.It must be ensured that every citizen can lodge with it a complaint of corruption, favouritism and nepotism against the Ministers including the Chief Minister without being required to pay a heavy fee which he may not be in a position to pay etc.

2. Soon after Captain took power, he appointed a retired High Court Judge who, we were told, would entertain complaints of the public and dispense justice.Some shady past of this retired judge himself got exposed and he had to quit. And that was the end of the promised justice to the common man. The government has taken one and half years to constitute even the District Grievances Committees. It is a record, in a way. Another record is that no representative of Akalis has been included in these committees. Such denial in case of the main opposition party is unjustifiable and it has never happened before.

It needs to be stated frankly that as time passes more and more people are concluding that Captain's 'fight against corruption' is selective and not intended to reduce corruption to the maximum extent at all levels. Motivaton seems to be different. As far as we are concerned, we welcome every fight against corruption at any level and whatever the motive.We do so because it will do, at least, some good. At the same time, we cannot and do not lose sight of the fact that when fight is very selective it cannot but help the corrupt who are the targets.It is of utmost importance, therefore, that strong public opinion should be created to fight against corruption of every type at all levels.

However, Badal too needs to answer one question. More than once he has boasted of "his men" in the administration of Punjab at the highest level. He has been claiming that from them he gets to know all the plans of Amrinder against him. This means he has been misusing his power as Chief Minister and violating the basic norms of parliamentary democracy and even the Constitution.

I should think that he can be tried for that. Be that as it may, why does he not collect evidence against Amrinder and his Ministers and go to a Court or Central Vigilance Commission controlled by his allies and get them exposed and punished?

Or, is Badal interested only in a Congress-Akali compromise that each when in opposition may accuse the other-in-power of high corruption but not proceed against him when the roles are reversed as being done in Nagaland.

An Appeal to Upright Akalis with a Conscience

The Akali Dal (Badal group) leaders are threatening to set Punjab on fire if Badal is arrested, even though it is not certain when Badal would be arrested, if at all. These threats completely violate the traditions of the Akali movement which had arisen to fight and did fight successfully to liberate the Sikh Gurudwaras from the clutches of Mahants who had become British agents. The spirit which moved them and inspired them to make great sacrifices would not, tolerate any corruption, much less corruption of the very high Badal scale.

In the earlier stages of the anti-corruption campaign of Chief Minister Amrinder Singh, the media gave the impression that at least some sections of the Akali Dal felt bad when the doings of one Akali Minister after another got exposed. Later it became known that Chief Minister Badal had not only recommended the then Chairman of the Punjab Public Service Commission to be made member of the Union Public Service Commission on the ground that it would help him personally as well as politically, but he had in fact pressed hard his friend, Prime Minister Vajpayee, to do so. Some say had he (the former PSPSSC Chairman) not been arrested for only a few days more, Badal's wish would have been fulfilled. Be that as it may, no Akali leader asked Badal to quit politics and at least to pray to God and to the people of Punjab to forgive him. Even then, by now the Akali leaders and activists had become so thick-skinned that they did not react even when corruption to the extent indulged in by Badal's most favoured SSP Pherurai and its most dangerous and anti-national character got exposed.

I regret to write that Chief Minister Amrinder Singh too has contributed to this situation. His too frequent pronouncements about Badal have created the impression that he has some personal scores to settle with him. The withdrawal or hushing up of some alleged corruption cases without telling the public anything; refusal to proceed against some bureaucrats and police officers known to be corrupt; failure to ensure at least lowering of the level of the ongoing corruption in various departments; refusal to deal with the corruption of some BJP Ministers in the Badal Cabinet, etc have created the impression that Amrinder's fight against corruption is selective. Two wrongs, however, do not make one right. Every upright Akali having courage of his conviction, should have criticised the Congress Government for all this and much more but should not have forgiven Badal even when he has been exposed as perhaps the most corrupt Chief Minister of India and as one who has contributed a good deal to make the Punjab bureaucracy and administration too perhaps the most corrupt in the country. It calls for some introspection by such Akalis that they too do not join in the corrupt lot threatening to put Punjab on fire.

Despite all the negative aspects of Amrinder's anti-corruption campaign, it will do some good if he takes it to its logical conclusion especially if he ensures confiscation of all ill-gotton properties of those declared corrupt by the courts. If the courts only send them to jails but don't confiscate their properties, there will be no remorse or heart-searching on their part and on the part of their kins. I know of one (corrupt) officer who had once said: "I will have no regret if I am killed for all that I have done. I have made enough money/ wealth/property that even my grandchildren will live in luxury without having to do anything."

I appeal to the upright Badal Akalis with a conscience to denounce the calls being given for setting Punjab on fire and support even Amrinder's one-sided selective fight against corruption. At the appropriate time they can launch a fight against the corruption of the Congress. I for one, will fully support it.

Communists and Corruption

Marxist ideology says that a just society in which there is no exploitation of man by man is possible. But this possibility cannot become reality without bitter struggles—economic, political, ideological etc and many sacrifices. This ideology therefore attracts those with lot of idealism and also desire to serve the exploited and the down-trodden. It is therefore natural that ideologically mature communists should be muchless prone to become corrupt than politicians belonging to bourgeois and petty bourgeois parties. This was proved beyond any shadow of doubt when the first-communist led Governmentof Kerala with a majority of only 2 in the Assembly could not be thrown out of power by winning over two MLAs though huge amounts were offered and despite the fact that there was no anti-defection law at that time.(Namboodripad Ministry was dismissed in 1959). There are many other facts which prove this. We will mention only two more.

Comrade Achutha Menon of the CPI as Chief Minister of Kerala proved to be totally incorruptible and also totally above nepotism and favouritism. No communist Minister (there have been many in States and two in the Government of India) has been involved in any Hawala kind like scandal. Comunists of India have proved that the maxim "power corrupts and absolute power corrupts totally" is not correct. However, as we shall see later power does tend to corrupt and absolute power tends to corrupt absolutely.

Notwithstanding what has been stated above, Indian Communists have not fully realised the necessity of fighting corruption. There has not been adequate realisation amongst them that corruption is not on a moral question. Thousands of crores of rupees are allocated in every year's budgets for development projects and for poverty alleviation programmes. Many researchers have come to the conclusion that only about10-15 per cent reaches the beneficiaries. Of the rest very big part lines the pockets of corrupt politicians and bureaucrats.Many development works exist only on papers. Many more are executed with defective materials purchased at prices much higher than the correct prices of even the best materials. Corrupt teachers may deliver any number of lectures to their pupils on virtues of honesty but by example will in fact train them in the art of corruption which they can indulge when they grow up. It is not necesssry to give more examples to prove that it is as much necesssry to fight corruption as it to fight for *Roti*, *Rozi* and *Makaan*.

The task of fighting corruption has been neglected also by Communists-in-power. Left Democratic Government of Kerala had started well by setting up a Lok Pal (Its name was perhaps different) before which any citizen could lodge any complaint of corruption against any Minister. He had to pay a very nominal fee and deposit a small amount which would be forefeited only if the complaint turned out to be frivilous (and not merely unproved). Many other steps which needed to be taken were, however, not taken. For instance, no communist led state Government has enacted legislation requiring all Ministers and MLAs to lay every year on the table of the House statements of their assets and those of their families. Like-wise, no legislation has been enacted for confiscation of properties proved to be the result of corruption.

If even a totally upright person does not fight corruption, neoptism and favouritism amongst others, he is likely to fall prey to the tendency to become corrupt especially when he is in power... It needs to be stated that in Parliamentary democracy, even effective leaders of opposition parties have some power and the clever amongst the ruling corrupt bourgeois politicians and bureacrats are keen to oblige them. In the Punjab Assembly I found that quite often when opposition MLAs began speaking about corruption and nepotism of some Minister, Dr. Kewal Krishan would shut them up by asking: "Should I tell the type of requests the MLA on his feet has been coming to me?" Here is my own experience. Ones I phoned the Head of a department in Amritsar district to bring to his notice a very genuine grievance of the peasants of Khurmanian, one of the villages in my constituency. I had not known that this officer was in the process of interviewing candidates for some posts as the head of a committee. When I told him my name he immediately asked me: "Sir, give me the name of the candidate in which you are interested."

There are more than one factor which make communists fall prey to corrupt practices because proneness of human nature is not consistently resisted. One is undue importance which has been given to seats in state legislatures and Parliament at this stage of revolution and hence keenness to maintain and increase vote-banks even at the cost of principles. Comforts and power which an MLA and MP gets increases the proneness. Another factor is that some Communists believe that making money for the party (i.e., for the revolution) by unethical means is moral from the class viewpoint. More often than not such communists can end up making money for themselves and their families too by such means. Such communists in fact are following in the foot-steps of the Congress immediately after freedom was won.

Late Comrade Ajoy Ghosh as General Secretary of the CPI often used to emphasize that Communists must not make electoral agreements with communal parties as that would give them credibility and thus strengthen communalism. This very correct thesis was violated both by the CPI and the CPI(M) not only in relation to the Akalis but also the worst communal party, i.e., the BJP, worst because it is controlled by RSS of which the political objective is to establish Hindu theocratic state in India (and towards that end to use whatever power it may have at any time to saffronise education, history etc and even the armed forces. This in fact is the real hidden agenda of the BJP which is being implemented ruthlessly. CPI(M) once made electoral agreements with BJP/Jan Sangh in U.P. etc on the ground that it was necessary to defeat the Congress. CPI joined United Front Government in 1967 in some states along with Jan Sangh though a minority was opposed to it.

Chacha Kesari, President of the Congress, speaking at a rally in Amritsar held to observe the Golden Jubilee of Indian Independence had put forward the thesis that "Communalism is more dangerous than corruption." This was done obviously to justify electoral alliance with Laloo Prasad of Bihar which "the Congress was wanting to make. I had then written against this thesis. I had also expressed the hope that Communists would not adopt it. It is still my view that this thesis is as wrong as the thesis that hepatitis-B is more dangerous than cancer. Unfortunately, CPI as well as CPI(M) adopted Chacha Kesari's thesis to justify their embracing Kings and Queens of Corruption in India in the Lok Sabha elections held in October 1999.

The above drift has done immense harm to the left in the country on which today depends the future of the country. Gone are the days when no Communist MLA could be bought. Some other evils which have gripped almost all non-Left parties have entered Communist Parties too. Corruption in the CPI(M) which is ruling 3 states is by no means negligible. Nor is the CPI free from it. All this is one of the factors responsible for erosion of the influence of the Communist movement instead of its rapid growth for which objective situation is ripe.

Both the CPI and CPI(M) must do all they can to get rid of this weakness. They owe this not only to the Communist Movement of India but to India herself. The mess in which the bourgeois rulers have landed India is aweful. And it is getting worse and worse. Unless a strong Left emerges in the country and also moves forward to build a left-democratic secular front which can win power to be able to bring about radical transformations in the national economy and civil society, future of our great motherland cannot but be very bleak.

Weaknesses which CPI and CPI(M) have to overcome are many. In relation to corruption, following tasks should be Minimum:

(a) A purification campaign should be launched to restore the health of the party. Both parties should once again be in a position to claim that no communist MP, MLA, Councillor, Sarpanch, Panch etc. can be purchased or even won over. Party candidates should be ready to lose elections rather than try to win them by using various types of unethical means.

(b) If there is corruption of such a nature as can rally people to fight against it, initiatives must be taken to organise people for struggle. An example would be some development work in which use of sub-standard material can prove dangerous for public. Another instance would be enbezzlement in school funds at the cost of student and their education. If communists are conscious of the need to mobilize people to struggle on such issues, they will come across many.

(c) Fight against corruption in Parliament and Assemblies must be much more than hitherto. This fight should include fight for concrete laws, e.g., obligatory declaration of assets once a year; law for confiscation of ill gotten properties, amending the definition of "public servants" to cover not only MPs and MLAs but also Mayors, Presidents of local bodies, Sarpanches, etc. Communist MPs, and MLAs must struggle to bring into existence really effective Lok Pals etc.

(d) Concrete cases of corruption involving Ministers or ex-Ministers must be taken to existing anti-corruption institutions like Lok Pals. This must be done even if the Ministers or ex-Ministers involved belongs to a party with which Communists may be having some electoral adjustments or agreement. No pact or agreement must compromise the fight which the Communists are expected to wage against corruption.

(e) Communist MPs, MLAs and leaders must not intervene to save/ protect corrupt officials/contractors, etc, whether they are big or small people. In cases in which possibilities of culprits being reformed are there, we may plead and try for punishments which are not extreme.

(f) Local Bodies controlled by Communists must be totally free from corruption or atleast to the maximum possible extent

There is no doubt that even today people recognise that as far as Communists are concerned, they are better (even, much better) than other parties. However, no good Communist can or should feel satisfied with this certificate.

Vital Question Before CPI and CPI (M)

When CPI and CPI(M) made an electoral alliance with AIADMK for Assembly elections in Tamil Nadu, many in these two parties felt uncomfortable for following reasons amongst others:

(a) It was an alliance without an agreed common minimum programme committing the two communist parties to support each and every AIADMK candidate.

(b) It was an alliance with a party led by Jayalalitha, the Queen of Corruption, desperately wanting to come back to power to scuttle various corruption cases against her.

In the past, such electoral alliances were sought to be justified on the ground that communalism is more dangerous than corruption and hence to defeat the bigger danger, it was correct to ally with corrupt but secular parties. This is a very fallacious argument. Corruption is not only a moral question. Corruption at different levels siphons off huge amounts meant for poverty alleviation, health care, education, etc, etc, into the pockets of corrupt politicians, corrupt bureaucrats, etc, Corruption results in rickety buildings, bridges, etc, coming up and this not unoften costs many lives. Corruption in the matter of purchase of weapons etc, for the armed forces endangers the security of the country. In view of all this, to argue that corruption is not as dangerous as communalism, is incorrect. It is like arguing that Hepatitis B is more dangerous than cancer. In the case in question, even this argument was really not available.

DMK is not a communal party and is as secular as AIADMK. True, in the election DMK was allied with BJP which however matters very little in Tamil Nadu. In any case, AIADMK too had been in alliance with BJP and his again crossed over to BJP-led NDA in run to 14th Lok Sabha. I am not pleading that communists should allied with DMK whose Chief too is a corrupt politician. If necessary, communists should fight on their own with some local adjustments which should be quite open.

The real argument for unprincipled alliances is that seats in Assemblies matter and without such alliance, Lok Sabha seats cannot be won. In the first place, seats no doubts are important but not at the cost of principles and thru opportunism. Secondly, mass movement is more important than seats. Thirdly, opportunistic tactics may get some seats for some time but they lead to erosion of mass base of the Left making them so weak that non-Left parties would, at some point of time, not see any advantage for themselves in electoral alliances with the Left. In UP for instance, alliances with late Chaudhary Charan Singh's party got CPI some seats for sometime but led to liquidation of its strong base amongst agricultural labourers in districts like Azamgarh. Choudhary Charan Singh was a leader of kulaks and was considered an enemy by the agricultural labourers. Moreover, if communists can make unprincipled alliances for some immediate gains, how can they prevent their followers from joining bourgeois parties with a similar objective.

Million dollar question is: for what reason Communist ranks don't speak up against opportunism. Marx had said: "Doubt everything". Communist leaders have so misinterpreted the correct organisational principle of Democratic Centralism as will help teach the ranks: "Take as gospel truth whatever comes from the top. Even if you have doubts, raise them only at the proper place and time". Only a new interpretation of this principle will change the Stalinist mind-set.

Be that as it may, what was more shocking was the fact of Comrades Har Kishen Singh Surjeet and AB Bardhan both declaring that Jayalalitha having secured the mandate of the people, had every right to become Chief Minister. Question is more moral than legal/ constitutional. Why CPI(M) and CPI leaders could not express the opinion that Jayalalitha should ask her party to elect someone else as its leaders?

Both the CPI and the CPI(M) need to debate the following questions:

(a) Have they been fighting adequately corruption of the bourgeois Governments?

(b) Have they been fighting corruption in the Left led Governments?

(c) Have they been fighting corruption inside their own parties?

What organisational changers are needed to ensure curbing of growth of corruption in the Communist parties? And what should be done to ensure nipping in the bud tendency of corruption to grow.

In my opinion, neglect of this task will prove dangerous. Communists are no longer regarded as incorruptible though even today they are considered better than others. It will not be long before even this impression melts away unless Communists pay proper attention to this vital question before it is too late.

VIII

A View of Religion based Politics

State and Religion : A Lesson from Pakistan

We have in our country persons and forces that want India to be a Hindu Rashtra. We have elements which want Muslim majority Kashmir to secede from India so that it can become an Islamic state. We have also groups which want a Sikh state (Khalistan). All such elements, forces and groups propagate that the salvation of the people lies only in a state based on religion.

We have in our neighbourhood such a state—Pakistan. When India became free in August 1947 after partition, India became a secular state while Pakistan was established as a theocratic state. Both swore by democracy and federalism. To what extent has theocracy helped Pakistan and its people? Here is what Zulfikar Ali Bhutto said about what happened in Pakistan during the first 30 years of his existence:

> "Pakistan was established on 14th August, 1947, as an Islamic Federal Democratic State... the first military coup d'etat of General Mohammed Akbar Khan was attempted in 1951. The second quasi-military coup came in October 1954, when Ghulam Mohammad dissolved the sovereign Constituent Assembly of Pakistan. The third quasi-military coup d'etat came in October 1955, when in total violation of the Lahore resolution of March 1940, provincial autonomy was abolished and One Unit foisted on West Pakistan"

"In October 1958 came the hard stuff: the military coup d'etat of General Ayub Khan. In March 1969 came the military coup d'etat of General Yahya Khan. In March 1973, the Brigadiers' military coup d'etat was scotched. On 5th of July, 1977, came the existing military coup d'etat. That means that in thirty years of the existence of Pakistan there have been—(a) two attempted military coup d'etats; (b) two quasi-military coup d'etats; (c) three full-fledged military coup d'etats. (From ***If I am Assassinated***)."

It may be added that besides all this, Pakistan broke up into two countries—Pakistan and Bangladesh.

When the present military dictator of Pakistan seized power, he gave a solemn assurance that power would be handed over to elected representatives of the people within three months. Nearly four years have passed since then. Not only have elections not been held, but Zia-ul Haq has categorically declared that there will be no elections in the near future, that not elections but the establishment of Nizam-e-Islam in the country is the primary task. He now promises transfer of power to the people only when "the objective of Islamisation and revival of Islamic values" has been achieved. Unless these are achieved, there will be no transfer of power from the present Government (***Patriot***, April, 1981).

Let us now see how Islamisation has actually worked.

An important practical step towards Islamic financial and tax systems was the introduction of Zakat tax. Overnight, towards the end of June, 1980, Pakistanis with more than Rs. 1,000 in bank saving lost 2.5 per cent of their money. The sum was deducted by order of the Government for redistribution to poor Pakistanis.

This 'Islamic measure' evoked strong opposition and reaction in the name of Islam itself. This can be seen from a report by Kevin Rafferty in the ***Observer***, London, reproduced in the ***Tribune*** of July 29, 1980. It says:

"Among the fiercest critics of the way the *zakat* was levied are some devout Muslims. 'It is a reversal of the principle of

> Islam', one commented. Though every Muslim who has the means is supposed to give *zakat*, the giving is a matter between him and his God. The first obligation is to the poorer members of your own family. After that you are supposed to remember your servants. And only after that, if you have anything left, do you give to the state treasury for donation to the poor. What the Government has done is to turn the obligation upside down. It is almost as if it has decided to play God. The next thing to watch will be how the money collected is distributed. It could easily turn into a means of political patronage....
>
> "As an example of cynicism, prevailing about the move, the Finance Minister, Mr Ghulam Ishaq Khan, told a close acquintance that the loss of 2.5 per cent was no real hardship 'as anyone interested in making money would not keep it in saving accounts. It is highly unlikely that many of Pakistan's big businessmen keep much money in bank deposits...The heart of the problem is whether the Government can force worldly people to become religious—and whether it is prepared to wreck the economy in trying to make them." (***Tribune***, July 29, 1980).
>
> Another important measure to "Islamise" the economy was the introduction of interest-free banking with effect from January 1, 1981. Instead by receiving interest which has been forbidden by almightly Allah, depositors would split profits or losses with borrowers. Eventually interest-bearing accounts would be phased out. (***Indian Express***, January 3, 1981).

In March 1981, it was reported in the ***Link*** magazine of New Delhi that the Pakistan Government would continue to demand interest on its own deposits!

Let us now take an example of Islamisation of the social life of Pakistan. Popular TV compere in Karachi, Mehtab Chauna, was sacked under orders from Islamabad for her persistent refusal to keep her head covered with a *dupatta* while presenting popular stage shows for youth on television. According to a PTI report from Islamabad, this stirred a wider debate on the rights of women in the context of the current Islamisation drive in Pakistan. The report says:

> "Meeting at a national conference called by the Zia regime, the women turned round to declare that discrimination against them was un-Islamic and their rights had been buried under customs alien to Islam.
>
> "A suggestion made by General Zia himself that separate universities should be established for women at Karachi and Lahore was rejected saying women there were using co-educational Institutions effectively. Delegates demanded education relevant to the 20th century..
>
> "The women were particularly concerned at press reports that a 1961 law putting a check on indiscriminate polygamy might be repealed at the instance of the Minister of Law and Religious Affairs which declared it un-Islamic...." (***Tribune***, November 24, 1980).

One of the earliest, Islamic measures to be introduced by the Zia regime, related to punishment for adultery, theft and drinking. In actual practice this had been utilised by the military regime to carry out severe and barbaric repression against the people. This will be clear from the following press reports:

(a) "Military courts were busy sentencing protesters against Mr. Butto's execution. Sentences ranged from six months to one year's imprisonment or 5 to 10 lashes. The Courts specified that women or infirm demonstrators could be lashed sitting down.... (***Patriot***, April 9, 1979).

(b) "There is at present the well-known case of Ali Hyder Shah, a Sindhi student sentenced to death by a military court. His crime? He organised a protest by Sind University Students against the rape of a woman medical student, Shirin Soomro, by the local Martial Law administrator in Nawabshah in the province of Sind.

"The protest led to serious clashes with the police. Hundreds were arrested and Hyder was sentenced to death. The University itself is almost closed by the military authorities. The local wags claim that military officers and policemen are the best educated in Pakistan since they spend too much time in Sind University.

"Soon after Zia assumed power in 1977, over a hundred striking workers were shot dead in the Punjab city of Multan. Hundreds of trade unionists have been whipped and given heavy imprisonment.." (Tariq Ali in the ***Guardian*** reproduced in ***Indian Express***, January 20, 1980).

(c) "Islamabad, April 15 (AP)—Pakistan's military regime yesterday stepped up its campaign against dissidents, sentencing persons to be imprisoned and flogged for political offences...

"Five were found guilty of meeting to create dissatisfaction against the army and to plan demonstrations to mark the January 5, brithday of Mr Zulfikar Ali Bhutto.

"Two persons were convicted of inciting students to boycott classes and shout anti-regime slogans by a military court in Hyderabad..." (***Tribune,*** April 17, 1981).

Last but not least, it needs to be pointed out that Nizam-e-Mustafa (Islamic rule) of Zia has been characterised as Un-Islamic by many important political and religious leaders in Pakistan. These leaders have expressed the view that "Islam does not permit one-man rule or dictatorship and so the General's Government, his well-publicised Islamic programme notwithstanding, cannot be considered as Islamic....Jamait-ul-Ulema-Islam chief, Maulana Mufti Mahmud, who as the President of the nine-party Pakistan National Alliance (PNA) spearheaded the anti-Bhutto agitations in 1977 and cooperated with the military regime till Bhutto's execution, is now a bitter critic of Gen. Zia. The General's is one-man rule which is neither democratic nor Islamic, he says.... "What forms the crux of the controversy is an apparently inspired theory that democracy is un-Islamic while the Presidential form of government, as General Zia claimed, was nearer to Islam. This theory has been rejected by all important political leaders, including the Jamat-I-Islami which has always supported Gen. Zia." (***Indian Express***, August 7, 1980).

Such have been the results of Islamisation of Pakistan carried out on the basis of the theory that Muslims are a nation and that religion and politics are inseparable. Here is the lesson which a former Chief Minister of Baluchistan has drawn from experience: "Look, I want to reiterate that there is no commodity like an Islamic nation. It has never existed and it cannot be artificially created in the name of our holy-scripture—The Quran. Those who talk of an Islamic nation or a Muslim nation are committing a heinous crime against the various nations and nationalities which subscribe to the Muslim religion." (Quoted in ***Patriot***, June 4, 1981). To this we may add: "There is no commodity like a Sikh nation or a Hindu nation either."

Shaurya Samriti Samaroh

The Shauraya Samriti Samaroh organised by the RSS at Amritsar on 29.1.2003 was yet another proof that the RSS and its political Front, BJP are out to distort history to suit their ideology and the aim of establishing a Hindu Rashtra in India, i.e, a Hindu theocratic State with Hinduism as the official religion (a la Muslim theocratic State of Pakistan—with Islam as the official religion).

It was announced that at the time of India's partition about 55 years ago, Muslim goons carried out a mass massacre of Hindus and RSS activists had saved a large number of them. Nearly six hundred such activists or their successors would be honoured at the function by RSS Chief KS Sudarshan.

The fact is that a section of Muslims on the one hand and a section of Hindus and Sikhs on the other, had been seized by communal madness. They were joined by anti-social elements and such elements as wanted to weaken the two countries. In West Punjab, victims were mostly Hindus and Sikhs while in the East Punjab, victims were mostly Muslims. Even children were killed and women were raped. Trains carrying Muslims to West Punjab and Hindus to East were set ablaze and all in them burnt to death. All sensible people in India and Pakistan have been pledging to work to ensure that such a thing would never happen again. They would recall and take inspiration from the fact that many Hindu and Sikh families saved the lives of many Muslim families and many Muslim families saved the lives of Hindu and Sikh families—risking their own lives in each case. Helping the refugees too was not the monopoly of any one organisation. (If an RSS-controlled Government remains in power for some more years, we are likely to find the above false version in our history text books without any mention of madnes as well as sanity amongst both sides resulting in killings by goons and saving families by sane persones, risking their own lives.)

Altogether distorted version of what happened in 1947 was propogated before and at the function. And this in Amristar which had witnessed massacre of Muslims and Sikhs on a large scale as also many Muslim families being saved by Hindus and Sikhs. This was not even taken note of, not to speak of drawing any lesson for the future.

Obviously the aim of the Samaroh was to create anti-Muslim hatred to be able to achieve the openly declared aim: We will do in the whole of India what we did in Gujarat. Of course, the RSS Chief talked about Gujarat at the function at Amritsar. He asserted that (large-scale) violence (including killings, burning alive of Muslims, raping of Muslim women, etc) after the higly condemnable Godhra incident was altogether spontaneous. This was an open admission that there was a total failure on the part of the Gujarat Government to do anything to prevent genocide of innocent Muslims. Actually, all this had been organised by RSS Pariwar with the Government and the state machinery backing it. Be that as it may, I have no doubt in my mind, that neither Hindus nor Sikhs of Punjab will go anywhere near Moditva or even touch it with a pair of tongs. Nor would his assertion that everything that happened in Gujarat was organised by ISI to defame Hindus would wash.

As regards criticism of Muslim Madrasas, it is possible that some or even many may be teaching fundamentalism. But there are quite a number of educational institutions being run by RSS which too teach religious fundamentalism. Both deserve to be banned.

It is a very old thesis of RSS that Sikhs are Hindus and that Sikhism is not a separate religion. During 15 long years of terrorism, Khalistani terrorists exploited this thesis for trying to convince patriotic Sikhs that they should support the demand for Khalistan. They would draw the attention of the patriotic Sikhs towards this thesis and then say: "In a united India, Sikhism will cease to have any religious identity of its own and will be absorbed by Hinduism". In fact RSS has consistently refused to recognise facts which are as under:

Any two religions including Hinduism and Islam as well as Hinduism and Christainity have much in common. However, Hinduism and Sikhism have more in common than any other two religions as both these religions took birth on Indian soil. Sikhism began with Guru Nanak Dev Ji's efforts to fight such negative aspects of Hinduism as the caste system. By the time of the 10th Guru, Sikhism emerged as a separated religion. Free India's Constitution recognised it as such. Insistence on Sikhs being Hindus, only widens the gulf between the two. It gives birth to the cry: "Sikhs are not Hindus."

At the Amritsar Samaroh of 29/1/2003, RSS Chief put forward his thesis in a slightly modified form to deny any separate religious identity of Sikhs. He declared: "All Sikhs are Hindus and all Hindus are Sikhs". This according to him clearly established co-identity of Hindus and Sikhs. Strangely, the RSS chief himself negated this thesis of his when he declared that every citizen living in "Hindustan must be identified as a Hindu" denying even Muslims and Christians, any separate religious identity. To leave no doubt in any one's mind, he declared that "Muslim, Parsis, Christians, Sikhs, etc were wrongly identifying themselves as religious minorities". Its real meaning would be clear from the following:

Guru Golwalkar had openly written that aim of RSS was to establish a Hindu Rashtra in India and that such non-Hindus as would not Hinduise themselves would be treated as second class citizens. Finding that overwhelming majority of Hindus in India were secular minded favouring every one having freedom to profess and worship according to his own religion or religion of his choice but State having no religion, they began arguing that "Hindu" meant "Indian" while Hinduise meant Indianise. Thus every one living in India was/is Hindu. On the face of it, the arugment is ridiculous and would not convince anyone. Vijay Kumar of Hind Samachar Group of papers through a signed editorial had once made a fervent appeal to Deoras during his visit to Jalandhar as RSS Chief at the time, to adopt "Bhartya Rashtra" instead of "Hindu Rashtra" as the goal of RSS. Reply of Shri Deoras was an emphatic "No, that would never be done."

The present RSS chief wants neither Sikhs nor Muslims, Parsis, Christians, etc to claim to be a religious minority because he too is loyal to teachings of Golwalkar and wants all of them to Hinduise themselves or be treated as second class citizens a la non-Muslims in Pakistan. If a big majority of Hindus were to follow the RSS path, it would surely lead to India's disintegration. Hopefully this will not happen. All patriots must want to ensure that.

A few words about KS Sudarshan's criticism of Jawaharlal Nehru. Even saffronised historians will not be able to deny that during India's struggle for freedom, RSS was on the side of the British rulers on the ground that main enemy were the Muslims. Another undeniable fact in that Hindu communalists were the first to claim that Hindus were a separate nation. Mohd. Ali Jinnah followed them to say the same thing differently when he put forward the two-nation theory and declared that Muslims were a separate nation (and therefore must have Pakistan). And yet RSS Chief made the fantastic assertion that Nehru was a protégé of the British and perpetuated British rule even after their leaving the country. Any one has the right to criticise Nehru and even Gandhi but the criticism should at least appear to have a molecule of logic. And why should a great man like RSS Chief stoop to so low as to make a totally false allegation against an ordinary citizen like the writer of these lines that he had got RSS leaders arrested many a time!

Never Minimise RSS Threat

Many were shocked at the way Kalyan Singh became Chief Minister of UP for the second time by making a large number of MLAs of other parties to defect to BJP and giving ministerial posts to all, many of them worst type of well-known criminals. Their shock was greater when Advani and even Vajpayee openly tried by using the Kalyan Singh strategy on Delhi-scale to have majority in Lok Sabha after IK Gujral resigned. That they did not succeed, is another matter.

(a) Not New

Actually there was no reason for anyone to be shocked. As long ago as 1979, the year when BJP was born, Advani had said in an interview published in the RSS Hindu weekly ***Panchanaya*** that "in India a party based on ideology can at most come to power in a small area. It cannot win the confidence of the entire country- neither the Communist party nor the Jan Sangh on the basis of ideals." (Quoted by Girish Mathur in an article in *New Wave*)

Since neither the Jan Sangh nor its successor, the BJP gave up its objective of being in power in Delhi, Advani had indirectly made clear in 1980 itself that BJP would have to use means other than ideals to seize power in Delhi. And what these other means are should now be clear to all.

BJP claims that after coming to power they will revert to value based politics. They should know that they can fool some people all the time, all the people sometime but they cannot fool all the people all the time. Congress has had absolute power in the whole country for more than 40 years. BJP has been in power only in some states for less than a decade and half and for a very short period in the Centre as a part of Janata Party. And thereafter for 6 years it has ruled India in the garb of NDA. BJP is now not behind but much ahead of the Congress as far as corruption is concerned. They came to power with the help of Jayalalitha, the Queen of Corruption besides many others who do not even deny that politics for them is a profession for minting money. Any yet, we are asked to believe that a BJP government dependent on them will clean up public life. We never had a doubt that if ever a BJP led government would be formed, its would be busy covering up their corruption as well as the own. Anyone who believes that BJP wants power to give clean public life is living in a fool's paradise.

(b) Power for What

What does the BJP want power for? To get a correct answer, one has to remember that BJP like other members of the Sangh Parivar is controlled fully and completely by the RSS. They make no secret of it except on the eve of elections. More than once, Advani and other top leaders of BJP have declared openly that they are bound to carry out the RSS orders. And that means orders of the RSS Guru because there is no internal democracy in this semifascist organisation.

BJP in fact is the open political front of the RSS for realising its objective of *Hindu Rashtra,* i.e, a Hindu theocratic State. No RSS Guru is prepared to drop this objective. And no BJP leader can dare go against the RSS. As already noted, a few years ago Hind Samachar Group of papers editorially appealed to the then RSS Guru, Deoras, to change the objective to "Bharti Rashtra". Quick came the reply from Guruji himself that would never be. And here is what the Hindu Raj would be like:

"The non-Hindu people in Hindustan must adopt the Hindu culture and language, must learn to respect and hold in reverence Hindu religion, must entertain no idea but those of the glorification of the Hindu race and culture, i.e, they must not only give up their attitude of intolerance and ungratefulness towards this land and its age long tradition but must also cultivate the positive attitude of love and devotion instead—in a word they must cease to be foreigners, or may stay in the country wholly subordinate to the Hindu nation, claiming, deserving no privileges, for any preferential treatment not even citizen's rights." (***We or our Nationhood Defined***: M.S. Golwalkar)

(c) Methods

Some of the methods resorted to so far to march forward to the objective are as under :

(i) Communal riots, especially Hindu-Muslim riots in States in which BJP is not in power, whether initiated by RSS or by Muslim communalists. RSS has been found responsible for such riots by more than one commission.

(ii) Re-writing history books etc so as to poison immature minds of school students as was done by the first Kalyan Singh Government in UP.

(iii) Demolition of Babri Masjid for which the first Kalyan Singh Government of UP of the BJP leadership is responsible primarily even though they were helped in the job by Narasimha Rao Government which deliberately refused to act though it was its duty to prevent the demolition which could surely be done if it had the will to do so.

What will a BJP Government of India do to further the cause of establishing Hindu state in India.

(i) It will manage infiltration of media by RSS men as was done by Advani when he was Minister for Information and Broadcasting in Janata Party Government. The media will then become a weapon to propagate RSS style Hindutva.

(ii) It will also manage infiltration of para-military forces and even the Army by RSS men. This is not a far fetched idea. RSS men were consciously recruited into UPPAC when a Jan Sanghi was the Home Minister of the State in 1967. Some of these as UPPAC officers murdered a large number of innocent Muslims near Meerut. Consequences of infiltration of the Armed Forces by the RSS will be many times more disastrous for the country.

(iii) Construction of Ram Mandir at the site of demolished Babri Masjid in Ayodhya and demolition of Masjids in Varanasi and Mathura and may be more elsewhere. Vajpayee may say that Mathura and Varanasi are not on their agenda. Advani does not want to leave any doubt in the minds of his followers. So he adds: "as yet" to what Vajpayee says. Other members of the Sangh Parivar go further and openly declare that demolition of Mathura and Varanasi Masjids is very much on their agenda. And the RSS Guru is equally emphatic: "No objective is going to be given up though at a particular time some may not be spoken loudly by BJP leaders (for tactical reasons)."

Let us not forget that India has more Muslims than any other country in the World except Indonesia. There are large number of people belonging to many other religions. BJP in power in the centre will try to establish a Hindu State in India and reduce all those who refuse to become Hindusied to second class citizens by methods like the above. I concede that it will try to keep India united with the help of an Hinduised Indian Army. But given the size and diversity of India, that is an impossible task. Inevitable result will be disintegration of India.

Let those who want India to remain united do all they can to ensure that BJP is not able to seize power at the Centre. If India is to remain united, it has to be a secular state. All those who stand for a theocratic state in India or even in any part of India must be opposed. Every Indian must have the right to profess the religion of his choice but neither the Indian State not any state of India must have any religion.

IX

Kashmir Problem

Lessons of Punjab have Relevance for Kashmir

Terrorism is a world-wide phenomenon. As a weapon, it has been sought to be used by those whose political objectives are just as well as by those whose political objectives are patently retrogressive and even blatantly anti-people.

Such ruling classes as have no scruples and are ever ready to use any means to further their selfish class or group interests make use of terrorism and terrorists when it suits them and denounce them when that serves their purpose better. The ruling class of the USA is a typical example of this. All sensible people capable of seeing beyond their nose abhor this ugly phenomenon and wish to see its end.

Circumstances and conditions which give rise to terrorism in different parts of the world and even in different regions in a vast country like India are different. Methods used by terrorists in different countries and even in different regions of a country are not entirely the same. However, there are many common style operations all over, for example, use of terror to prove the "superiority" of terrorists over the state, extortions, kidnappings and keeping persons as hostages, etc. There is also the fact that nowhere terrorism can operate without some mass base which they acquire because of genuine or perceived grievances of the people or of a sizeable section of the people. From all this it follows that in the fight against terrorism anywhere lessons of fight elsewhere can prove useful provided that difference in conditions and circumstances are not lost sight of and lessons are not applied mechanically.

Are there any lessons from Punjab which can help the fight against terrorism in Kashmir? In our opinion there are. Here are some. For long the Government of India and its nominees in Punjab pursued a policy of battling the terrorists on the law and order front on a limited scale, to be followed by attempts to make a deal with the terrorists or a section of them. This policy always proved counter-productive as had been predicted and warned by the Left. An outstanding example of this was the Black Thunder Operation which yielded very good results. However, the same were completely lost when the fight on the law and order front was stopped after the Operation and instead efforts were started to make a deal with a section of the terrorists with the help of Jasbir Singh Rode even though the backbone of the terrorists was far from broken as yet. The big success achieved in Punjab came about only when it was decided to relentlessly continue the anti-terrorist front till the backbone of the terrorists was broken. In Kashmir locals have started helping securiy force to combat trans-border terrorism. If this trend rises, terrorism can be ended for good.

In Punjab often in the name of bringing the misguided youths to mainstream, "boys" were released from jails en masse. Invariably, a big majority of them rejoined the ranks of the terrorists as soon as they were released. The Left in Punjab was as keen as anyone else to save as many youths gone astray as possible. It was however clear that apart from individuals successes here and there, a real breakthrough would be possible only when the backbone of the terrorists is broken and when it becomes clear to all that terrorists could not succeed. Here too there is lesson for Kashmir.

A lesson which Kashmir policy-makers must learn from Punjab is that negotiation with the agitating outfits—unexceptionable in principle and quite necessary to settle grievances, genuine or perceived—do great harm if they are undertaken at a wrong time, i.e, when the signal given would be that the government is yielding and may agree to their separatist objective in one form or another.

In fighting terrorism in Punjab, one of the things which has paid dividends is the fact that conscious efforts were made by the Army in the second stage not to do anything that would give accretion once again to the dwindling mass basis of terrorists. This must be don in the case of Kashmir too. Firing into the funeral procession of Moulvi Farooq during Mr Jagmohan's tenure, burning down of mohallas in retaliation for killing of some Jawans more than once and during the regimes of various governors, are instances which prove our contention. Special efforts were made in Punjab to train the Army as well as the para-military forces in this regard. And the Army after this training went all out not only to fight the terrorists without being prominent in this respect but also to help the people in various ways in rural areas. Such a policy now seems being followed in Kashmir. In any case, this must be done.

It is veritably proven that even such terrorists as start on the path of terrorism with noble motives join hands with anti-social elements and themselves degenerate into worst types of hooligans and anti-socials unless they give up terrorism well in time. This happened in Punjab too. By the time Beant Singh government came to power and started an all-out fight, supporters of terrorists in districts like Amritsar had turned against them because by then they were not merely extortionists, killers but had also become rapists who demanded girls as a matter of right even from families which had helped them. This helped the security forces a lot because people began helping them, even though the security forces dealt with the terrorist killers with no holds barred. The process of degeneration and consequent alienation of terrorists taking place in Kashmir too seems to be paying the dividends.

It was realised in Punjab that even though help of Army and paramilitary forces would be indispensable, without the Punjab police going into action against Khalistani terrorists it would not be possible to beat back the terrorists. The Punjab police is overwhelmingly Sikh. There was a time when a good section of it was helping terrorists out of sympathy or out of fear. Another section was not willing to act because of the fear that a terrorist leader was likely to become Chief Minister of Punjab. There was lot of conflict between the Punjab police and the paramilitary forces. First Riberio and then K.P.S. Gill did a lot to motivate the police force. Beant Singh removed the fear that a Manochahal or a Mann would be put into power in Punjab. The Punjab police then went into action bravely and all-over. J & K public is fully married up with armed force and doing well.

There are some lessons of a different type also which Kashmir policy-makers must learn from Punjab.

First, elections and formation of the Beant Singh Government in Punjab has helped because along with the terrorists, Akalis made the mistake of boycotting the elections. It was a blessing in disguise. Majory of people including promilitant organisation participated in 2002 Assembly elections dislodging Abudulla dynasty from power. Karan Singh abstained. Return of Pandits is still a distant dream. However, this has to be realised if peace and normally have to become stable and lasting.

Second, in Punjab political process did not come to a halt even when terrorists ruled the state. The Left campaigned even in the terrorists ridden rural areas losing many lives. The Left continued this till it became absolutely impossible for some time. Off and on, terrorists on the one hand and the Hindu communalists on the other did succeed in bringing about tension and situation of near riots in some towns. All political parties of Punjab and above all the Left and the working class successfully intervened to save the situation. A large number of committed political activists did not leave Punjab.

Third, when all-out fight against terrorism was started after Beant Singh took power and necessary powers were given to the police, no steps were taken to ensure that at least avoidable excesses against the innocents were stopped. Such police excesses in Punjab have been many. A section of the police believed that since they had brought peace to Punjab (which is only a half truth and hence dangerous), they had the right, not only to make heaps of money but also to rule Punjab. The presumption increased its alienation. Undoubtedly Mr K.P.S. Gill, is a supercop as far as fight against terrorism is concerned but his policy has a negative side too and this is the theory that excesses against and even killings of innocents, is the price which has to be paid by a people fighting against terrorism. The need to prevent avoidable excesses to the maximum possible extent is overlooked on the false plea that any attempt to do that will demoralise the police force. This mistake should be avoided in Kashmir.

Fourth, there was fear of re-emergence of terrorism in Punjab because nothing was being done to resolve political problems by exploiting which terrorists were able to acquire some mass base. Had this been done earlier, Punjab would not have suffered for 12 long years. In Kashmir this mistake was made on a much bigger scale. BJP has in fact been helping the terrorists of Kashmir by demanding abrogation of Article 370; by its contribution towards demolition of Babri Masjid; by being a member of a 'parivar' whose head and boss is determined to convert India into a Hindu Rashtra. The Congress party did the same when it failed to resolve the problem of adequate autonomy for J & K and for Jammu and for Ladakh within J & K.

Finally, two factors—role of mass media in Punjab and Kashmir—and vote-bank policies of the two major political parties are of great significance. While the first needs to be taken up separately, the latter has to be nailed for having contributed a lot towards the rise of terrorism in Punjab. It is high time that Kashmir is treated as a national issue by all political parties which stand for unity and integrity of India. A million dollar question is: are our political parties capable of sacrificing their immediate and partisan interests for the sake of the country? People can and must make them do that.

Kashmir and Right to Secede

Rulers of Pakistan fly in the face of too obvious facts when they continue to deny that they are training and arming the terrorists in Kashmir or are giving them any other material help and thereby interfering in the internal affairs of India. At the same time, they openly declare that they will give them maximum moral, political and diplomatic help. They justify this on the ground that Kashmiris have the right of self-determination including the right to secede from India. The same right was also talked about a lot in connection with what was going on in the USSR. It will, therefore be worthwhile to examine this question at some length.

One country may conquer or annexe another country with the force of arms and treat it as its colony, as an enslaved country. People of the latter country are bound to fight in one form or another for their freedom. The colonial country on finding the freedom struggle of its colony becoming irresistible may offer it a somewhat better or substantial status within the empire and may even try to force it to agree to it. This cannot be justified and the people of the enslaved country must have the right to complete independence, that is, the right of self-determination including the right to secede. India took its stand on this right when it demanded complete independence and rejected Dominion Status.

In the Russian Empire of the Czar which was a prison-house of nations, the non-Russian nations were virtual colonies. For a successful fight against the Czarist regime and for revolution, the unity of the Russian and the non-Russian people was necessary. Lenin also held the view that after the Revolution it would be in the interests of all to stay together out of free will and completely voluntarily. He and his party conceded the right of self-determination upto secession but advocated that the right should be exercised to remain together. In actual practice, some nations (countries) decided to secede while others decided to form/join the Union of the Soviet Socialist Republic.

Having exercise the right to remain together at the relevant time, did a nation/country reserve its right to secede at a later stage? And if it did, would it be free to secede whenever it would like? Would it not be necessary to take into consideration the big changes that may have taken place in the intervening period, as for example, the integration of the economies, the migration of people of other ethnic and linguistic groups, etc.? What would be the procedure to raise the demand to secede and what would be the procedure to decide it?

These and other allied questions were raised for the first time in the USSR in late eighties. They have relevance for the rest of the world too. They need to be debated and decided by the people in many countries. In the USSR, these questions were relevant even in relation to the three Baltic States which joined or were annexed by the USSR less than half a century ago. Assuming that they were annexed, it would seem certain that the people of the three Republic preferred to be annexed by the USSR to the only other alternative existing them, that is, of being annexed by Hitler Germany.

Let us now come back to Kashmir and India. Kashmir was never a separate country. It was part of one country called India though artifically divided by the British rulers into British India and so called Indian States ruled by princes called Maharajas, Nizam, Nawab, etc—who in fact were British stooges. Kashmir was never colony of India. In fact the whole of India was a British colony.

When forced to quit, the British wanted to divide India not only into two parts (India and Pakistan) but into dozens. Every prince was given the right to decide whether his state would join India or Pakistan or become independent. Quite a few princes were for independence—playing the British game. The people foiled their game. The Maharaja of Kashmir was for independent Kashmir. The Pakistani rulers wanted to grab Kashmir by capturing Srinagar with the help of the raiders. It is the people of Kashmir led by the National Conference who defeated the game of the raders by resisting them and by making the Maharaja sign the instrument of accession to India. On its part, India agreed to give a special status to Kashmir. Article 370 of the Constitution also provided that changes in this status must take place only with consent of the people of Kashmir.

In other words, both constitutionally/legally as well as morally Kashmir opted against joining Pakistan or becoming independent. Constitutionally as well by the will of its people, Kashmir became a part of India—except for the fact that a part of the State remained under the illegal occupation of Pakistan.

A point is bound to be raised. In the UNO India agreed that the question of accession be decided afresh by a plebicite. Many may be of the opinion that it was a big mistake on the part of India to have taken the issue to the UNO. It may also be true that India made this mistake under British influence and in fact played into the hands of the British. The fact, however, remains that India did agree to plebicite. But then this was to take place after Pakistan fulfilled certain conditions, as for example, withdraw all its forces. It never fulfilled these conditions. Moreover in 1971, the two countries signed the Simla Agreement and agreed to resolve all disputes, including Kashmir, mutually, peacefully and bilaterally. To harp upon the UNO resolution and to help the 'militants' is gross violation of the Simla Agreement and is clearly an interference in India's internal affairs.

One important question remains: can a part of a country/ nation demand the right to secede? It cannot be disputed today that India is not only a country but a nation—at least a nation-state-in the making. At the same time it is a multi-lingual or multi-national country. Besides their Indian identity, the people in India have a Bengali identity or a Marathi identity or a Gujarati identity or a Kashmiri identity, etc. Indian unity and Indian identity will not become strong if these different national or sub-national identities are sought to be underminded or are not allowed to develop.

Do nationalities/sub-national groups—linguistic groups have the right to demand secession at any time? Let us assume that they have, that at least the Kashmiris have it? The procedure for demanding and deciding the demand by ascertaining the will of the people and the procedure for ascertaining this will have to be first agreed upon. Terrorism cannot be accepted as a legitimate weapon to decide this matter or to ascertain the will of the people. Are the Kashmiri Pandits and the Kashmiri Sikhs not Kashmiris? To force them to migrate through terror and to compel sizeable sections of others to ditto what the terrorists say, is to negate the right of self-determination. Terrorism has to be opposed tooth and nail and peace restored. If neighbouring Pakistan renders help of any kind to such "freedom fighters", it violates not only the Simla Agreement but also the civilised norms of relationship between two neighbouring countries.

Some in the Pakistani ruling circles are out to help "Our Muslim brethren in Kashmir". Nothing could be more hypocritical. Why does their concern for Muslims evaporate when riots and killing take place between Muslims who migrated from India to Pakistan, and Sindhis and Pathans and Afghans—all Muslims. The Pakistani rulers would do well to heed world public opinion, stop helping the terrorists of Kashmir (and of Punjab) and sit down and negotiate in a peaceful atmosphere under the Shimla Agreement. Apart from this, the rest of the matter is entirely an internal affair of India which we hope will get resolved in a peaceful atmosphere to the satisfaction of the people of Kashmir as well as of the country as a whole. It requires wisdom on the part of all concerned.

X

Random Thoughts

Student Movement in British India

During my student days at Lyallpur, Lahore, and Bombay, I had a privilege of being a member and an active worker of the All India Student Federation, the premier organisation of Indian students. Its Golden Jubilee celebration has given me an opportunity to recall with pride the many sided activities of the AISF of those days. But let us first have a look around us. India is proud of the good work being done by Romesh Chandra, President of the World Peace Council to save humanity whose very existence will be in danger if a nuclear world war were to break out. Not long back, a news appeared in the press that the military dictator of Pakistan was not allowing Mazhar Ali Khan that fearless fighter and journalist who would not betray the people of Pakistan and the cause of Indo-Pak friendship under any circumstances to go abroad for treatment for his serious illness. Many an Indian felt as if the life of a very dear and near one of their was in danger. As India's Ambassador to the USSR for many years, Inder Kumar Gujral won laurels for the work he did to strengthen Indo-Soviet friendship which has played a vital role in strengthening Indian independence and in defeating imperialist efforts to foist neo-colonialism on our country. In the Lok Sabha, Late Geeta Mukherjee used to forcefully represent the cause of Indian women heroically fighting against rape and other atrocities, for equal rights and against their social and economic exploitation.

They and many other prominent, dedicated and self-sacrificing public workers of our country today took the path of service, struggle and sacrifice through the AISF as its members, activists and leaders. They include prominent trader unionists like Homi Daji, A. B. Bardhan and M.S. Krishan. Many big names today in the field of art, literature, education, films etc. too were in the AISF during their student days.

Members and activists of the AISF of today have good reasons to be proud of their heritage.

Persons of my age were in the AISF when India groaned under the jack boots of the British imperialist rulers. Fight for freedom was the first and most sacred tasks of all patriotic Indians. Without first winning independence, there was no question of building a strong, and prosperous India which would be able to take its rightful place in the comity of nations. Without first getting rid of the colonial yoke, there could be no question of clearing the way for a society in which there would be no exploitation of man by man and in which there would be no poverty, hunger, child labour, unemployment, illiteracy, etc. A free India was the first precondition for creating a society in which education would be within the reach of all and not the preserve of the few. It was the AISF which mobilized Indian students of those days to join hands with the Indian people in the fight for freedom and to thus discharge the duty they owed to the Motherland as its small but privileged minority having education. Students rallies on 26th January every year to take the independence pledge used to be much bigger than the Congress rallies in many cities of the country. Most progressive and Left-minded leaders in the Congress used to gladly accept invitation to address student gatherings on the independence day. There used to be students demonstrations and even strikes to protest against repression against the freedom struggle. When political prisoners went on hunger strike inside jails for better conditions, students led by the AISF would hold demonstration in their support and also for demanding their release. When the British put on trial officers of the Indian National Army (INA) founded by Netaji Subhas Chandra Bose, students in their thousands marched in streets all over the country to record their powerful protest.

It was the revolt in the armed forces started by the ratings of the Royal Indian Navy (RIN) that shook the very foundations of the British rule in India. It was the RIN revolt which made the British realize that they had now no alternative but to quit. When the British rulers threatened to crush the striking ratings and when orders were issued to the British Warships to sail for India, students alongwith the working class came out on the streets in support of the ratings despite most barbaric repression let loose by the government. The RIN ratings were also helped by the AISF in collecting funds, etc. The ratings in revolt had hoisted the Congress, the Muslim League and the Red Flags over their ships. Except for a few leaders like Aruna Asaf Ali, they were let down by top leaders of even the Congress, who called upon them to surrender, students along with the working class stood by them and thereby made further big contribution in ending the British rule in India.

Over many years students had learnt that their future lay in being united with the common people, above all with the working class and the peasants. Every conference of the AISF and of its provincial units used to have big placards and banners calling for and hailing "workers, peasants and students unity"! The AISF also taught the students to serve the people in various ways. A most outstanding example of this was the work done by the AISF in connection with the 1943 famine in Bengal, which killed lakhs. AISF delegations from various provinces went to the famine-stricken Bengal, saw the havoc played by it, went back and reported to the mass of students. The massive scale on which relief—in cash as well as in kind—was collected and sent to Bengal was unprecedented.

In normal times activists of the AISF in many places ran night schools and adult education centres to impart literacy and some education to industrial workers and other illiterate people.

The Indian student movement can be proud of the fact that is has always been on the side of progressive forces—on national and on even international issues. Students had responded in a big way to Jawaharlal Nehru's call for solidarity with Spanish Republic against fascism and with China against the Japanese aggression. Much of the credit for this goes to the AISF.

To weaken the freedom struggle, the British rulers encouraged communalism and communal riots. Students led by the AISF took their position along with those who fought against this game of imperialism. Besides "Workers, peasants, students unity", another watchword of the student movement of those day was "Hindu Muslim unity". Another glorious tradition of the AISF need to be recalled. It has been a member of the International Union of Students (IUS) and the World Federation of Democratic Youth (WFDY) from the day these world organisations of students and youth were founded. AISF has been taking active part in their work and has made good contribution in this respect. It is also not without significance that the first AISF representative to work in the WFDY and the IUS headquarters at Paris and Prague respectively were girls—Vidya Kanuga and Vimla Bakaya.

While it is heart warming to recall all this it is necessary to remember another very vital aspect of the work of the AISF of those days. The mass of students looked upon it as their own organisation. They paid for its funds besides paying regularly the membership fee. They respected and loved the AISF leaders. This was the result of the fact that the AISF and its units paid the greatest possible attention to the day-to-day needs, demands and rights of students. Mass of student were mobilised to fight for these. They were not told "Let us first win freedom and then all problems will be solved". Militant struggles were fought against the detention system, against increase in fees, for democratic unions in colleges and universities etc, students were mobilised for such demands as "mother-tongue to be the medium of instruction" etc. The colonial character of the education system was exposed. The relationship between problems of students and the colonial economy of those days was explained and the need for freedom emphasised. But the tasks of mobilising all including the least conscious (politically) for their day-to-day demands was never neglected.

Nor was this all. Good students used to be mobilized to help in their studies such students as were academically weak. Incidentally the top leaders of the AISF units generally used to be at the top in their classes and examinations also. And this helped a lot to win respect for the AISF.

Last but not the least, some words about the unity of students and the AISF. For many years the AISF was the only organisation of Indian students. When rival and parallel organisation came up, the AISF refused to become sectarian. It waged a persistent struggle for students unity. One of the factors because of which AISF remained the strongest organisation of Indian students despite many efforts to weaken it, was work for students unity.

Situation today is very much different from what it was when people of my generation were students. Number of educational institutions has increased many-fold and so has the number of students. Class composition of students is also different. Some changes have taken place in the system of education. And yet many of the old problems remain. Education is quite expensive. It is not yet within the reach of all. Many text books continue to contain untruths and distortions introduced by the British—especially on the question of Hindu-Muslim relations. Educated youth faces unemployment. Everybody talks about the need of a job-oriented education system. But nothing come of it because we have a crisis-ridden capitalist economy which cannot be job oriented. Powerful vested interests who wield political power stand in the way of basic socio-economic changes without which problems of today cannot be solved.

Notwithstanding the radically different situation today, a few lessons from the history of the AISF can help the student movement of today. It is to be hoped that the present leaders of the AISF will look into this aspect.

Trade Union Movement

From factory workers trade union movement in India has engulfed white collar employees, employees in the service sector, Government employees, employees working in the State Electricity Boards, those in hospitals and educational institutions including doctors, school teachers, college teachers and university teachers, etc. It has dug deeproots in the private sector as well as public sector. It has been growing in the unorganised sector too. Despite weaknesses resulting from the divisions in the trade union movement in India, it has many achievements to its credit in the field of bettering the living and working conditions of workers/employees and in the field of social security as well as in field of fighting for and protecting trade union rights. Nor is this all. It has done well also in the field of service to the nation. The struggle waged and won by the AIBEA for bank nationalisation is an outstanding example of this. Another outstanding example is the glorious fight which the working class of Punjab waged against terrorists. Of course all round achievements would have been much bigger but for split in the trade union movement of India. Nor is the disunity its only weakness. There are many other ailments too. It is not my intention to make any theoretical analysis of the same. All that I will try to sustain is to point out to these by giving examples from my own experience and memory. In fact, this is only an attempts to focus attention on the need to note these, to analyse them and to search for remedial measures. I remembered that many many years ago, during a general strike in Amritsar, all of a sudden a report spread like wildfire that a worker had been killed. Later on report was found to be false and had been spread by someone who felt that the tempo of the striking workers needed to be kept up through such a report. During review of the strike done at the appropriate time, the issue was hotly debated. Our conclusion was that it was not correct to adopt such means, that such methods would do much harm in the long run even if sometimes they seemed to result in some temporary gain.

Again quite long back, a worker was dismissed from a textile mill in Chheharta. The allegation was of stealing some grease from the mill. I was asked by the trade union activists in the mill to hold a gate meeting and to rouse the workers to wage a struggle for the reinstatement of the dismissed worker. Not a few were surprised when I wanted to find out whether the allegation was correct. It was not an easy job to convince the leading workers of the mill that it must be admitted that the worker had done a wrong thing and that the demand must be against the extreme punishment. Settlement was arrived at when the management agreed to treat the worker as retrenched (without the right to re-employment) and to pay the worker accordingly. It did not weaken the Union. On the other hand its prestige amongst the general public went up.

Another incident. It happened 40 years ago in our strongest mill in Amritsar. Having won many demands through strike and struggles, workers and their leaders got addicted to using the strike weapon too lightly and too frequently. One day, one leader of the mill committee of the Union came to me and narrated a small altercation between a worker and the manager and somewhat objectionable behaviour of the Manager or some such thing. It was asked: "Should we stop work as a protest"? Without batting on eyelid, I said: "Go ahead". This time the employer decided to fight to the finish. The strike lasted for months. Thanks to some favourable unexpected factor coming to our help, we came out of it not at all badly. But I had learnt the lesson. Strike weapon must not be wielded too lightly and decisions must be collective in the appropriate body.

It has been my feeling that we have not paid adequate attention to the housing problem of the industrial workers. During a particular period, however, we did campaign for houses being built by the Government for industrial workers. We had good achievement too. We came across an unexpected phenomenon. Quite a few workers not needing houses for themselves applied and got them allotted, being eligible. They then gave possession of the same to some others including non-workers for consideration. It also happened that some rightful occupants after sometime "Sold the occupation rights" to some non-eligible persons. I thought such unethical practices would prove harmful for the Trade Union movement itself besides being bad for the country. We discussed and evolved a slogan: "The Department must have one person (care-taker) for every colony whose duty must be to report the needs and problems of the colony as well as to lock up any house vacated by its rightful owner or to report immediately any illegal occupation". It remained a slogan only and the unethical practice referred to above continued.

Pratap Singh Kairon was the Chief Minister of Punjab. Patwaris of Punjab went on a strike. Their demands were more than just. And yet the Government was able to crush the strike very easily. Reason was utter lack of sympathy for the Patwaris amongst the rural population. Reason was alleged widespread corruption in the department of which Patwari had become the symbol. Peasents sided with the Government. The same thing happened once with the strike of the employees of the State Electricity Board.

Public sympathy is vital for every struggle of the working class. It is much more so where strike directly and immediately hits the public, e.g, in sectors like transport, education, banking, electricity, etc, etc. Trade Unions in these sectors need to constantly review whether they are doing all they can to ensure that their members have a correct and courteous attitude towards the public in day-to-day dealings. Also, whether whatever possible is done to make the public aware of the injustice to the workers/employees which may be forcing them to resort to a strike/struggle and of the fact that before deciding upon a strike all other methods had been exhausted. In my opinion, too frequent strikes however just the cause in the service sector, cannot but do harm to the trade union movement. Not long ago, this wrong tendency seemed to be very much there in the banking industry. There are other things which alienate public opinion, e.g, filthy slogans, night Jagratas before houses of officers inconveniencing entire colonies and neighbourhoods; manhandling of officers, etc.

Widespread corruption including at levels directly affecting consumers is an important cause which tends to alienate general public from employees. More than once leaders of trade unions called upon trade unions to fight corruption in Government services in particular. This was very much appreciated by the public. Results however have been poor. There has also been an interesting upshot. Not a few trade union leaders in these fields don't see any corruption of even the most corrupt officers as long as they cooperate with the union in the matter of say transfers and such other matters. However, when an officer is or becomes non-cooperative, his corruption is discovered and even made a big issue. Corruption is becoming a very big menace and even a danger for our people and our country. Trade Unions of Government employees and in service sectors need to pay serious attention to "tasks of Trade Unions in the fight against corruption."

Recent emergence of some new wrong tendencies as a result of crude economism and/or populism need to be taken note of.

In Punjab, the High Court has set aside many appointments made by the Government as these were made in violation of the rules and not on merit. Fresh appointments were ordered to be made on merit and in accordance with the rules. In some cases, some specific instructions were also given, e.g, for reducing the marks for "personality" for "general knowledge" or whatever you may call. Those thrown out were not deprived of chance of being considered in the new interviews ordered by the High Court. And yet in some cases, they formed ad-hoc Unions and started agitation for being kept in service. Most of the Unions and Associations of Government employees have backed them up. This obviously is a very dangerous and alarming signal. May be it is result of trade union rivalries. But that does not make it less dangerous and harmful.

Another tendency emerged in a big way during the bye-election to the Punjab Assembly from the Giddarbaha constituency in Faridkot district in 1995. Unions and Associations of Government employees led by leaders having links with some opposition party or the other held rallies at Giddarbaha with state level mobilisation. At these rallies highly exaggerated demands were raised/reiterated, Government denounced for not conceding them and employees called upon to work for the defeat of the Congress (I) candidate. They were countered by rallies of employees organised by Congressmen at which concession were announced (to be implemented after the voting had taken place) and then explicit and implicit appeals were made to the employees to work for the success of the Congress (I) candidate. Very negative and disruptive effect of such struggle tactics and methods to get demands accepted on the unity and organisation of employees is not at all difficult to imagine. This however did not seem to concern the leaders. The fact is that neither any demands have been conceded nor any of the special concessions announced have been implemented.

Last but not least, question of many holidays has attracted the attention of the media and also of the people. India in fact is a land of holidays as far as Government employees are concerned. And the number of holidays keeps on increasing. More and more holidays are being demanded in honour of some great man, Rishi, Guru, pir, martyr, leader of some particular caste, etc. State Governments at least in Punjab too, are willing to oblige. Holidays are also declared when some VIP dies. If this trend continues, serious and even irreparable damage to work culture in country will be the result. Leaders of Unions instead of educating employees about why this trend is very wrong and dangerous follow a tailist policy. It is high time that a new national policy for holidays is evolved. There should be 4 or 5 national holidays in the year. In addition, the employees should be allowed 5 to 6 restricted holidays of their choice. Reasonable number of causal leaves, medical leaves and earned leaves of course should be there. No holidays must be declared when any VIP dies except one each in case of death in harness of Prime Minister, President, Vice President or Chief Minister. In some other cases, half-holiday may be given locally only to those wanting to join cremation. However bitter may be the struggle for power between different political parties, on certain issues consensus is the need of the hour. Question of holidays is one of these.

Statistics, Truth or Lies

Do statistics tell the truth or Lies and even Damn Lies? Here are some of my experiences:

(a) There was a Congress Government of India. A claim was made that percentage of population below poverty line had decreased. The claim did not tally with the ground realities. I had gone to Delhi for a meeting. There I visited a distant relation of mine, some one from the family was a clerk or an Assistant in the statistical department of Government of India. I asked him: "At what level are statistics doctored to suit the Government". He said: "Surely not at my level"! When I pressed hard, he said "At a much higher level than mine". He would not go beyond that. However, what he said was enough for me.

(b) Once official figures released during Vajpayee's Government indicated a substantial decrease in the percentage of people below the poverty line as compared to the earlier year! Drum beaters of BJP-led Government were jubillant, What good work Government led by Atal Ji had done"? However, even the bourgeois newspapers were not taken in. Some editorially pointed out that fall was entirely due to the change in the method of arriving at the figure. In other words, the fall had been manipulated to be able to claim that the policies of the NDA Government had led to decrease in poverty even when reality was just the opposite.

(c) Latest example involves even the topmost leaders of the NDA Government who have been claiming a very big achievement on the basis of the recently released UNDTP's Development Report 2001. This report (HDR) ranks India 115, which is significantly higher than the 128th rank given in HDR 2000. On the basis of it, it has been claimed by officers and Ministers that living standards in India have improved significantly. The balloon has been punctured by an associated professor of economics, IIT, New Delhi. He has pointed out that HDR 2001 has removed 12 countries from its main list "because of non-availability of reliable data". (HDR 2001 has 162 countries as opposed to 174 countries in HDR 2000). Eleven out of these 12 countries had an HDI rank higher than India in HDR 2000. Had these countries not been removed from the main list. India's rank this year would have been only 126, hardly an improvement over last year's rank at 128". Nor is this all. For instance, he also shows that "Statistics given in this year's report are strictly not comparable with what was given in last year's or earlier reports". The professor concludes by saying that the excitment generated by the report "is totally uncalled far." (***New Age*** August 26, 2001)

(d) When the Annual Budget is presented in the Punjab Vidhan Sabha, every MLA gets a very fat book called "Statistical Abstract of Punjab". Comrade Hardev Arshi MLA has been kind enough to supply me this book every year—latest relating to the year 2000. I consulted once this book for the year 1999 or 1998. I wanted to ascertain the total number of students in Punjab in Government schools as well as in non-Government schools and in primary classes, middle classes, etc. I found that separate figures for Government school and non-Government school were not there. It was also not clear whether the figures given related to all schools in the state or only the Government schools or only Government schools plus aided schools. I found that figures given were of no use in relation to the purpose for which I had looked up the Abstract.

(e) On another occasion I looked up the Statistical Abstract of Punjab to find out number of students doing PhD and of those studying in post-graduate classes. I felt that figures given could not be correct. I consulted Dr Harish Puri of GNDU. He was emphatic that figures were wrong to an absurd extent.

(f) People of the whole country made tremendous sacrifices during the struggle for Indian independence. It is true that Sikhs/ Punjabis have made more sacrifices than proportion of their population in the total population of India. People of some states too can make the same claim. However, Chief Minister (Badal) alone has been claiming again and again, that independence for India was won by Sikhs/Punjabis. This amounts to an insult to the people of rest of India. Badal has been quoting figures of those hanged and those sentenced for life but only selectively e.g, Ghadar Movement, convicts in Andaman jail (Kala Pani), etc. More than once through my articles I asked Badal to mention the year in which freedom struggle started and then give figures for the period beginning that year upto 14/8/1947 with detailed split up. His Public Relations and Information Department could easily do this job. But why should they do it? They are not supposed to collect and disseminate truth. They are meant to select/doctor/distort statistics to suit their political bosses. The above examples are enough. Lesson is obvious. Take statistics, especially official ones, with a pinch of salt.

Incidents from My Political Life

A friend has asked me to narrate some of the incidents of my political life which I may be often re-calling for one reason or the other. Here I pen down a piece to comply with the wishes of my friend.

(a) It was many many years ago, not very long after my wife and I had settled down in Chheharta. We were living in a one-room rented quarter in Naya Naraingarh. With such quarters on both sides, there was one 20 feet wide street. During summer one tandoor used to be put up in the street. And house-wives would bake chapatis in this tandoor. One day I was told by my wife, Vimla Dang, that there was some trouble about this. Some one had demanded that two families—one belonging to scheduled castes and one to backward castes—should have a separate tandoor. There was hot discussion going on. We called a number of tenants who were working in different mills. They agreed that the demand was very wrong. They also told us that in the Canteens of their mills they all took tea and sometime ate food too together and nobody bothered about castes of different persons, etc. However they pleaded their helplessness in the matter of convincing their women folk. A meeting of all the women was then held. Vimla spoke to them at length and tried to convince them how the caste system worked against the interest of workers and other common people including women, etc. All except two agreed that the tandoor common for all should continue. An agreement was then reached that the common tandoor would be open to all and the two dissenting house-wives could have a separate tandoor of their own if they so liked.

The above helped me to understand that the original belief of the communists that with industrialization of India, caste system would automatically disappear was rather simplistic and that prolonged ideological struggle against the caste system is essential.

(b) A factory in Chheharta closed down and service of all workers except a Chowkidar were terminated. The management took the position that it was a case of closure on account of circumstances beyond their control and hence workers were entitled to only 3 months wages in lieu of their services and not 15 days wages per year of service as retrenchment compensation.

The dispute was referred to the Industrial Tribunal. (There were no Labour courts then). I argued that it was a case of retrenchment as the machinery was still there; there was also the chowkidar and the factory would most likely be restarted with new labour. The case was decided against us. It was held that retention of a chowkidar to look after the factory could not mean that it was not a case of closure but was a case of retrenchment. Later on I discovered that in a judgement of Supreme Court it had been held that even if was a chokidar was kept in employment, it would be case of retrenchment. I felt very bad that I had not found this ruling before I argued the case.

(c) A young girl Rani (not her real name) had worked as helper in our house. She belonged to a scheduled caste, was good looking and was extremely well-behaved, honest and civilised. She was about 20/21. One day I learnt that she had run away with her boy-friend etc. I later learnt that that the two were deeply in love; that the parents of girl were not willing that they should get married and that resulted in the two disappearing. Parents of the girl approached the police. As both were adults, police told them that it could do nothing and that they (i.e, the parents) could go to the court if they so liked and if ordered by the court the police would try to nab the girl and produce her before the court. They approached me and desired that I should request the police to help. I told them that they were in the wrong; that they had the right to try to convince their daughter but she had the right to take the final decision. Finally girl's parents got their whole mohalla to support them and to request the police to bring the girl with the assurance that parents would not harass her and would only try to convince her. A police official sought my view. I told him, if police felt like agreeing to the request of the mohalla, it might. Later on, I learnt that the girl had been traced, had been handed over to the parents who had beaten her up a lot and that she had committed suicide by jumping into a well. There was another version too but that did not seem to be true. The body had been cremated very quickly. This incident weighted my mind a lot for long as I had not been able to foresee the possibility of what really happened and preventing the same. I even felt that to some extent I was also responsible for the death of Rani. Of course, I drew appropriate lesson for future and that has been of great help.

(d) One day I was working in Ekta Bhawan, Chheharta in my office. Three persons—one of them bleeding profusely from a head injury came to see me. They were from a village in Amritsar district. I was told that they had been attacked by some anti-social persons and that the police was not registering a case. I rang up the police officer concerned and requested that action in accordance with law be taken against the culprits. Next day, a big group from the village came and told me that they had acted to prevent a murder by those who had come to me. I got an independent enquiry made. The second version turned out to be correct. I learnt the lesson that to get the truth it was necessary to hear both sides to a dispute as what may look apparently correct may turn out to be wrong.

(e) Once editor of a quarterly published from Chandigarh asked me to write an article on one year of Akali-BJP ministry led by Prakash Singh Badal. It was a long article dealing with the unlimited corruption in Government, I had also mentioned a case in which some IAS officers were the accused. The Chief Minister had succeeded in ensuring that the case was delayed to a maximum possible extent though his efforts to get it dropped had failed. One accused was his Principal Secretary. One was the Chief Secretary and there were one or two more. I had said that one of the accused was known to be highly corrupt. That was also the public view in general. Chief Secretary had been promoted and made Chief Secretary by Badal superceding 6/7 seniors. In the case in question he had very likely passed some erronious order. I had been of the opinion that he was a good officer. On the basis of experience, I had known that as Secretary earlier and even as Chief Secretary he was more helpful than many others in the matter of removing genuine grievances of people and ensuring justice. I was of the opinion that he was not corrupt even though some of the faction of top bureaucrats to which he belonged were corrupt in my opinion. Considerations on the basis of which groups of bureaucrat get formed don't include "personal honesty" or otherwise.

The Editor took the liberty of editing my article mainly to improve its English etc. In case of the paragraph in which virtual hushing up of this CBI case was mentioned, the Editor introduced the name of the Chief Secretary as "a most corrupt officer". When I read it, I was very much upset. I wrote a letter to the Editor protesting against the "addition" made. I had hoped that the Editor would make amends in the subsequent issue. When he did not, I thought of writing to the Chief Secretary conveying my regrets and also explaining the facts. Somehow I drifted. And this weighed on my mind a lot and for long. I may be able to recollect more of the type. Just now however I would like to narrate only one more concerning my personal life.

Vimla and I were married in 10/4/1952 at Bombay. The marriage party consisted of only four, if I remember correctly younger brother Jagdish, eldest and youngest amongst my sisters and a brother-in-law of mine. The marriage was dowryless. The reception for the newly-weds was a big one. I have often regretted that I let the entire expense to be met by the family of the bride instead of 50 per cent of the expense being contributed by our side which would have been gladly done if I had suggested and insisted. Marriage, of course, was under the Civil Marriage Act. I was told that we could get the Marriage Certificate by paying Rs. 5 only in addition to the fee for services of the Marriage Officer. I said: "I don't think any of us would need it."

Party Press

Long back I wanted to write an article about party press. I had in mind the press of the two communist parties. It was in the days of Gorbachev when under influence of his ideas a debate had started about the need of renovation of Marxism as well as of "Leninist principles of party organisation". I did not come across any discussion about the way the communist press had been functioning and how it should.

It was in this background that some controversy started about the refusal of the official organ of the CPI (M) to print a rejoinder which the famous economist K.N Raj had sent it for publication. Raj had written some article. It was published in some other journal/ paper, which I think was not official organ of any party. ***People's Democracy*** (CPI (M)'s weekly organ) had carried an article strongly criticising the views of K.N Raj. It was to this article that K.N Raj had sent a rejoinder. CPI (M) justified its refusal to print it on the ground that the organ of political party was meant to propogate the ideology and views of that party and therefore it could not be forced to print views contradicting the official views of the party.

I for one could not agree. One can understand no party leader or activist being allowed to oppose a mass movement or campaign of the party. An official organ of the party may not also print articles opposing the party policy or programme. However, on theocratical and ideological matters not to allow any difference of opinion to be aired can only harm inner-party democracy. Airing of differences can be allowed on policy matters too provided differences are expressed in a healthy manner. Not to print reply of a leading economist whose views had been criticised in the party organ and that too/of an economist friendly to the Left, seemed to me to be totally incorrect. Suppose, K.N Raj had complained to the Press Council of India. One wonders what would have been the verdict of council. In any case, the debate which would have started in the media would have been quite interesting. It would have to deal with question of rights of an official organ of a party vis-à-vis freedom of press.

This brings me to what has provoked me to pen this piece now. That is an observation made by the Press Council of India in the course of the guidelines for print media issued by it on 19th July, 1999 and carried by the press on July 20, 1999.

It reads:

"The press is not expected to indulge in canvassing of a particular candidate or party. If it does, it shall allow the right of reply to the other side also." (***The Tribune***, July 20, 1999).

This raises more questions than it answers. Official papers/ journals of parties like the CPI and the CPI (M) will surely canvass for the party candidates through articles, editorials, etc. Ask them not to do that, would be on the face of it quite wrong. Of course, their papers will not black-out news of public meeting of other parties and of speeches made by their prominent leaders, etc. But will that mean complying fully with the Press Council directive! "It shall allow the right of reply to the other side also"? Most likely, not. In that case, what exactly does this directive of the Council imply? Press Council may consider the desirability of clarifying the matter.

Perhaps a discussion is needed as to what freedom of press means for papers which are official organs of parties, what special rights, if any, such papers can be allowed to have, etc. Party press must not be and in fact cannot afford to be party Gazettes. At the same time, party press, it seems to me, cannot be required to run exactly like non-party papers in every respect. Also, it needs to be ensured that the right of readers of party press to get truthful information, is not curbed or suppressed. How all this can be ensured is, the million dollar question.

Class Morality Versus Universal Moral Values

A controversy has been going on among Marxists for some time now about universal moral values and the concept of class morality. One view is that all morality is class morality. And whatever serves the interests of the working class and of revolution is moral. Further, in case of conflict between what is in the interests of the revolutionary class and any of what are regarded as "universal moral values", the former should prevail. There are others who argue that there can be no real conflict between the class morality of the working class and universal moral values; that there is a relationship of dialectical unity between the two. It is further argued that giving precedence to universal moral values is a non-class concept and must be rejected. There is the other view that certain universal moral values are there and have to be observed for the very existence of human society. It is further held that in case of a conflict between the (immediate) interests of the working class and these universal, moral values, the latter should prevail and the same should not be sacrificed.

The dominant view amongst Communists has been the former view i.e, all morality is class morality. This view has drawn strength from the undoubted fact that all moral values are not eternal; many change. This has been well brought out by Anatoli Butenko in the ***Theory and Practice of Real Socialism***. He writes: "What was just under certain conditions, became its opposite, unjust, under different conditions and vice versa. Thus in primitive society, with its low labour productivity, warring tribes killed their prisoners. This was considered just because no sustenance could be provided for them. Later, when human labour began, it came to be considered unjust to kill prisoners of war. In conditions of low labour productivity and dearth of basic necessities, the principle of egalitarian distribution (wage levelling) is socially just, as it serves to support man, the main productive force. In other conditions, this same principle is socially unjust, as it rules out any incentive to raise labour productivity..."

Many more examples can be given to prove that many concepts of morality and justice change with changes in society. However, this does not prove that all morality is class morality and that there are no universal moral values at all. Some have been drawing the wrong conclusion that there can be no universal moral values.

Marxist-Leninists have been always emphasising that the interests of working class and its party are incompatible with narrow class egoism and narrow-minded policy-making, it generates. Further "the charges levelled against Communist ideology claiming that it engages in politicking; that it banishes ethics from politics are non-sensical". Lenin himself had insisted that a Marxist politician should possess high moral qualities—force of conviction, a keen sense of justice, devotion to Communist moral ideals, etc. According to Lenin: "honesty in politics is the result of strength; hypocricy is the result of weakness". Also : "Morality serves the purpose of helping human society rise to a higher level and rid itself of the exploitation of labour". Further, "use of coercion when it can be avoided is unacceptable and at times even criminal from the moral stand". From all these and other writings of Lenin, one thing is clear. Lenin attached great importance to moral values. At the same time it has to be admitted that there are things in his writings which appear to mean that all morality is class morality. Gorbachev, in one of his articles, quoted Lenin to show that the latter had stood for subordinating class interests to universal moral values. A top leader of the CPI(M) asserted that Gorbachev had quoted Lenin out of context and had even distorted him. Be that as it may, absence of adequate emphasics on universal moral values was perhaps due to the fact that these were by and large being observed in the society as a whole even though "we live in an age of commerce when the bourgeosie have no scruples about trade in honour and conscience" (Lenin). Some time back the Russian press reported that many postmen dumped or destroyed their entire dak instead of distributing it. It is almost certain that such a thing never happened in Russia of Czars and during the period about which Lenin wrote the above.

Whatever one's view about the relationship between Communist class morality and the universal moral values, in my opinion, the thesis that all morality is class morality, has led and will lead to erosion of universal moral values. If all morality is class morality, whatever is in the interests of the working class is moral.

Interests of the working class are represented by the party. Whatever is in the interests of the party is therefore moral. Who decides what is in the interests of the party and what is against it? Ostensibly the majority, but actually by the leader because the leader is supposed to represent the majority. In case of a party in power, the leader can order liquidation of any number believing that their remaining alive with their views is against the interests of the party and the working class. And he can do this without any burden on his conscience. I think this is what happened in the Soviet Union of Stalin's period.

Many wrong things in gross violation of universal values can take place and can be done against differing comrades even in non-ruling parties. Let me give examples which I have witnessed.

- Comrades whose views may be considered harmful for the class and the party and therefore wrong are kept down or out by undemocratic means and by subverting inner-party democracy.
- Use of double standards, unjustified discrimination and giving of special facilities and favours to favour those who side with the leadership (and therefore "serve" the cause of the revolution). These methods are also used to win over comrades in disagreement.
- Discouraging and even curbing independent thinking on the ground that it is necessary that views harmful for the class/party do not gain strength.
- Introduction of a spy system including censoring of letters inside the party.
- Carrying on of the inner-party struggle by putting out false news and reports against comrades who may be considered to have the potential of becoming a threat to the "revolutionary leadership". This is done with the help of friendly and obliging journalists and without taking the responsibility for such news and reports. Invariably those who indulge in this practice tell

lies and deny having fed the press with false news and reports. The beneficiary journalists of course can point-blank refuse to reveal their sources.

One example of methods worse than the above keeps on haunting me even though it is many years old. One leading Comrade in one district of one state was considered a hindrance in the way of installing loyal district leadership. Various types of methods were used to isolate him. When normal methods did not succeded it was alleged that he had illicit relations with the wife of another Comrade. The husband of the lady himself strongly refuted the allegation. Notwithstanding this, however "evidence" was produced and an atmosphere created which "convinced" almost every member of the body competent to take action. Action was taken. Some years later, the key and supposed eye-witness in the case blurted out to one friend, very privately, of course, that in fact the incident had been fabricated. The matter of course could not be reopened because the admission made was strictly "private". The couple, victim of "class morality", left the party. This incident is one of the few which have been weighing on my mind the most.

It can be argued that such instances take place not really because of the class morality concept but mainly because of petty ambitions, etc. That is quite possible. But the thesis that everything which helps the class is O.K, does play a big part in at least rallying support for patently wrong and immoral methods.

We are living in a period of parliamentary democracy. The main front for Communists has to be the mass front, the front of struggles. Parliamentary front has to be secondary. Even then winning elections is very much in the interests of the class. For that raising the political and class consciousness of the voters through economic, political and ideological struggles is very important. That however is a long-term affair. Keeping the voters happy for winning the next elections may be necessary and that would be "in the interests of class". For that purpose, tendency to adopt methods which are obviously and patently wrong is increasing. For instance, it is not very uncommon to give wrong and clearly false certificates for proving eligibility for various concessions and facilities such as loans, grants, old age and widow pensions, etc, etc. Bogus voting during elections is now indulged in by the Left also. The argument is: "since others do it, if we don't indulge in it we cannot win elections even if we may be the strongest party in the constituency". During the Panchayat elections in Punjab held during 1993 and 1998 every party in the contest, even though contesting as independents, had booths to provide (illicit) liquor to voters.

A very important and rather difficult question arises. Must such universal moral values as truth, honesty, etc be observed always and under all circumstances? As we have seen above, Lenin considered coercion to be immoral and criminal except when it cannot be avoided. Many anti-Communists would assert that this in fact is a formula to justify coercion. But then Gandhiji, an apostle of non-violence, too visualised cases in which resort to violence would be correct and justified, e.g, by a woman whose modesty and honour are threatened. It is the practical experience of the writer that often peaceful strikes, struggles of workers are sought to be smashed by violent methods; by anti-social elements engaged by the employers and to defeat this game retaliatory violence by workers against these anti-social elements becomes essential and even unaviodable. During the British rule, Congress legislators took (false) oaths of loyality to the crown when their open and declared aim was to wreck the reforms. This could not be and was not considered immoral by the Indian people. More examples can be given. On the one hand, as we have seen, the concept that anything that advances the revolutionary cause is moral leads to very wrong practices. On the other hand, there are occasions, when universal moral values cannot be adhered to. How and where is the line to be drawn, is the important question. May be those who speak of dialectical unity between working class or communist morality and universal moral values can enlighten.

Index

D

P

Q

R

S